Making
Sense of Society

Making Sense of Society

POWER AND POSSIBILITY

Alex Khasnabish

Fernwood Publishing
Halifax & Winnipeg

Development editing: Fiona Jeffries
Copyediting: Brenda Conroy
Text setting: Jessica Herdman
Cover design: John van der Woude

Printed and bound in Canada

Published by Fernwood Publishing
32 Oceanvista Lane, Black Point, Nova Scotia, B0J 1B0
and 748 Broadway Avenue, Winnipeg, Manitoba, R3G 0X3

fernwoodpublishing.ca

Fernwood Publishing Company Limited gratefully acknowledges the financial support of the Government of Canada, the Canada Council for the Arts, the Manitoba Department of Culture, Heritage and Tourism under the Manitoba Publishers Marketing Assistance Program and the Province of Manitoba, through the Book Publishing Tax Credit, for our publishing program. We are pleased to work in partnership with the Province of Nova Scotia to develop and promote our creative industries for the benefit of all Nova Scotians.

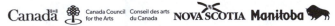

Library and Archives Canada Cataloguing in Publication

Title: Making sense of society : power and possibility / by Alex Khasnabish.
Names: Khasnabish, Alex, 1976- author.
Description: Includes bibliographical references and index.
Identifiers: Canadiana (print) 20210354054 | Canadiana (ebook) 20210363150
ISBN 9781773630960 (softcover) | ISBN 9781773635385 (PDF)
Subjects: LCSH: Social sciences—Research—Canada—Textbooks.
LCSH: Social structure—Research—Canada— Textbooks.
LCGFT: Textbooks.
Classification: LCC H62.5.C3 K53 2022 | DDC 300.72/071—dc23

CONTENTS

For Indra and Eshan, for a better future

ACKNOWLEDGEMENTS

This book wasn't easy to write but doing so taught me a lot along the way. Perhaps more than anything, I learned a protracted lesson in humility. No matter what we think we know, there is always so much more to learn. A contribution that feels monumental to us individually is still incredibly modest more broadly. This doesn't mean it's not a worthy contribution, particularly if it's in the service of collective liberation and in hopes of making the world a better place. So much of the modern university has been conscripted in service of prevailing relations of ruling that we rarely stop to think about research as a process of guided inquiry animated by curiosity. This act of rigorously and critically exploring our world is crucial to acting powerfully, intentionally, and meaningfully in it. I hope learning with this book provokes your sense of imagination and possibility. I hope it gives you some ideas and tools to explore your world with the intention of making it more just, peaceful, and liberated.

This book would never have been written had there not been a publisher looking for a different kind of textbook about social research and social justice. Thanks to Fernwood Publishing for always being willing to publish radical books about social justice and social change. In particular, I thank Candida Hadley, Errol Sharpe, and Fiona Jeffries, the editors I worked most closely with in bringing this book into being. Your patience, encouragement, critical engagement, and expertise were invaluable. Thanks also to all those friends, colleagues, and comrades who so graciously agreed to contribute the interventions that appear in this book. I'm also deeply appreciative of Brenda Conroy, copyeditor, and Jessica Herdman, publishing assistant, and all the other staff at Fernwood whose hard work made this book a reality. My sincere thanks to the anonymous peer reviewers, whose kind words and careful engagement with this manuscript gave me the opportunity to improve it.

Finally, my deepest love and gratitude to my partner and kids for encouraging, supporting, and generally putting up with me. Candida, Indra, and Eshan, you are my gravitational centre and always remind me what's really important in this life. I'd be remiss if I didn't at least shout out my furry companions — Foosa, Skippy Jon, and the Kitten — who kept my lap and shoulders warm during the hours it took to write this book.

Introduction

BEYOND THE SILOS
Toward a Social Justice Social Science

This book isn't another standard introduction to sociology and anthropology. There are lots of textbooks that aim to usher students into the hallowed halls of various academic disciplines. These books are produced, factory-like, by every major corporate publisher. Most of them are pretty good in terms of basic content and certainly do the job of introducing students to core concepts and methods. But they are also often cookie-cutter products, created with generic, modular flexibility in mind and with "tailored" content dropped in to suit national contexts. They also tend to reproduce the same tired "dead white guy" disciplinary histories.

This book aims to do something different. Rather than assuming there's something valuable and necessary in these disciplinary approaches and their histories, this book looks at the utility and importance of social science research today. It examines the roots, analytical frameworks, methods, and concepts of this practice, but its primary purpose is to critically explore what social research is, what it does, and what it is and isn't good for now. This book doesn't attempt to create new disciples for the academic disciplines of sociology and anthropology. Many who read this book won't go on to advanced study in the sister disciplines or work in the university. The following questions drove my desire to write this book: What's valuable about social research that people can take with them and use in all their diverse journeys? What does the act of intentionally investigating our lived realities make possible? What can we know that we don't already and what can we do with that knowledge? More crucially, what's useful and important in social research that we can use to build a more just, democratic, and peaceful society? What does the act of rigorously, intentionally, and critically exploring our world offer in the pursuit of addressing the problems that plague us? As I hope to show in this book, the answer is: quite a lot.

BEYOND THE SILOS

The world as we know it is not in good shape. Human-driven climate change threatens our very survival on this planet, while novel diseases wreak havoc on increasingly urbanized, precarious, and impoverished majorities. As a species we have never possessed such technical prowess or produced so much wealth, and yet rarely in history has that prowess been so squandered or wealth so unjustly distributed as they are now. Humanity faces a crisis complex of global proportions, but we do not confront these crises in the same way, with the same resources, or with the same expected outcomes in all areas of the globe. On top of it all, it hasn't taken our experiment in mass, industrialized, capitalist civilization very long to enter into crisis. That doesn't bode well for how it will weather current crises or those to come, particularly because it is their source. Given the complexity and interconnectivity of our modern ways of living, shocks to them can have incredibly widespread and acute effects, as 9/11 and the "War on Terror," the 2008 financial crisis, and the COVID-19 pandemic all illustrate. Imagining a time when it was possible to have easy faith in the idea of progress, that the future was necessarily going to be better and brighter than the present, is increasingly difficult. Despite the knowledge, technical skill, and resourcefulness of humanity, we live in a time awash in pessimism and a self-fulfilling belief in the inevitability of collective decline. Conspiracy theories proliferate, spreading virally through digital channels, and the spectre of fascism looms over us again as people lose faith in dominant institutions, power relations, and worldviews.

But is the future necessarily darker? Are we collectively doomed to disastrous decline like some B-rate zombie apocalypse film? Are comfort and security achievable only through individual success, accumulation, and consumption? Is collapse inevitable, or are alternative futures available to us? Are social problems like rampant wealth inequality, white supremacy, and misogynist violence solvable?

The act of critically, rigorously, and intentionally investigating a given phenomenon is what research is. It rarely provides us with simple or easy answers, but without it our world is a mystery, and we can't act effectively. This book introduces tools that can be of significant use in figuring out and then acting in the world. I'm not interested in convincing you that social research, or the allied disciplines of anthropology and sociology that form its root system, is the best or only way to explore the world. But the tools it provides us have been tested and proven useful, if not unproblematic.

As I show in this book, we abandon our critical capacity for evidence-based exploration at our peril. While we are right to be skeptical of ruling-class stories about our current, deeply broken world order, the solution to the problems we face does not lie in gut-reaction mysticism or baseless social media–fuelled conspiracism. It lies in our collective capacity to rigorously make sense of our world and to figure out common solutions to the challenges that confront us. Our social worlds are not made up of atomized individuals pursuing their narrow self-interest. Society isn't just the sum of all our individual actions. It's a product of social relations and institutions, and those are things we can explore and understand. If we can do that, we can act on them in better informed and more effective ways.

The focus of this book is on critical, contemporary social research rather than any specific discipline, although the legacies of anthropology and sociology feature prominently. These sister disciplines make up the foundations of this book, and we explore them as we move forward, but this book intentionally crosses borders rather than respects them. While the university is still, for the most part, divided into disciplines as a way of organizing knowledge and education, it has become increasingly common to see the boundaries between disciplines blurring. That's happened for many reasons, some exciting and worthy, some cynical and convenient, but suffice it to say that many students today find themselves learning across disciplinary traditions rather than restricted to them.

While it's not true for all disciplines, socio-cultural anthropology and sociology have grown increasingly closer since their inception more than a century ago. While die-hard disciplinary warriors may continue to fight border skirmishes, many practitioners agree that these two scholarly fields share much more than they don't and look increasingly similar. We have many of the same intellectual touchstones, look at many of the same problems, and draw on the same basic methodological toolbox. Many institutions, including my own, unify anthropology and sociology in a single academic department with a curriculum that grows from both disciplines. So it makes sense to look at what social research conducted from this widely shared foundation looks like and what it offers.

Another reason to write a book like this is less academic and more political. Like all modern schooling, postsecondary education is a powerful social institution enmeshed in dominant power relations. This doesn't mean that institutions like schools, universities, and colleges are nothing but a tool of ruling-class domination, but they're certainly not innocent in terms of their role in maintaining the status quo. Schools of all kinds are training, credentialing, and sorting machines. While it's a nice bit of liberal mythology that education is a "public good" and a key aspect of social uplift, modern schooling in the Western world came into being not out of a grassroots demand but at the behest of capitalists who wanted to ensure that workers-to-be were being prepared socially and technically for the work world. Schools are critical institutions in cultivating capitalist work discipline and disciplined social subjects, which means coming to know and internalize the norms and values appropriate to the context. Under white supremacist, heterosexist, patriarchal, settler-colonial capitalism, such norms and values include hierarchy, competition, hyper-individualism, status obsession, profit-seeking, predatory accumulation, and conspicuous consumption. This is of course not all that education offers us, but this is its foundation under prevailing ruling-class relations.

The segregation of knowledge into discrete, bounded, and policed fields is one way of cloistering it and keeping it in the hands of the credentialed experts rather than opening it up democratically to all. Like any practice, academic disciplines are not necessarily bad in and of themselves. After all, we do have to organize knowledge and the practices it relates to in some way, whether we're talking about food preparation, dancing, martial arts, or science. At the same time, remaining blindly faithful to increasingly porous boundaries doesn't serve either the pursuit of knowledge or the uses to which learners might put it. Where it makes sense, we need to bring different ways of knowing into dialogue with each other as a way of expanding our own capacity to explore and live decently in the world. This book encourages a more dynamic approach to critically investigating our social worlds by considering the shared legacy of anthropology and sociology and its promise in light of the socio-political, economic, and ecological challenges we face today.

SOCIAL RESEARCH FOR WHAT?

What is seen as worthy of learning and the way in which it is learned are not universal or inevitable, nor are they arbitrary or accidental; they are deeply influenced by the interests of those with the most power and authority. It's no accident, for example, that the school day mirrors the typical waged work day, that students are encouraged to compete for scarce grades and accolades, that forms of discipline and reward structures in schools mirror those in wider society. Education isn't a neutral act; it's deeply vested with power and interest and is directed at producing what those with the most power see as appropriate social subjects. We always have to question the values and orientation at the heart of it. Even the way we organize knowledge and learning is affected by these power relations. In trying to push past a disciplinary focus on anthropology and sociology, I'm not trying to do away with conventional academic disciplines or cheerlead for trendy but often hollow calls for greater trans- or inter-disciplinarity. My ambition is more humble and more radical. I focus our exploration on what makes social research worth doing here and now. I introduce people to the act of intentionally, transparently, rigorously, and critically inquiring into our world and show them why such work matters and what we might do with it.

This book is about contemporary social life and how we investigate it. It's also a book that is fundamentally concerned with building a better, more just, peaceful, and liberated world. Research isn't a politically neutral act. Accepting the status quo is not more bias-free than challenging it; it's actively complicit in reproducing and legitimating it. That doesn't mean all research is or should be activism, but it does mean that, as social researchers, we have always to be mindful that the ways we identify, explore, and talk about social issues has implications. It also means we must be critically aware of and responsive to the fact that the very act and conditions of research are shaped by prevailing power relations and the interests behind them. What do we see as a social crisis in desperate need of attention and resources and what doesn't make the cut? Who gets identified as a "problem" population in need of surveillance and intervention? What kinds of suffering are written off as the unavoidable if unfortunate fruits of progress? How do we know what's realistic or possible when it comes to alternatives to the social problems that plague us? These questions and so many more point to the fact that research and its results are inherently political.

As we explore the methods and theories that animate social research, we also have to keep excavating its politics. This means figuring out who gets to ask the questions and do the investigating, who and what gets studied, and who does what with the results. This book introduces you to the core elements in the study of contemporary social life, drawing on the allied disciplines of anthropology and sociology. It also asks you to consider what we do with social research and what interests are served in doing it.

In this journey you won't just hear from me. In each chapter you will read short, critical interventions from a diverse array of scholars and practitioners that highlight important contemporary concepts related to the chapter's theme. These interventions not only introduce key concepts from anthropology, sociology, and, more generally, critical social research but also highlight how making sense of society through critical, grounded investigation gives us the ability to act more effectively, collectively, and justly in it. The core theme of this book is that critical social research offers us tools of considerable value in addressing the crises that face us and in building a better society. These are not the best or only tools we need to survive the present and build a better future, but they are important. It's the purpose of this book to show you how and why and what we can do with social research for social justice.

1

BECOMING HUMAN

Diversity and Evolution

Co-authored with Anthony Davis

What does it mean to be human? What are humanity's origins and how do they inform how we understand ourselves now? Was there a clear point in our past when we became human and, if so, what does that mean? Is humanity a destination that we were always moving toward, or is it better thought of as a point in a process of change and becoming? What is the relationship between our species' biology and our social life? Before digging into some of the pressing issues confronting us today, it is vital to understand who we are as one species among many others on this planet. In so doing, we can tease out the elegant relationship between our biological evolution and our *sociality*.

For those of us with ready access to Internet-based media, particularly those of us ensconced in enclaves of relative comfort and security in the *Global North*, there is an increasing tendency to consume our media in silos. We tend to stick to what we know and like, what our social networks know and like, and what reaffirms our values, convictions, and conceptions. Social media is often accused of creating opinionated echo chambers rather than diverse opportunities for communication and engagement. This effect isn't limited to our social media platforms and can even be seen in institutions like the university and the way it produces knowledge about the world. As we progress through the education system, we are encouraged to focus ourselves, specialize our knowledge, and produce expertise with great depth in one area but very little breadth or connection to others. In an environment structured by the capitalist logic that orders society as a whole, academic disciplines and their practitioners are set against each other in a contest for resources, attention, accolades, influence, and prestige. This fuels an unending cycle of conflict and competition that produces a lot of heat but very little light with respect to the social issues and problems at hand.

This has important implications for the story of our human origins. Humanity is neither an exclusively biological nor social state of being — it is both at once. We can't tell the story of who we are as a species without contextualizing that in the web of relationships with environments and other forms of life that make up our existence on this planet. Without letting go of the always important details, when we step back and seek to make connections between different aspects of our collective existence and experience, we are operating according to a *holistic perspective*. By bringing the biological and the social together, we shed critical light on both, and we are able to see our evolutionary journey as a constantly unfolding, never-finished, bio-social feedback loop set in the midst of a diverse ecology of which humanity is only a part.

NATURE VERSUS NURTURE?

Where do our potentials and problems come from and how do we come to know them? Are we born or taught to be who we become? This is more than an abstract debate. The way we understand our social behaviours and their origins profoundly informs how we think about dealing with them. If we understand competition, violence, hierarchy, and domination as pure expressions of our biological makeup, coded into our DNA, then there is no point doing anything to address or ameliorate their social manifestations, including wealth-hoarding, child and slave labour, war, poverty, authoritarianism, sexual predation, and so much more. If we are hard wired to be vehicles for these drives, doing anything to change them or their expressions would be futile, wasteful, and even counter-evolutionary, a denial of our very nature as a species. On the other hand, if we understand phenomena like these purely as products of our social environments, it is easy to lay the blame for them at the feet of the system, some amorphous monolith that looms above us and makes us dance like puppets on strings. While this second perspective has the advantage of not biologically mystifying the nature of domination, exploitation, and oppression, it is just as guilty of positioning an all-powerful force above us and obscuring how social relations are structured and sustained.

Stories seeking to naturalize domination, exploitation, and oppression at inter-personal and global scales have ancient roots in human societies. While pseudo-scientific narratives are frequently deployed in their justification today, justifications for these behaviours have also been expressed in mystical, religious, and philosophical terms. However, simply because domination, exploitation, and oppression exist doesn't make them right, natural, or inevitable; such power relations are only one possibility of our human sociality among many. In addition, it is not enough for these power relations to be imposed on people; they have to be seen as legitimate if they are to endure and to shape people's behaviour and expectations.

In the social sciences, the long-running contest between those who believe human behaviour is determined by our genes and those who contend that it is driven by the environment is known as the "nature versus nurture" debate. Those who come down on the side of "nature" (our genes and physiology determine behaviour) are known as *biological determinists*. They interpret every social problem, issue, and activity as little more than an effect of the supposed underlying human compulsion to carry on our genetic material through offspring. One of the biggest challenges to biological determinism is that the relationship between our genetic information (genotype) and the ways it's expressed through observable traits (phenotype) is not simple. Most traits are the result of a complex interaction between multiple genes and environmental factors (Mehta 2014). While it may be tempting to interpret all social events as if they were somehow unfiltered expressions of our biology, that view is not borne out by genetic science.

One problem of biological determinism is that it explains the status quo in near-mystical biological terms. No geneticist would argue that there is a gene for hierarchy, rampant accumulation, rape culture, war, exploitation, or any number of other social problems in the same way that genes that control eye colour or skin pigmentation. Yet this is what biological determinists argue. They seek to naturalize forms of domination, exploitation, and oppression that are profoundly unnatural. The attempt to explain and legitimate social injustices by recourse to imagined biological causes is known as *social Darwinism*. Despite its name, it has very little to do with the theory of evolution proposed by Charles Darwin and everything to do with the misapplication of scientific knowledge in defence of existing relations of power and privilege.

On the other hand, those who come down on the side of "nurture" (environment determines behaviour) are known as *social determinists,* and they argue that people are basically blank slates impressed upon by the social environment into which they are born. For social determinists, there is no human nature outside of our sociality, and all our activity, potentials, problems, and issues come back to the social context. While this perspective has the advantage of not mystifying and biologizing social issues and power relations, it tends to deny our material, biological existence entirely. While humans as a species are not simply drones carrying out subconscious biological imperatives, our material realities clearly shape our opportunities and potentials. For example, the work of caring for one another is central to our human existence, whether it's raising children, caring for elders, preparing food, or any number of other emotional and physical activities involved in sustaining ourselves on a day-to-day basis. This labour – referred to as "social reproduction" – is a necessary part of our continued existence individually and collectively. We literally cannot get on without it, as anyone who has been forced to go without such care can attest to. But this biological imperative tells us nothing about how this work gets done, by whom, and under what conditions. These are all social questions.

Under patriarchy, a social relation that privileges men at the expense of women, this critical work of care is overwhelmingly performed by women. This is not because women are essentially more nurturing or inclined to such work than men but because it benefits those with power to sustain this exploitation. Under patriarchal social relations, all men in some way benefit from the oppression and exploitation of women, not just abstractly but in concrete, material terms. Such exploitation would appear, rightly, as profoundly unjust without the justifications provided by recourse to women's supposedly natural role as caregivers, a rationalization that, like a house of cards, is built on a variety of shaky assumptions and essentialized notions that reflect rather than explain the way the world is. All kinds of phenomena are rooted in our biological necessities and realities, but these are run through and given shape by dominant social relations. We cannot retreat to some mysterious, primordial biological truth to explain our social problems and possibilities, but neither can we ignore our biological and material needs when seeking to understand why society works the way it does and how we might arrange it differently.

BASIC PREMISES IN THE STUDY OF HUMANITY

While it is a mistake to reduce social issues to mere effects of our biology, it is equally wrong to imagine that we are free-floating identities constructed by society. It is impossible to understand humanity without considering the social *and* biological terms of our existence. Perspectives that encourage us to understand discrete phenomena relationally and in context can be described as holistic. Rather than reducing everything to a single source or factor, this perspective encourages us to attend to the way that relationships structure our lived realities. From a holistic perspective there are six basic insights about the human condition that are vital to keep in mind as guideposts for our explorations of human social activity:

1. Human beings are and have always been members of the biological universe.
2. Biologically, humans are mammals and members of the scientific classification.
   Kingdom: Animalia
   Class: Mammalia
   Order: Primates
   Family: *Hominidae*
   Genus: *Homo*
   Species: *Homo sapiens*

3. As in all biology, humans have been shaped in essential ways by the dynamics and forces of evolution.
4. As for all biological organisms, humans require energy to survive and flourish (i.e., food).
5. As for all mammals, humans sexually reproduce.
6. Humans have developed distinctive and complex forms of social relations, organization, and cooperation — we call this "culture." While culture emerges, in part, to satisfy these basic requirements, it is in no way limited to them.

These six basic guideposts remind us that humanity is not a collection of disparate individuals but a species implicated in a much larger web of life that is globe-spanning in nature. Our existence on this planet is shaped not only by our own capacities and limitations but by the ways we interact with other forms of life and the environments we inhabit. For example, all people need food, water, and sleep to survive. The ways in which we secure, prepare, and consume these things varies incredibly not only across time and geographical distance but according to prevailing power relations, systems of oppression and exploitation, cultural traditions, and ecological context.

It is simple enough to say that without food, water, and shelter human survival is impossible, but it is a more complex proposition to explore how and with what consequences these essentials are secured. Shelter may be essential, but does that mean urban sprawl is inevitable? Food is unquestionably necessary for human survival, but does this mean fast food or any given fad diet is an unproblematic expression of this need? Similarly, while humans reproduce sexually, does this mean that every individual has to produce biological offspring or that reproductive heterosexual sex is the only legitimate form of human sexuality? These fundamental needs are profoundly shaped by the context in which they are set, contexts which are never free from the operation of power. One thing we can take from this is that human nature, while rooted in fundamental realities relating to our biological evolution as a species on this planet, is not very natural at all.

HUMAN EVOLUTION

People are not just social beings; we are also biological entities inhabiting a material world and shaped as a species over millions of years by the forces of evolution. *Evolution* is a term that describes the changes in heritable characteristics in biological populations over generations. While the idea that one type of biological organism could descend from another stretches back millennia, the contemporary formulation of the theory of evolution is attributed to Charles Darwin (1809–1882) in his famous work, *On the Origin of Species* (1859). Evolution doesn't try to explain the origins of life on the planet; it is instead a compelling analytical framework for understanding how life has changed and developed over time.

Evolution does not refer to a process of organisms becoming better over time, nor does it imply that superior organisms survive and evolve while inferior ones die out. Changes in genetic material in living organisms are produced through mutation and the reshuffling of genes during sexual reproduction, resulting in offspring differing in minor ways from their parents. These changes are random, but the evolutionary process is not. As Darwin describes in his theory of natural selection, changes that provide offspring with a better chance of survival in a given ecology allow them an opportunity to reproduce and carry their genetic material forward to successive generations. Darwin did not understand the mechanism responsible for imperfect copying of heritable traits; that would come through the pea plant experiments of Gregor Mendel (1822–1884), which laid the groundwork for the modern study of genetics. Darwin did, however, offer the critical insight that evolution is a process of random change in heritable traits over time and that the traits and organisms which endure are those which facilitate survival and, ultimately, successful reproduction in a specific environment. Evidence supporting evolution as an explanatory framework for the development of life on Earth comes from the fossil record, comparative anatomy, and molecular biology and is incredibly robust.

The phrase "survival of the fittest" is often mistakenly associated with Darwin's theory of evolution and is misunderstood to mean that the "most superior" organisms survive and dominate the natural world. The phrase was coined by English philosopher and political theorist Herbert Spencer (1820–1903), who came up with it after reading *On the Origin of Species*. Spencer took ideas from Darwinian evolutionary theory and mapped them onto dominant social, political, and economic power relations, using them in an attempt to justify existing forms of injustice and inequality. Social Darwinism is the name given to this ideological justification of the socio-political and economic status quo, which appropriates concepts developed through the study of how organisms successfully reproduce themselves and pass on heritable physiological traits.

Societies are not living biological organisms; they are complex constructions made out of relationships, institutions, and ideologies. The earthly biological universe of which humanity is a part is not a war zone but an incredibly complex, interconnected web where adaptability, not supremacy, is the key to survival. Social Darwinism is not only wrong in its ideological justification of power but in its conception of the phenomena at hand. Spencer's influence would not endure, and disciplines like sociology and anthropology would quickly reject social Darwinism as bad social science and little more than a smokescreen for domination. As we will see in chapters to come, this would hardly mark the last time scientifically suspect and ethically bankrupt theories speaking the language of "biological difference" would be rolled out to endorse all manner of social violence, oppression, and exploitation.

So, what does this all mean for us as humans on this planet? Simply put, it means that our existence is interwoven with the ecologies we inhabit. Ecologies are not just environments, backdrops against which life goes about its business. *Ecology* refers to the web of relationships between an organism and its environment. Focusing on ecology instead of environment allows us to better see our embeddedness in these webs of life. It is impossible to understand the human evolutionary journey and its implications without thinking about it ecologically (discussed in greater detail in Chapter 7). This is even more important in an era of climate crisis driven by human activity. Evolutionary changes in the human species not only facilitated our collective survival, they also opened possibilities for our social coexistence and closed others. This is not to suggest that biology determined our social life on Earth, only that these changes in context served as the foundation for two of our species-defining traits: sociality and cooperation. In this section I focus on three significant hallmarks of human evolution that are critical to understanding humans as biocultural organisms.

The Earth is approximately 4.54 billion years old, with recent evidence suggesting that life may have emerged as soon as the planet cooled enough to hold water – as early as 4.3 billion years ago. If we go far enough back, we can trace all life on Earth to a single ancestor. The history of our own species, *Homo sapiens*, is far more recent. The genus *Homo*, encompassing modern humans and our extinct relatives and ancestors, is a member of the taxonomic primate family *Hominidae*, otherwise known as the "great apes" or *hominids*. We share this great ape family with three other genera: *Pongo* (the Bornean, Sumatran, and Tapanuli orangutan); *Gorilla* (the eastern and western gorilla); and *Pan* (the common chimpanzee and bonobo). Humans and chimps are the most closely related of all the great apes, with humans and our ancestors diverging from chimpanzees on the evolutionary timeline between 5.6 and 7.5 million years ago. The term *hominin* refers to the group including modern humans, extinct human species, and our proto-human ancestors but excluding the other great apes. The earliest member of the genus *Homo* is *Homo habilis,* who dates to approximately 2.8 million years ago. This means that in the scope of life on Earth, a span of more than 4 billion years, modern humans and our ancestors take up less than 3 million of those years. *Homo sapiens* evolved between 350,000 and 260,000 years ago, and our ancestors who ended up populating the planet left Africa a mere 50,000 years ago. The story of humanity is an eye blink in evolutionary terms.

EVIDENCE AND INTERPRETATION

Before delving into some of the unique features that define our human evolutionary journey, a few words about evidence and its interpretation are in order. Paleontology, evolutionary anthropology, archaeology, paleoecology, and genetics are the research fields most closely associated with the search for evidence concerning human and proto-hominin biological evolution, social behaviour, and material presence. Often working in collaborative teams, researchers seek material evidence such as fossils, tools, paleo pollen, and recoverable DNA as data sources to describe and situate the developmental history of humans and our proto-hominin ancestors.

Unavoidably, certain characteristics of this evidence place important limitations on what can be inferred from it. First, the scientific search for this evidence has been underway for only a little over a hundred years. While growing, the volume of evidence remains sparse and incomplete. Fossils are difficult to find and, even when unearthed, are mostly fragments of skeletons. Teeth and parts of large bones are the most likely anatomical features to be fossilized. Similarly, the recovery of usable ancient DNA is extremely challenging. Evidence associated with humans and our proto-hominin ancestors is also limited by the fact that any tools or materials made from plant fibres, wood, or animal skins is unlikely to fossilize and survive in the record. Such limitations obviously restrict what we can know and what we can infer. Material evidence such as fossils, for example, cannot tell us much about social organization, intra-/inter-group relations, and gender relations, but it can allow some careful, contextual inferences concerning most likely associated social relations. Evidence doesn't speak for itself; we make sense of it based on knowledge frameworks that are themselves indelibly marked by dominant power relations.

Another characteristic of evidence interpretation is that until recently, essentially all research in this area had been conducted by white men. In some key respects this has shaped the interpretations of evidence. For instance, their research and backgrounds informed a Eurocentric male interpretation of fossil evidence as supporting the presumption that our proto-hominin ancestors featured male dominance as expressed in evident sex-based dimorphism. That is, the finding that males were, on average, larger than females produced presumptions that males were dominant. Yet the accompanying fact that proto-hominin dimorphism is remarkably less present among most great apes and deceases across time was ignored until recently, as was the fact that relative largeness does not necessarily or naturally translate as dominance. Alternative interpretations not conforming to a patriarchal view of the world could challenge the unquestioned presumption of male dominance within Eurocentric societies and that male dominance is simply a fact of human nature (see Larsen 2003). Knowledge production is never innocent of power relations.

It is always important to keep in mind that science practices and evidence interpretations, as human activities, are impacted by researchers' cultural and social backgrounds, including belief systems that frame what is taken for granted. Perhaps one of the most egregious and obvious illustrations of this is found in the presentation in evolutionary "trees" of humans, often looking very Northern European in ancestry, as the apex beings derived from an evolutionary process that moves from simpler earlier forms to the most developed current form. Of course, the evidence does not support the notion that human beings (*Homo sapiens*), existing for around 300,000 years, are better adapted as a species than either our ancestor *Homo erectus,* which existed for a million years or more, or our even older ancestor species *Australopithecus afarensis* and *Australopithecus africanis,* which likely existed for well over 2 million years.

Finally, considerable comparative emphasis is placed on the relation between humans, our proto-hominin ancestors, and the other hominids – the great apes such as chimpanzees, bonobos, gorillas, and orangutans. For instance, it's now known that modern humans share well over 98 percent of their DNA with modern chimpanzees and bonobos, establishing the evolutionary kinship of these great ape species. Yet DNA analyses have clearly established that our proto-hominin ancestors diverged from those of chimpanzees and bonobos somewhere around 6–7 million years ago. Of course, chimpanzees and bonobos have experienced their own evolutionary processes, quite independent from that of proto-hominids and modern humans, and these processes remain largely unknown. So, the extent to which observations of modern chimpanzee and bonobo organization and behaviour can provide insight on early proto-hominin and human organization and behaviour is extremely limited, to say the least. Despite this, it is not uncommon to find inferences drawn from such observations about how great ape behaviour and organization reveal something about human nature. It is extremely important to avoid anthropomorphizing nonhuman behaviour and organization, especially those of the great apes. To do so diminishes the remarkable independent evolutionary history of these species while also distracting thinking from the need to understand on its own terms the evolutionary history of humans and our proto-hominin ancestors.

OUT OF AFRICA

The scientific consensus today based on the best available evidence is that humans originated in Africa and dispersed from there to populate the entire world. This theory, known as the *recent single-origin hypothesis*, holds that *Homo sapiens* developed in East Africa between 400,000 and 200,000 years ago. From there, at least two dispersal events occurred, one between 130,000 and 115,000 years ago via a Northern African route and the second following the Toba super volcanic eruption roughly 75,000 years ago and following a southern route. It was the second dispersal event that led to humans populating the world. Archaic humans (*Homo erectus*) also migrated out of Africa in a dispersal event beginning somewhere around 1.9 million years ago. This earlier dispersal wave is thought to have left little to no trace on modern human populations, but it did give rise to other hominin groups, including *Homo neanderthalensis* and Denisovans (*Denisova hominins*), who would, in turn, later both interbreed with and be replaced by *Homo sapiens*.

While genetic and paleoarchaeological research continues to shed light on this fascinating period of hominin existence and many details will undoubtedly be filled in and, perhaps, change with the addition of new information, the overall picture of our *hominin* and proto-hominin origins is clear and remarkable. We are a single, highly adaptable, and extraordinarily social species that is both world-changing in nature and world-spanning in range. That said, humans are not especially impressive physical specimens. We lack tough hides, large teeth or claws, the ability to see in the dark, and any number of other physical traits that make for impressive predators. Capitalist mythmaking aside, we are not a species characterized by our rugged individuality; our survival individually and collectively depends on our capacity for sociality, cooperation, and problem-solving. So, from an evolutionary perspective, what explains our global reach and our unsurpassed role, for good and bad, among other living species as world-shapers?

TEETH AND DIET

Humans and our proto-hominin ancestors have several unique and distinctive anatomical characteristics. These range from cranial and dental features, through attributes of shoulder and hip joints, to characteristics of hand, foot, and pelvic bones. For instance, the earliest fossil evidence, essentially because teeth are most likely to be preserved, points to changes in the size, characteristics, and distribution of teeth as denoting the appearance of our proto-hominin ancestors. Particularly notable is the reduction in size of canine teeth and the dominance of large, flat molars, designed for grinding. These changes are significant because they point to changes in early proto-hominid diet and behaviour.

The reduction of canine size suggests that these teeth were no longer required for aggression and threat aversion displays, while the dental dominance of large grinding teeth denotes dietary dependence on foods such as ripe fruits and other plant material. The dental evidence associated with proto-hominids clearly shows that these were not raw meat eaters as the teeth simply are not made for slicing muscle fibre; a lot of energy-intensive chewing would be required to ingest and process any quantity of raw meat. Some consumption of insects, grubs, worms, and decomposing animal flesh was a possible source of high-quality protein and food energy for our proto-hominid ancestors, but the extent to which this was the case is unknown. Fundamentally, what these changes in dentition show is that our proto-hominin ancestors consumed a diverse diet.

BIPEDALISM

Many of the distinctive human and proto-hominin anatomical features are associated with the fact that proto-hominins developed into a fully bipedal great ape. Indeed, bipedalism and its anatomical consequences clearly distinguished proto-hominin species from all other primates, so much so that these anatomical consequences often determine whether fossil finds are classified as proto-hominin or otherwise. These qualities also draw the direct ancestral linkage between the fossil evidence and modern humans.

The scientific consensus today is that our proto-hominin ancestors were well on their way to becoming full bipeds by 4 million years or more ago (e.g., *Australopithecus afarensis*) and that bipedal locomotion was adopted and evolutionarily enabled rather quickly. The existing fossil evidence shows that bipedalism preceded any notable increases in our proto-hominin ancestors' cranial capacity. We were walking upright on two legs before the explosion in brain development that also stands as one of the defining characteristics of our species. Available data shows that the cranial capacity of early bipedal proto-hominins was not much different than that of contemporary chimpanzees, at around 400 cubic centimetres. It is important to keep in mind that proto-hominins, with direct ancestral linkages to modern humans, were much more like great ape primates in ecological conditions and behaviour than like modern human beings (see Stanyon, Consigliere, and Morescalchi 1993).

Bipedalism and its consequences are at the core of our species becoming human. Employing techniques such as pollen analyses from lake-bed core samples, paleo-ecological research shows that the environments where bipedalism came to be were landscapes featuring extensive forests broken up by open areas with many lakes and rivers. These environments provided proto-hominins with opportunities to access diverse resources for food energy, in trees, on the ground, and in and around water-linked ecosystems. The processes that favoured adopting bipedalism must have featured extremely advantageous benefits for accessing food energy resources within the paleo ecosystem, particularly since bipedalism came at a considerable risk of becoming food for much faster and stronger quadruped predators.

Ordinary humans can run, on average, about 18 kilometres per hour (km/hr). Usain Bolt, to date the fastest human on record, attained a maximum speed of almost

48 km/hr. These foot speeds are remarkably pedestrian compared to those of predators such as hyenas (60 km/hr), tigers (64 km/hr), African wild dogs (71 km/hr), and lions (81 km/hr). These predators and their ancestors employ extreme bursts of speed to take down their prey. Early bipedal proto-hominins were small-sized beings, estimated at well under 50 kilograms in weight and not much over a metre in height, and would have had little chance to outrun most predators. Bipedalism requires and develops relatively strong lower body muscularity but at the price of much weakened upper body strength, meaning a diminished ability to climb quickly into trees as a way of avoiding becoming food.

So, what did bipedalism offer to make the cut from an evolutionary perspective? One idea about an advantage of bipedalism suggests that the standing posture provided early proto-hominins with the ability to see predators in hiding and thus to avoid them. Yet, a broken forest landscape would provide predators with many out-of-sight hiding places. So, what could possibly explain the ways and means proto-hominins survived and thrived? It is most likely that proto-hominins found safety in numbers. That is, they lived and moved about in large social groups that cooperated to provide mutual protection while foraging for food on the forest floor and along shorelines. Notably, adopting bipedalism came with anatomical changes in arm length (shortened), hand and finger shape favouring grip efficiencies, and shoulder structures. These features enabled proto-hominins to become much more efficient and accurate throwers than evident in any other ape species. It is possible that this unique capacity was employed early by proto-hominin groups to deter predators and provide time for escape. Speed isn't everything (see Richmond and Berbesque 2001).

REPRODUCTION

Becoming fully bipedal is also associated with significant consequences for another important proto-hominin physiological process: the female reproductive system and fertility cycle. Among most mammals, including the great apes, female reproductive fertility is marked by estrus. Through a variety of physiological signs, including vulva swellings, vaginal emissions, and scent profiles, quadruped females signal reproductive fertility to potential mates. This is an extremely efficient system that pretty much assures that fertile females will conceive when ovulating. In human females, and likely their proto-hominin ancestors, this is reversed, with the time of ovulation hidden and the time of infertility marked (see Gangestad and Haselton 2015).

Physiologically, becoming fully bipedal likely meant that estrus no longer worked effectively among proto-hominin females. Bipedalism resulted in female reproductive organs becoming tucked out of sight within the pelvic floor. Among proto-hominin females, sexual maturity also brought with it the development of secondary characteristics, particularly breasts, which are absent among the other quadruped, knuckle-walking great apes. The fullness of proto-hominin breast form mimics a condition as if the female is permanently lactating, unlike non-proto-hominin ape females, wherein the breasts fill out only when actually lactating. The in-front location of this secondary sex-linked attribute during female sexual maturity would clearly signal their physiological reproductive capacity. Taken together, bipedalism and its associated reproductive changes suggest that proto-hominins had to adopt a practice of frequent copulation over the course of the female cycle in order to produce offspring.

A final, major anatomical consequence of bipedalism concerns changes to the proto-hominin pelvis. Adopting bipedal locomotion required that the pelvic ilium turn inwards, tilt upwards, and narrow somewhat, changes required both to support an upright posture and motion and to support the internal organs. For female proto-hominins, this also meant a narrowing of the birth passage. While this might not have been much of an issue for the earliest proto-hominins with their modest-sized skulls, it would become a major issue for fetal development and birthing once proto-hominin skulls began to grow in capacity and shape. It is likely that at some early stage, female proto-hominins began giving birth to developmentally immature infants that were physically dependent on their mothers, and possibly all intra-group adults, for much longer periods of time than had been the case.

Taken singularly or all together, these attributes would have had incredibly meaningful consequences for proto-hominin social relations and organization. Reproductive success — the ability to produce future generations and propagate the species — in these circumstances would have necessitated a larger population of males and much more frequent and closer social interactions between females and males. Uncertainty surrounding female fertility would have necessitated this by itself, requiring as it does more frequent and regular sex across the reproductive cycle to produce offspring. Further, it is likely this necessity would underwrite and reinforce social cooperation among groups of proto-hominins, particularly as proto-hominin females had to become receptive to frequent copulation (see Marlowe and Berbesque 2012).

Significantly, and with implications for contemporary patriarchal myth-busting, the reproductive requirement for frequent sex, randomly distributed over female reproductive cycles, also meant there was not any biological necessity favouring male dominance and the so-called "alpha male complex." Choices made by females with respect to sex partners were likely a major driver in the anatomical changes and behavioural features noted above. Preference for less aggressive and more involved males was likely an aspect of female choice, especially given the fact that they had to interact more regularly and intensively with males. Contrary to contemporary myths about the desirability of so-called "alpha males," the behavioural attributes associated with them would have presented few advantages for both individual females and species reproduction overall. For instance, females providing the requisite care over increasingly long periods of time for physiologically dependent infants must have fostered a preference for female-male and intra-group cooperation. Without this basic sociality, our collective survival would not have been possible. In such a context, males more prone to pro-social behaviours, like sharing food resources, were likely preferred and chosen for sex. Of course, these features would exert a selection feedback effect on physiological and behavioural attributes through female exercise of choice in mates.

CRANIAL CAPACITY

The physiological and behavioural changes surveyed so far preceded significant increases in proto-hominin cranial capacity and the bolstered intellectual abilities with which they are associated. While increased brain size and complexity understandably garners a lot of attention when it comes to understanding our human evolutionary journey, it's critical to recognize that these other unique attributes are intrinsically linked to the development of sociality and cooperation among our proto-hominin ancestors. As we've seen, these physiological changes could only prove to be advantageous in a pro-social, cooperative context, whether in terms of accessing food energy, providing security and mutual aid through large group living, or assuring species' survival through reproduction. Rather than seeing these evolutionary attributes as the bedrock for sociality and cooperation, or the reverse being true, we need to appreciate these changes as intertwined and mutually constitutive of each other. Some researchers suggest that the reproductive requirement for frequent and randomly distributed sex as well as increasingly dependent infants may have encouraged the development of new social bonds between at least small groups of reproductively mature males and females. The work involved in maintaining such intense bonds and complex social relations, in turn, likely fostered increasing complexities and densities in neural connectivities, thereby putting in place the foundations for becoming the "brainy" great ape.

The next notable anatomical development unique to humans and our proto-hominin ancestors once fully bipedal was the gradual but dramatic expansion in cranial capacity. The fossil evidence indicates a gradual increase in cranial capacity between around 4 and 2 million years ago. It is presumed that this expansion was accompanied by enhanced cognitive abilities to engage with ecosystems for the purposes of extracting food energy and assuring reproductive success. The first simple stone tools that have been found are associated with this period, indicating our proto-hominin ancestors' greater capacity to intentionally shape the means with which they engaged their environments. This stone technology remained essentially unchanged over at least a couple of million years, although it is useful to recall there is no fossilized evidence of technologies using materials such as plant fibres and wood. This should not be taken to mean that such materials weren't used to make various sorts of tools and implements, only that they cannot survive in the archaeological record.

About 2 million years ago the species *Homo* appears, distinguished by a notable jump in cranial capacity and other anatomical features. This growing brain required a disproportionate share of available food energy. In modern humans, the brain by itself requires and consumes over 20 percent of all daily food energy intake. Growing and sustaining such an organ required greater access to and dependency on high quality food energy, both in terms of protein and caloric intake. This likely meant increased consumption of both animal protein and a broader array of nutritionally rich plant foods such as seeds, nuts, and tubers. It is apparent that our *Homo* ancestors accomplished this and in the process transformed our species' evolutionary experience and dynamics. The primary question is what provided access to the quantity and quality of food energy required to grow and sustain the brain?

According to the evidence found to date, the key to unlocking this transformative development is proto-hominin control and use of fire, particularly for cooking meat and plant material. Our ancestors were the only primate, let alone mammal, to achieve control over and use of fire. It is likely that we'll never know who first controlled fire and directed it toward purposeful use or where in sub-Saharan Africa this first occurred. But there is no question that the path of hominin biological evolution and social development was revolutionized through this achievement; it is unlikely that we would be here in our present form were it not for this. It is interesting to speculate on how this happened. At some point our proto-hominin ancestors connected several dots about the transformative impact of fire on foods such as meat, nuts, seeds, and tubers. Perhaps scavenging soon after a fire provided experience with at least partially cooked meat and roots and cracked nuts. Developing a preference for such food sources, our proto-hominin ancestors, likely beginning with female preferences and mate choices, opened the door on access to new sources of high quality protein and caloric energy —precisely the food energy sources required to grow and fuel the brain. At some point, one or more groups recognized that fire was the key and that they could use fire to access the preferred foods, perhaps first by intentionally setting fires.

Our immediate proto-hominin ancestor, *Homo erectus*, is associated with the earliest evidence concerning intentional control and use of fire, over 750,000 years ago in Northern China. As carbon does not fossilize easily, finding earlier incontestable evidence of control of fire is challenging. Fossil evidence for *Homo erectus* itself extends back in time over 1.5 million years, so, it is likely this proto-hominin ancestor achieved control and use of fire well over a million years ago. The jump in cranial capacity and the presumed associated development of increased intellectual capacity and neural complexity from *Homo habilis* through *Homo erectus* to *Homo neanderthalensis* and *Homo sapiens* could only have been realized through sustained access to qualitatively superior nutrition, in all likelihood enabled through the control and intentional use of fire.

Cooking meat and plant material with fire unlocks enormous nutritional resources and benefits. Cooking gelatinizes meat collagen, enabling our proto-hominin ancestors with their dominant grinding teeth to consume much more meat than had been previously possible. Cooking denatures food proteins, making them much easier to digest efficiently and thoroughly. In addition to meat, cooking also softens other foods, especially those high in carbohydrates and starches, and in the process increases their digestibility. Thus, cooking provides a jumpstart on the efficient extraction of food nutrition, the condition required to grow and fuel the brain.

Becoming dependent on a cooked food diet also likely resulted in a couple of other notable changes for our proto-hominin ancestors. One is that the digestive tract shrunk notably. Shorter small intestines were required for the work of digesting and extracting nutrition from cooked food. Increased use of cooking and the related energy and nutrition extraction efficiencies would also have greatly reduced the amount of time proto-hominins had to spend foraging for and consuming food. This would leave much more time for social interaction, building social relationships, and nurturing physiologically immature infants. Cooking food would also likely have enhanced opportunities for and the necessity of cooperation and sociability within hominin groups (see Wrangham 2009).

Control and use of fire preceded by at least hundreds of thousands of years the technical ability to "make" fire at will (for example, using flints). Once fire dependent, our proto-hominin ancestors must have developed ways and means to keep fire going and available. This was accomplished well before the emergence of our species, *Homo sapiens*, in sub-Saharan Africa around 300,000 years or so ago. Anatomically, all *Homo* species have been fully bipedal with shared overall physiological characteristics, including an expanding cranial capacity that, by the time *Homo sapiens* emerges, has exceeded 1400 cubic centimetres. Ever more intensive emphasis on social relations stressing intra-group cooperation, sharing, and interaction has also become embedded in ever more complex neural connectivities, underwriting the development and emergence of the distinctive qualities that have translated into "becoming human."

As we've seen, the available material evidence indicates that becoming human was a gradual process stretched over a huge span of time. For example, the stone tool assemblages associated with the earliest of *Homo sapiens* fossils remain basically unchanged over the initial 150,000 years after our species appears. This is often referred to as the "sapiens paradox." Even though possessing a large and distinctive brain, little technical innovation and symbolic expression in material remains is evident over almost 50 percent of our species' known existence. While a curiosity, it is likely that this initial period featured further development of the neural connectivities that would eventually enable elaboration around 100,000 years ago of symbolic expression, including the development of speech.

These qualities include sentience (self-awareness), the cornerstone of consciousness, as well as the bewildering array of capacities and experiences ordinarily assayed as expressing emotions and intelligence, including speech. The full attainment of sentience and consciousness is often associated with evidence of symbolic expression in forms such as body adornments (e.g., shell necklaces) and painting (e.g., cave art). Perhaps the fullest expression in the available evidence of having arrived completely as human beings is the practice of burying the dead. Our species and associated *hominin* cognates are the only species that intentionally and ceremonially disposes of its dead. Whether through burials or other means, the intentional and ceremonial disposal of the dead expresses a deeply profound acknowledgement of the complex and meaningful social, personal, and emotional interconnectivity of the living and the deceased, often so meaningful that various grave goods were interred with the deceased. Intentional interments are associated in the evidence with *Homo neanderthalensis* disposals as well as those of *Homo sapiens*, meaning species in addition to *Homo sapiens* had attained similar levels of self-awareness and complexities of intra-group relations, likely extending back in time over 500,000 years or so.

Of course, consciousness and sentience have a sharp-edged underbelly: awareness of mortality both for oneself and for all others with whom one is connected. Ceremonial disposal of the dead says as much about the meanings for the living arising from awareness of mortality as it does about the connections experienced through life in relations between the living and the dead. Here we can also see a full expression of that cognitive, emotional, and social quality that in many ways distinguishes hominins, and particularly *Homo sapiens*, from all others – empathy. The capacity to relate to the experiences of similar beings in behavioural and emotional ways fully expresses the intensities and dynamics of the sociality and cooperation that mark the processes of becoming human and of being human. Behaving cooperatively, engaging socially, and expressing empathy are all core aspects of being a fully integrated participant within the social group and in social life.

Becoming human is a consequence of the interplay of biological and social processes that have enabled an essentially small-sized, slow-footed, less dimorphic ape to develop extremely sophisticated social, emotional, and cognitive capacities as the means to satisfy the food energy and reproduction requirements of life. It's a notable part of this story that it is likely that female preferences drove the selection and reproduction of desired anatomical and behavioural attributes, which, in turn, enhanced our ancestors' reproductive success as well as access to and consumption of food energy. It is likely that the female preference for socially cooperative behaviour and food/resource sharing behaviour would have diminished the usefulness and expression of male intra-group and inter-sex aggressivity (see Jones and Ratterman 2009; Small 1993). Common interest, mutual aid, and cooperation within large groups of proto-hominins positioned our ancestors to develop the means to become human cognitively, socially, and emotionally.

WHAT ABOUT CULTURE?

Understanding humanity's place in the biological universe is necessary to appreciating where we've come from and where we could be headed as a species. But biology is not destiny, and while the evolutionary path we've travelled provides the foundation for who we are and what we might do and become, this is true only in the narrowest sense. For example, as humans we cannot live without food or water, survive in a vacuum, or fly without technological assistance. Outside of these restrictions, there is an awful lot of possibility. The history of human habitation on this planet is defined by an incredible range in experiments in social, economic, political, and cultural life together, and it's important to recognize that the way our lives are organized now is only one possibility among many. While it often seems to us as though the social world we inhabit is normal, natural, and inevitable, that perception is the result of the powerful effects of being socialized into a given set of social relations, not the consequence of us tapping into some species-specific destiny that we are fulfilling (or not). Culture is a term often used as shorthand for all that humans do together outside of bare survival and the biological foundations and limits of our existence. At its most general we might think about culture as encompassing the worldviews and lifeways of self-consciously constituted human social groups. In other words, *culture* is the shared conceptual framework and corresponding material practices belonging to a group of people who understand themselves as a distinct collective.

At the beginning of this chapter, I list six basic premises relating to the study of humanity. The sixth premise relates specifically to culture, which I described as the "distinctive and complex forms of social relations, organization, and cooperation" humans have developed over time and space. This collective, social work of meaning-making is one of the essential, defining characteristics of humanity. Making meaning together isn't work that people do on the side of more important activities; it's central to them. As we saw in the exploration of our becoming human, the social and biological are not neatly separate spheres of life; they weave back and forth across each other. There is no way to understand how humans as a species have gotten where we are today without taking on this holistic perspective. Critically, this means that the common work of creating "distinctive and complex forms of social relations, organization, and cooperation" is something people do together rather than something we have or possess. Culture is more like making music together than putting on a coat. For it to exist, we must *do it* together instead of imagining we can just adorn ourselves with it.

The world we are born into is already a cultural space, but while we may be born into culture, we are not born with it. Enculturation is the process of learning the cultural codes appropriate to a given social context, a process that begins at birth but can also occur later in life if an individual transitions from one context to another. Unlike formal schooling, the process of learning culture is both ubiquitous and often informal and implicit. Children and other newcomers to a given society aren't given culture manuals, decoder rings, or flowcharts to figure out daily life. They are inducted into culture, first by kin and other caregivers and later by a wider range of people involved in the complex and unfolding process of bringing people into shared social, symbolic living spaces. Frequently, significant stages in achieving cultural competency are marked by what social scientists call "rites of passage," a term for symbolically significant events through which individuals are expected to pass in order to successfully take on new statuses, roles, responsibilities, and freedoms. Think everything from graduations, birthdays, and weddings to surviving in the bush for days entirely alone and unequipped and sports-team and fraternity hazing.

Culture is dynamic and differentiated. People struggle over it, and these struggles change and shape it. Sometimes these changes are driven by people trying to conserve, resist, or change the status quo. This is the work done by social movements, which we consider later in Chapter 8. Sometimes these changes are driven by forces, circumstances, and actors external to the prevailing social order that challenge its ability to continue with business as usual.

For example, gender roles in North America today are not the same as they were a century ago, and we can be assured that a century from now they will be different again. When significant numbers of women in the Global North entered the ranks of the waged workforce during World War II to keep the economy going, most did not do so with the consciously radical intention of smashing patriarchy and ending gender-based oppression. But the act of masses of women working for wages nonetheless produced profound reverberations within society, and when the war ended many women refused to be re-domesticated and return to the sphere of home and hearth. The entry of some women into the ranks of the waged working class did not translate into women's liberation in some unqualified way, but it did contribute to a fundamental shift in gender roles, the social division of labour, the economic land-scape, and more. It is a mistake to imagine culture as homogenous, timeless, and unconflicted. Like living ecosystems, a change in one area can produce unpredictable changes in others.

Culture is material and symbolic; it is the food we eat, the clothes we wear, the dwellings we inhabit, the media we consume, the technologies we make use of, and the physical way we shape and engage the world around us. It is also highly symbolic; it is concerned with the ways we organize our social relations — our relationships with other forms of life and the values and norms that underwrite our understand-ings, expectations, and experiences of reality. Anthropologist Clifford Geertz (1973) famously described culture as "webs of significance" that people spin and in which they are suspended. Geertz's web metaphor for culture points to both the central im-portance of the work of public, contextual meaning-making for human groups and the fact that people are the active agents carrying it out. It also draws our attention to the fact that while people make culture, we cannot possibly be aware of every strand of it or recall how and why it came into being.

Rejecting theories that locate culture as some kind of "'superorganic' reality with forces and purposes of its own" or the "the brute pattern of behavioral events we observe … in some identifiable community or other," Geertz urges us not to try to pin down some specific definition of it but to focus on what it means, what the sig-nificance of public acts of meaning-making are in a given context (1973, 10). The work of making meaning in society is something we are constantly engaged in and has been an enduring hallmark of the social life of *Homo sapiens* for hundreds of thousands of years. From ceremonial burials, body modifications, and cave paintings to viral memes, organized sport, and struggles over who we are and how we remem-ber our past, human societies are nothing if not meaning-making ecologies. This culture work is carried out relationally, is always in-progress, and is never free from challenge and contestation.

All this work of investing our collective social life with symbolic meaning is pro-foundly shaped by the way power is exercised and distributed in the social group. Culture work is in no way free from the relations of oppression, domination, and ex-ploitation that mark the larger social context in which it is situated. People fight over social values, norms, and roles. They work together for change and struggle against visions of society they disagree with. The work of social meaning-making is a site of power and struggle, and it is also the glue that binds us together in communities of shared significance.

Too often culture is discussed casually or in popular media as if it's a thing to which people belong, a force or structure that shapes people from the top-down and in uniform ways. In this view, our culture slots us into neat and discrete identities and social orders, separating us clearly from those who belong to other cultures. The problem with this understanding of culture is that it makes groups seem much more homogenous and the differences between them much harder, fixed, and unchanging than they really are. Part of this problem comes from the conflation of culture with nation-states and modern nationalism; in this way of thinking cultural identity and citizenship are frequently collapsed. While this certainly simplifies things, it also introduces all kinds of problems into our ability to understand what culture is and why it matters.

It's obviously important that people invest meaning in and attribute significance to our social activity. We spend all kinds of time and effort telling stories, caring for each other, preparing and sharing food, and producing value through our labour. We probably spend an equivalent amount of time and effort discussing what it all means, what these activities could and should look like, and what kind of society they should contribute to. It isn't a one-way street between social organization and activity and culture work either. We don't go about carrying out our social activities and then map meaning on to them retroactively. We don't begin by doing and then move to thinking, nor do we move from thinking to doing. Our social activity and our culture work run through and are bound up with each other. The way we organize gender relations, distribute authority, settle disputes, and divide labour is also about the way we understand all these things and their importance. What kinds of work are most valued or degraded and why? Who does them and why? Which presentations of gender count as normal and acceptable and which do not? What counts as wealth and value? Why? What do we do with people who violate our norms and values? Who gets to decide what is normal and valuable? Who enforces these standards, with what tools, and with what consequences? Activity and meaning-making are clearly not separate.

This work of collective meaning-making that we call culture is most real and significant at the level of living relationships and social contexts. It makes sense that people who encounter each other with fair regularity work out forms of social relations, organization, and cooperation, and the symbolic orders that correspond to them, in the course of living together. When we pass these socio-symbolic codes on intergenerationally, they become culture, webs of significance that connect people to each other across time and space. This doesn't have to be a purely physical phenomenon, as digital media demonstrates, people make cultural meaning in virtual spaces and encounters too. The advent of the printing press in Europe in the sixteenth century similarly allowed for the possibility of widely dispersed people (or at least the literate local elites) reading, thinking, and feeling in common for the first time in a mass, reproducible way. By the same token, oral traditions vastly predate the printed word and have served as vital and robust vehicles for the geographical and temporal transmission of memory, meaning, and identity.

But there is something different, and decidedly more problematic, about trying to line culture up with the borders of modern nation-states. Political borders map very poorly onto the dynamics of culture as lived into being by human collectives. Nation-states are a form of political organization that has emerged only in the last few centuries, and while they dominate the global political stage today, they are far from the only way humans have organized their political lives. They are not simply scaled-up versions of some primordial, authentic, and grounded social life; they are political and bureaucratic institutions driven by specific interests and operating in the service of particular agendas, and their animating ethic is the centralization of political power and authority.

The borders of modern states have been imposed on pre-existing human groups with their own identities and forms of social, political, and economic organization. The modern nation-state of Canada, for example, was created as a product of British and French *colonialism* and the genocidal dispossession of Indigenous nations of their traditional territories and lifeways. All *settler-colonial* nation-states are products of this process of state formation, but that's not to say other states are not marked by similar forms of violence, displacement, and marginalization.

It's something of a national pastime for Canadians to fret over what Canadian culture is, particularly when set against the United States. But these settler-colonial anxieties are far less interesting than the recognition that Canada itself is an imposition on territory that was originally – and continues to be — home to diverse Indigenous nations. Where do these other lifeways and worldviews fit into the vexed narrative of Canadian cultural identity? And what of the waves of immigrants brought into the Canadian state, many of whom helped to build the very infrastructure of the state and yet are not regarded as part of the Canadian national identity as anything more than representations of its "multiculturalism"? Clearly, the nation-state isn't synonymous with culture.

The rise of modern nationalisms – the belief in specific, exclusionary, and authorized identities tied to the state and its true people – doesn't emerge from the ground up and the context of people's lives together. They emerge as ideological projects meant to bind people, most of whom will never encounter one another, to political, social, and economic projects driven by the power relations at the heart of a specific order. Benedict Anderson (2006) famously called this kind of collective identity tied to modern states *imagined communities* that serve to bind people together and to a specific set of interests through the use of various techniques and technologies. These imagined communities aren't spontaneous; they are elite-driven projects that are transmitted through a variety of forms, including national spectacles and holidays, standardized official languages, official histories of the nation and its founding, monuments and commemorations, sport, arts, school curricula, and so much more.

They are also sites of contestation and alternative-building as a diversity of individuals and collectives struggle over identity, memory, and the future from the ground up.

CONCLUSION

What makes us human? As this chapter explores, there is no one answer to this question and humanity remains a work-in-progress socially and biologically. From an evolutionary perspective, we are not even an end point in a journey; we are merely one possibility and stop along the way. What is so compelling in exploring the evolutionary journey of our species is the way the social and the biological intertwine and spin off each other. While there are core physiological changes that were critical to our ancestors becoming what we understand as human (bipedalism, large and complex brain, dexterous hands and diverse teeth), these changes were propelled by and feed into an ongoing experiment in sociality.

If we think about our biology from a species perspective, we might imagine it as a floor on which we collectively stand. That floor is our most fundamental capacities and our most basic needs. Beyond that foundation lies a vast expanse of possible ways that we might live together on this planet. Some of these ways are profoundly oppressive and exploitative; others point in the direction of collective liberation. We cannot tell one from the other by turning to convenient rationalizations steeped in pseudo-scientific myth-making that excuse domination, violence, exploitation, oppression, hierarchy, and inequality.

Those who seek to dismiss the possibility of building more just, liberated, and peaceful societies often tell stories about human nature that begin by accepting the status quo as normal and even inevitable. They then work backward from this premise, scouring for evidence of this naturalness in our evolutionary journey. Such accounts mystify social problems in a sloppy and simplistic biological idiom. They also betray a basic misunderstanding of how evolution works. We cannot trace any specific social behaviour, relationship, or institution to any specific gene. In fact, scientists are still puzzling out the complex relationship between phenotype (observable traits), our genetic information (genotype), and environmental factors. We are not simply unmediated expressions of our genetics; if that were the case social life would be much more uniform. As we discuss in chapters to come, the real danger is that social injustice and systemic violence, oppression, and exploitation are made to seem natural and normal when rendered in this supposedly authoritative scientific discourse. Not only is it bad science; it is bad science in the service of domination.

And what of culture? Making meaning is one of the defining traits of humanity whether in the form of cave painting, social roles and norms, high fashion, language, storytelling, systems of belief (religious and not), and more. But, as with our biology, problems quickly become evident when we try to impose this concept simplistically and monolithically on our social experiences. There are real problems with seeing culture as something that belongs to a neatly bounded and clearly defined group of people – and, ultimately, a thing to which people themselves belong.

One of the biggest problems is that this perspective reinforces a timeless, homogenous, unchanging, and monolithic sense of who other people are, what they do, and why they do it. This leads to easy and often problematic stereotypes of those others that become the basis for our actions in the world. People come together and make complex, symbolic, and diverse forms of social meaning and practice that can draw them together and distinguish them from others who practice and believe in different things. They devise frameworks for understanding the world, develop forms of organization that allow them to act together in a variety of common pursuits, elaborate belief systems that conceptualize what is good and true, and create a vast array of ways to communicate all this. This is what culture is — frustratingly ephemeral and manifestly concrete and ever-present all at once.

If we recall Clifford Geertz's description of culture as "webs of significance" that people weave themselves and in which they are suspended, we can study what these webs mean, how they're woven, and why they matter. As we explore in Chapter 2, our ways of coming to know the world are never free of the power relations, assumptions, and interests that advance them. This doesn't make them bad necessarily, but it certainly means they are partial, imperfect, and power laden. All systems of knowledge and their associated techniques and technologies are products of the context from which they arise.

We can study culture without treating it as if it is some mysterious force pulling people's strings or collapsing it into the system of nation-states that maps the world politically. Culture is run through by systems of power and wrapped up in relations of domination, oppression, and exploitation just as much as it can be a source of solidarity, resilience, and liberation. The socio-symbolic capacity for collective meaning-making and the material practices that accord with it are vital aspects of our existence as a species on this planet. Humanity's incredibly diverse and complex experiments in sociality would be impossible without culture as a tissue connecting and differentiating us. Culture is not destiny; it is not a discrete category into which we can simply drop masses of people for the sake of easy generalizations about the world. This means our work in trying to understand it and what it does in the world has to be careful, critical, and richly contextualized.

KEY CONCEPTS

biological determinism: the belief that our genes and physiology determine individual behaviour and mass social experience. Biological determinists interpret every social problem, issue, and activity as little more than an effect of the supposed underlying human compulsion to carry on our genetic material through offspring.

colonialism: the process of one people or power establishing control over another people and their territory with the aim of securing enduring relations of exploitation.

culture: the shared conceptual framework and corresponding material practices belonging to a group of people who understand themselves as a distinct collective.

ecology: the web of relationships between an organism and its environment.

evolution: the changes in heritable characteristics in biological populations over generations. While the idea that one type of biological organism could descend from another stretches back millennia, the contemporary formulation of the theory of evolution is attributed to Charles Darwin (1809–1882) in his famous work *On the Origin of Species* (1859).

Global North: less of a geographical concept than one denoting countries that share a set of socio-political and economic characteristics. The Global North is made up of the richest industrial capitalist countries, most of which are also liberal democracies. This group includes Australia, Canada, all of Europe, Israel, Japan, New Zealand, Russia, Singapore, South Korea, Taiwan, the United Kingdom, and the United States.

holistic perspective: seeking to understand discrete phenomena relationally and in context rather than by recourse to single causes.

hominid: the group including all modern and extinct great apes (humans, orangutans, chimpanzees, bonobos, gorillas, and all immediate ancestors).

hominin: the group including modern humans, extinct human species, and our immediate ancestors but excluding the other great apes.

Homo sapiens: a Latin term meaning "wise human" and referring to all modern humans.

imagined communities: a term coined by political scientist Benedict Anderson (2006) to analyze modern nationalism. Anderson's basic idea is that the nation is an imagined community because in even the smallest of them most members will never meet each other, yet they share an idea of belonging to the same community.

recent single-origin hypothesis: the scientific consensus today that humans (*Homo sapiens*) originated in Africa and dispersed from there to populate the world.

settler-colonialism: a form of colonialism where settlers from the colonizing power seek to replace the Indigenous population through genocide and forced assimilation and secure possession of territory. It is best understood as a form of colonialism where the settler never leaves.

social Darwinism: the ideological attempt to justify the socio-political and economic status quo was coined by English philosopher and political theorist Herbert Spencer (1820–1903), who took ideas from Darwin's evolutionary theory and used them in an attempt to justify existing forms of injustice and inequality.

social determinism: the belief that social environment determines individual behaviour and mass social experience. For social determinists, there is no "human nature" outside of our sociality, and all our activity, potentials, problems, and issues come back to the social context.

sociality: the capacity of individuals in an animal population to associate in social groups and form cooperative societies.

2

DOING SOCIAL RESEARCH

Intentionally Exploring Social Life

What comes to mind when you read the word "research"? Libraries? Laboratories? Sophisticated technical equipment? Elaborate experiments? Experts in lab coats? While we are taught to associate research with credentialed experts, sophisticated equipment and techniques, and highly specialized knowledge, at its most basic level it is the process of critically and rigorously inquiring into the world. While people may think that experiments, labs, and hypothesis-testing constitute research, much research doesn't involve any of these things. Research about social problems and issues, the focus of this chapter and much of this book, happens out in the world and in the messiness of people's daily lives. There is no "controlled environment," no "control group," and no hypothesis to prove or disprove. Social research conducted by anthropologists, sociologists, and practitioners in other related disciplines often explores phenomena that are complex, not clearly bounded, and experienced by people as part of their lived realities. Social research is not simply about describing phenomena like poverty, police violence, or homelessness. It examines what brings them into being, what their significance is for individuals and society, and how we might address them or, better yet, change the relations and structures that cause them to exist. At its best and most grounded, social research aims to take people's realities seriously.

While the world around us can seem entirely natural, this is the result of a process of socialization that begins at birth and is dedicated to fitting each of us into dominant social relations and providing us with the script we need to navigate them. However, we should not mistake the feeling of naturalness of the society we were raised in – if we do indeed feel it – for its reality. Accepting the status quo as natural is easier if we happen to occupy a position of relative power and privilege because no one wants to imagine their comfort is the result of unjust and exploitative relations. There are lots of problems with seeing our society as natural but not least is that we view every issue through the lens of our own experience and ideological perspective, regardless of whether we know anything about the matter or have any stake in its outcome. Even worse, the violence and exploitation that are woven into the structures of many societies are made to seem inevitable and their victims and beneficiaries as deserving. Unless we bring our capacities for critical, grounded, rigorous inquiry to bear on social phenomena, we run the considerable risk of accepting social relations that prey on the life, labour, and dignity of others.

In a very real sense, research is going on all the time and all around us. People do research whenever they have to figure something out that they do not already know the answer to. Whether it's a personal health issue, travel plans, accessing public services, or any number of other everyday issues, the process of formulating a question, gathering and analyzing data, and synthesizing an answer is the backbone of the research process. This isn't to say that all processes of inquiry are the same or that finding solutions to everyday problems is identical to running a large-scale research project investigating a pressing social problem. It is critical to recognize that simply because we all live in and help reproduce society does not mean that all our impressions of it are accurate or equally valid. There is a huge gulf between our individual preferences, opinions, and experiences, and the systematic, rigorous study of a host of phenomena, many of which we may never have experienced personally or know anything significant about.

I can drive a car or use a computer without having any understanding of how either machine works, and I can live as a member of society without understanding the power relations that drive it. This is not about uncritically or absolutely elevating certain forms of knowledge or practice above others; it is about recognizing the contextual nature of all knowledge practices and understanding the relationship between knowledge and technique in any given context. Dominant ways of exploring and making sense of the world – what in the West is called "science" – are both powerful and shaped by power relations. No scientific technique or technology allows us to simply peer into the nature of reality and see the truth of whatever phenomenon we might be interested in. Every form of knowledge, technique, and technology is part of a process of interpreting the phenomena we discover in our explorations. Since these forms of knowledge, techniques and technologies, and the interpretations of the world we derive from them are powerful and authoritative, shaped by power, and vested with specific interests, we need to understand and critically unpack all of this if we're not to simply reproduce the status quo and the relations of domination, exploitation, and oppression that constitute it.

Rather than seeing research as something only done by experts, it is important to acknowledge that we are all researchers any time we choose to seriously explore our world. Members of social movements, for example, do research as they struggle to understand and change the social relations and institutions responsible for inequality, exploitation, and oppression. Research isn't just about describing the world; it's about critically and rigorously exploring it so we can act effectively in it.

This does not mean research or knowledge is "objective," "value-free," or "neutral." As we explore in this chapter, from its inception, what we understand today as the scientific method has not been some universal set of truth-uncovering practices but an approach to inquiry and knowledge production with deep roots in a particular historical, cultural, and political-economic context. This recognition does not mean the scientific method or the extension of the Western European Scientific Revolution into the Western European Enlightenment were "bad" or "wrong," but it does mean these forms of knowledge-making are partial, limited, and connected to powerful social forces and institutions. What might be learned and achieved by bringing them into dialogue with other ways of learning about and exploring the world?

WAYS OF KNOWING AND THEIR CONSEQUENCES

As a starting point to any discussion about how and why we do social research, it's vital to acknowledge that we do not all understand and experience the world in the same way and that this has dramatic consequences for the ways we explore it. It is easy enough to acknowledge differences in perspectives between people on any given issue, particularly in capitalist societies where our ability to consume and the brand choices we make are trumpeted as identity-defining activities. Differences in opinion on a host of social issues from climate change to marriage equality to sexual violence to poverty are even encouraged so long as they are figured as "opinions" and not challenges to the interests of the powerful and the smooth operation of the status quo. But the kind of differences I'm pointing to here go much deeper and are not simply interpersonal in nature; they are systemic and power laden.

As we discuss in Chapter 1, parcelling the world into discrete cultural groups may be convenient, but it also imposes an artificial and problematic map of supposedly clear, discrete, timeless, and homogenous collective identities on people, particularly those seen as less than modern, rational, developed, and enlightened. This doesn't mean that differences between individuals and groups aren't real; humanity shares a world filled with diverse experiments in ways of living together. The problem is not with individual or collective identity and difference; the problem lies with who gets to name, study, and make sense of difference and who gets named, studied, and made sense of. Whose experience gets figured as the baseline, the "normal" against which other experiences are measured?

The practice of producing knowledge does not occur in a vacuum; it's deeply shaped by and essential to the power relations that structure our societies. The forms of knowledge-making that seem so dominant, powerful, and natural to many of us are rooted in specific histories, worldviews, values, and assumptions about truth and reality. This is especially true for those of us living in societies in and identifying with the civilizational project of "the West."

Theories about what is real, what the nature of being is, and what makes up reality are known as ontologies. Theories about what we can know, what knowledge is, and how we can gain access to it are known as epistemologies. No individual, collective, institution, or society functions without a theory of what is real and what is true and knowable. Yet these theories are so fundamental to human societies and our socialization into them that they recede into the background and become "common sense." The danger of this is that we run the risk of forgetting that our ontology and epistemology are only one possible way of knowing the world among many. When we posit our own theory of being and knowledge as universal, any other is seen not only as incorrect but as an existential challenge that must be confronted and overcome. After all, one theory of what is real and knowable cannot be universally true and admit that other such theories are equally valid.

As we discuss later in this chapter, this is not an argument for descending into total relativism where any position is just as legitimate as any other. I may indeed be free to have my own opinions about any number of issues or phenomena, but I must be able to convince others of their accuracy if I am going to move them to act. Assuming I am not an authoritarian bent on simply imposing my will on people, this means I need to offer evidence, analysis, and argument for my positions that others will accept, at least in part because they explain the phenomenon at hand in a convincing and robust way. This becomes more challenging when groups or individuals do not share the same perspective on what is real and what we can know. Nevertheless, some of the most interesting and productive opportunities for knowledge production emerge out of encounters between ways of knowing that seem at first to be totally at odds with one another. When we shut out other ways of knowing because they clash with our own, we fall easily into dogmatism, reproducing our own assumptions about the world because they serve dominant interests and sacrificing important opportunities for learning about each other and the world we share.

This is much more than a plea for diversity, tolerance, and understanding of a multiplicity of ways of exploring and coming to know the world. The real cutting edge here is that when one specific way of knowing the world, or *paradigm* (see Kuhn and Hacking 2012), is elevated to the status of universal truth, it denies not only other ways of knowing but the ways of life and the people with whom they are associated. In a world where capitalism has mapped coordinates of value through the lens of profit and accumulation on a global scale, claims to know who and what counts as real, worthy, and important of consideration are not neutral and entail profound consequences. For example, to a capitalist corporation involved in fossil fuel extraction, wealth is to be found in the fossil fuel itself, which needs to be located, extracted,

kind of what happened with christianism that shut down any other religious belief

transported, refined, and sold for profit to be realized. But what of the ecology that is disrupted and even destroyed in the process of extracting the fuel? What about the life – human and not – that inhabits the environment? What about the diverse lifeways that are implicated in that ecology and are threatened by its despoliation? "Wealth" is not some universal, unchanging concept; it is grounded in the systems of knowledge-making and social relations that people use to build their social worlds.

As Cree scholar Shawn Wilson (2009) argues, social research isn't about a thinking, empowered subject exploring an inanimate world of objects; it is about building and maintaining relationships between those involved in and impacted by the research process. This does not mean doing research that only says what people want to hear, far from it. It does mean that social research is not like research in a laboratory. It often involves and requires a willingness on the part of the researcher to personally get to know the people and contexts involved in the research and to be affected and even transformed by the research process itself. Wilson writes about an Indigenous research paradigm specifically, but his analysis of the process holds for other research paradigms as well, including the scientific one.

There are other approaches to research, particularly from feminist and radical political perspectives, that also emphasize relationship-building and social change as an integral part of the research process. Wilson's emphasis on relationships is significant in another sense too. He draws attention to the deep connections between the way research is practised and the worldview and value system that guides it. It's common to discuss the way one's epistemology (theory of knowledge) affects one's *methodology* (theory of study, how knowledge about the world is gained) in any given discipline and in any given research project. Wilson expands this to include a consideration of ontology and *axiology* (theory of value and morals, what it means to ethically move through the world). The Indigenous research paradigm Wilson explores highlights the reciprocal relationships between what we believe to be real (ontology), what we believe to be true and knowable (epistemology), what we believe to be right and ethical (axiology), and what we believe to be capable of investigating our reality (methodology). This relationship is of course also at work within any research paradigm, even the scientific model many take for granted as a bias-free way to explore the world and gain knowledge about it. But there is nothing value- or bias-free about any theory of what exists, what is valuable, what counts as knowledge, and what constitutes legitimate inquiry into it all.

THE EUROPEAN ENLIGHTENMENT, COLONIALISM, AND THE AGE OF EMPIRE

All knowledge-making practices are contextual and shaped by power relations. What context and power relations are most relevant to understanding how social science is carried out in the West today? Both Canada and the United States are settler-colonial nation-states, socio-political orders imposed by force, deception, and genocide on the Indigenous nations who inhabited these territories for millennia prior to the arrival of European colonizers and settlers. To understand our current context, we have to look back five centuries to Europe, where the feudal world was giving way to a massive social, political, and economic transformation that would eventually coalesce into capitalism. This isn't to suggest that capitalism is the most important system in shaping people's lived realities, but our ways of knowing the world are deeply intertwined with the ways we seek to make use of it. We discuss capitalism in greater depth in Chapter 7; the roots we're excavating now lie elsewhere.

As *feudalism* was reaching its limits in Europe, the elites sought to cobble together new ways of extracting wealth. Feudalism wasn't only an economic system, it was also a social and political order steeped in medieval, Christian ways of understanding the world. It was predicated on a fixed and unchanging order ordained by God and administered by nobles. However, new ways of exploiting land and labour required new ways of knowing the world. New forms of enclosure, exploitation, and wealth accumulation required understanding the world as a place in which humanity could actively intervene. The Western European Scientific Revolution is often narrated as a critical moment in human history that represents the triumph of rationality over superstition. It was also a moment where the world and its inhabitants were radically "disenchanted" (Horkheimer and Adorno 2002), separated from the religious worldview that provided order and meaning, and reinterpreted in light of a new ethic that not only opened paths to new freedoms and forms of understanding but also new forms of exploitation and domination.

The *European Enlightenment* is best understood as a social transformation spanning the seventeenth and eighteenth centuries in Western Europe. It extended and deepened many of the core principles animating the Scientific Revolution, which began in the sixteenth century. The period marks a series of profound changes in the fabric of European societies, including challenges to understandings of how the world and the universe are ordered, the nature and bases of political and moral authority, socio-political and economic systems, and the capacity of people to explore, make sense of, and exercise agency in the world. For those of us living in parts of the world today that are offshoots of European colonialism and empire-building, this historical moment marks the rise not only of what we would recognize as modern science but the social and political orders and institutions that we often take for granted.

None of this is to suggest that colonialism and imperialism are uniquely European or modern processes. For example, in the so-called "new world," both the Aztec and the Inca were imperial powers well before the arrival of European colonizers, conquering and absorbing an array of other peoples into their political and economic orders. There are also many permutations of colonialism, as many and as diverse as there are contexts to inhabit and people to enact them (see Veracini 2016). While it's common to think about European powers colonizing the rest of the world, the Arabs, Greeks, Egyptians, Persians, and Romans, amongst many others, established extensive colonies hundreds and even thousands of years before the birth of the modern era. While it's important to understand the specificity of our modern era, it is a profound error to see the dynamics animating it as unique.

Nevertheless, the Western European Scientific Revolution and Enlightenment mark the threshold onto what many consider to be the modern world. In the standard version of this intertwined tale, the Scientific Revolution and the Enlightenment are a pathway to reason and understanding replacing dogma and superstition. This is the story of progress liberating us from the shackles of tradition. Modern science comes to life in Europe during this period alongside modern forms of exploring and organizing social, political, and economic life. Notions of an unchanging, divinely ordered world where everything has its place are supplanted by new understandings of time as progressive and historical, with the world a place that can be understood and shaped by people.

This simple story of progress also has its dark side. As critical theorist Walter Mignolo (2011) argues, modernity and coloniality are two sides of the same coin. In the words of postcolonial scholar Gurminder Bhambra, "The world-historical processes of dispossession, appropriation, genocide, and enslavement" are "central to the emergence and development of modernity and its institutional forms," including the Western university and its academic disciplines (2016, 962). Emancipatory rhetoric aside, we need to understand that not all populations counted as "people," particularly as the age of European colonialism and *imperialism* truly accelerated in the sixteenth century. Whether we're talking about technology, the infrastructure of industrial society, biomedicine, economics, or politics, the defining elements of modern life are products of specific ways of producing knowledge about the world. These practices of knowledge making were deeply wrapped up in the Western European inter-elite scramble for land and labour on an increasingly global scale.

To put it simply, a world that was non-capitalist and organized around many civilizational centres prior to 1500 CE became increasingly capitalist and dominated by Western civilization for the five centuries after (Mignolo 2011). The tip of this global transformation, beginning in earnest in the sixteenth century, was Western European colonialism and inter-imperial squabbling. This is not to claim exceptionally laudatory or heinous status for the power players of this era or their descendants. It's merely the necessary work of excavating the roots of how we came to be who we are now. In the Western European heart of this burgeoning global order, as feudalism gives way to capitalism and the nobility to the bourgeoise (those who own society's means of production) as society's dominant class, forms of knowledge making most appropriate to this emerging order are invested in, developed, and authorized. While there is so much to unpack and explore here, for our purposes the most important point is that the modern age was ushered in by Western European colonialism, imperialism, and newly emerging capitalism. This would powerfully shape ways of understanding and acting in the world.

Running the risk of oversimplification, we can map the development of new ways of exploring and understanding the world in light of the needs of a new system of exploitation, enclosure, and wealth accumulation. As Gurminder Bhambra, Dalia Gebrial, and Kerem Nişancıoğlu argue, the Western university was a key site through which colonialism and colonial knowledge was "produced, consecrated, institutionalised and naturalised" (2018, 5). In the colonial heartland, universities were sites for the development of the intellectual architecture of colonialism, propagating racist theories and ideologically justifying dispossession and domination in addition to training would-be colonial administrators. In colonized territories, European institutions of higher education became an "infrastructure of empire," spreading Eurocentric forms of knowledge, suppressing Indigenous ones, and training a class of native collaborators. Not only this, universities in both the colonies and the colonial centres of power were literally built and sustained by the spoils of enslavement, dispossession, and plunder. Lest we imagine this as nothing more than sins of the past, even after the fall of Western European empires and their colonial projects, the institution of the university remains intimately tied to the enduring power relations that birthed them. The content of curricula, who teaches and researches, who gets taught about and researched, disciplinary conventions, and the interests centred and served remain thoroughly steeped in the legacies of colonialism and empire. The phrase "knowledge is power" may be a bit of a cliché, but it is nonetheless true that how we come to know the world is intimately wrapped up in how we see ourselves living and acting within it and what the material conditions of our power and privilege are.

GENOCIDE, DISPOSSESSION, AND SCIENCE

The story of Francis Bacon and his theory of "just war" is an important and illustrative example. Sir Francis Bacon (1561–1626) was an English philosopher, politician, and scientist who is widely regarded as the founder of the modern scientific method. He was also a central figure in developing a theory of "just war," which can be waged against all those "unavowed by God," in his text *An Advertisement Touching a Holy War* (1622). In the early seventeenth century, at a particularly delicate moment in England's history, nobles and the king struggled over control of wealth and political authority. With the threat of civil war looming, Bacon stepped in to offer both a release valve for intra-elite competition and a justification for the terror and brutality at the heart of colonial dispossession and imperial expansion. In this work, Bacon employs a notion of "monstrousness," developed in his scientific theories to construct a list of people who can be killed without offending Christian sensibilities. This list included Indigenous people, dispossessed commoners, women rebels, bandits and pirates, heretical Christians, and assassins.

Bacon's *Advertisement* was cast in mythological proportions. The European elite were represented as the mighty Hercules bringing order to the world while the monstrous, many-headed hydra stood in for all those resisting domination and exploitation (Linebaugh and Rediker 2000). Essentially, Bacon wrote the first modern justification of genocide. Each of the collective identities named in Bacon's *Advertisement* represents a threat to the imperial ambitions of England's elite and so must be neutralized to bring the new world into being. Indigenous people and commoners resist being dispossessed of territory and the communal lifeways to which it is connected. Women lead rebellions and food riots as the commons are enclosed as a critical step in the transition from feudalism to capitalism. Pirates and bandits threaten the circulation of currency and commodities and interfere with new forms of wealth accumulation. Christian heretics refuse to recognize church hierarchy and authority over religious experience and practise forms of egalitarian collective life that stand in opposition to elite authority. Assassins simply figured as quintessential boogeymen in the imaginations of kings and nobles, a shadowy threat plaguing elites otherwise shielded from the brutality and violence of Europe's transition to capitalism. Bacon's book offered a rationalist defence of genocide in the service of dominant interests, an example of scholars making knowledge useful to power in ways that continue today.

A similar narrative is present in the debate that took place in Valladolid, Spain, in 1550 between the Dominican friar Bartolomé de las Casas and the jurist Juan Ginés de Sepúlveda. The question they were considering was whether Indigenous people in the Americas were "natural slaves" or not. Troubled by reports of widespread and systematic brutality levelled at Indigenous people by Spanish colonists, the

Vatican organized this debate to provide a definitive line on the colonial question. If Indigenous people were "natural slaves," they had no souls to save and so colonizers could do whatever they wanted with them with no spiritual or legal consequences. If, on the other hand, they had souls, then they could be converted to Christianity and it was against God's law to dispossess, terrorize, and kill them. The Spanish colonial system depended fundamentally on the labour extracted by force from Indigenous people. The stakes of this debate, while dressed in trappings of religiosity and moral philosophy, were just as much about the material relations of exploitation, enclosure, and wealth extraction that made the colonial enterprise so lucrative and important.

The result of the debate was unclear with both sides claiming victory and neither seeing the outcomes they desired. While new laws were issued that were supposed to restrict some of the worst abuses of the colonial system Spain implemented in the Americas, the real impacts of these reforms were negligible given the distance between the colonies and the Spanish court. At the same time, it was clear that the issue of the rights of colonized peoples couldn't simply be dismissed. One of the most troubling outcomes of the debate was the eventual substitution of enslaved people stolen from Africa for Indigenous people in the colonial system. If European elites were uncertain about the humanity of Indigenous people, they seemed far less troubled by the brutalization of Africans through the trans-Atlantic slave trade.

One final story is worth relating here. As Marxist-feminist scholar Silvia Federici (2003) documents, the idea that the genocide, dispossession, and domination of Indigenous people by European colonial projects was the result of good faith misunderstandings or mistakes is a convenient myth that legitimizes the ongoing violence of settler-colonialism. Federici's focus is on the witch hunts that swept Western Europe from the fourteenth to eighteenth centuries. She documents how the terror techniques used by European colonizers against Indigenous people to conscript their labour, dispossess them of territory and wealth, and destroy their resistance were first developed and honed in the witch hunts. Historians (typically white, typically male) have largely written off the European witch hunts as the spontaneous results of superstition and crisis. Federici shows how they were a meticulously organized campaign directed by church and state and aimed at subverting a broad-based people's resistance to new forms of exploitation and domination.

To pull this resistance up by the roots, people's sense of solidarity and common ground had to be destroyed by encouraging them to blame not the elites but each other for their plight. The scale itself is staggering, with some estimating that over three centuries more than a million women were tortured and killed in the course of the witch hunts (Federici 2003). The elaborate propaganda, juridical, and carceral system required to sustain what should be known as the "women's holocaust" belies the spontaneity thesis. It also demonstrates how early modern forms of knowledge making, governance, and political and moral authority were central to making this mind-boggling violence possible.

There was an elaborate, meticulous, and refined brutality to the witch hunts that was exported to the "new world" as part of the colonial extraction of wealth and labour. We might think about this protracted process as something like a science of oppression in the service of exploitation. On both sides of the Atlantic, the Inquisition developed elaborate tests – often involving torture – to determine the guilt or innocence of suspected witches, heathens, and heretics (Federici 2003; Mies 1986). Rather than spontaneous eruptions of superstition that would fade under the light of reason cast by the Enlightenment, the witch hunts and the terror techniques the Inquisition exported to the Americas were intimately bound up with the creation of this new world order.

Today, this same logic is replicated in modern militaries' counter-insurgency doctrines as a critical technique for making the world safe for capital and powerful interests (see Price 2011). What this history shows is that the stories we tell about the world and those we share it with are never free of the power relations and vested interests at work in the social order we are embedded in. The forms of inquiry and knowledge production that we call science, including social science, are not free of this. Despite tales to the contrary, the Western European Enlightenment and the modern world it helped usher in did not result in a definitive move from backwardness and superstition to rationality and progress. Indeed, as these three short histories demonstrate, oppression and exploitation do not fade from the world with the rise of science. Instead, the idiom through which they are rationalized changes in accordance with these new norms. From the beginning, our forms of inquiry and knowledge production have been bound up with how we understand reality, our place in it, and what we want to do in and with it.

This complex interplay of ontology, epistemology, axiology, and methodology, set against the backdrop of a social world shaped by power relations and vested interests, is not an artifact of the past but a dynamic very much alive today. While it is easy and often tempting to look back in history and feel satisfaction that we know better now or dismiss such examples as judging the past by the standards of our present, these three examples show us a different truth. Authorized forms of exploring and coming to know the world are always bound up with the power relations and institutions that give them legitimacy. While it is easy to get lost in hyperbolic moralistic debates about "good" and "bad" research, researchers, and the knowledge and outcomes produced, they lead us away from the really important issues at stake and the questions that need to be asked. Whose life, reality, and interests are advanced by any given way of exploring the world? What interests are served by the ways knowledge is produced and the ends to which it is put? Who gets to arbitrate truth? Who gets to study and who gets studied? Why? And for what purposes?

A BRIEF HISTORY OF ANTHROPOLOGY AND SOCIOLOGY

Since the academic disciplines of anthropology and sociology are foundational points of reference in this book, it's useful to know something of their roots and development. Rather than telling a too-easy story about the "great men" of the disciplines and their intellectual biographies as a way of tracing the development of anthropology and sociology, it is considerably more useful to set these key figures, their ideas, and the development of their academic disciplines in a wider social and political context. While the university is often cast, romantically or disparagingly, as the ivory tower, a place removed from the messiness of daily life, the truth is that the university as an institution has always been connected to power. Whether as a place to cultivate social capital for society's elite, vocational training for the professional managerial class, or the research and development wing of corporate capital, the university, like other central institutions of modern society, is a key cog in the maintenance of the dominant order. This means that the interests and actors at the heart of that order also wield an awful lot of power within the university as an institution. This has direct consequences for everything from legitimate research topics to methodologies to funding and knowledge-communication models. This is not to say that this is all the university is, but we ignore the influence of these powerful interests at our peril.

Anthropology means "the study of humanity" and *sociology* "the study of the development, organization, and functioning of human society." Today these descriptions seem impossibly broad and ambitious but at the time of their emergence as fields of inquiry they reflected the modernist faith in exploring the world through the senses and systematically striving to make sense of it. By *modern* I'm referring to the historical age ushered in by the European Enlightenment, characterized by belief in reason, progress, and individualism and by the rise of the nation-state, capitalism, and the political institutions broadly associated with them. While the story that most often gets told about this period is that of the flowering of reason and social progress, neither are neutral or universal concepts. What they mean is shaped by those with the power to do so.

Just as the European Enlightenment challenged the conception of natural and social orders as divine and unchanging, the modern era it helped usher in wanted the world to be known, mapped, and quantified. This way of understanding the world in *empirical* and systematic fashion arose, not coincidentally, at a moment when new forms of extracting wealth and exploiting labour were being cobbled together. Indeed, the philosophical perspective known as *positivism*, which came to prominence in the nineteenth century, was ideally suited to a new era of enclosure, wealth accumulation, and profiteering. Positivism holds that truth and verifiable knowledge exist in the world as a consequence of natural and social laws and can be uncovered through empirical investigation and logical reasoning. Whatever the hierarchies and violence of feudal Europe, a world that was divinely ordained by God and whose nature was inherently mysterious and unknowable to humans was not a place in which everything was available for exploitation and commodification. Capitalism requires certainty and mastery over the world and its inhabitants; it demands a mapping of coordinates of value onto the world and all it holds in its quest for limitless profit-taking. Only a new kind of knowledge production could deliver this.

It's essential to recognize the difference between empiricism, the conviction that the world is knowable through sensory experience, and positivism, the belief that there are singular, eternal truths waiting to be discovered that are only knowable through sensory experience, reason, and logic. Empiricism remains an important principle at the heart of contemporary social research and a host of other scientific approaches to exploring the world and even the universe. As humans, we navigate and come to know the world through our senses, although rarely through them alone. Positivism asserts that only sensory experience, (Eurocentric) reason, and (Eurocentric) logic are capable of uncovering knowledge about reality. No other ways of knowing count. If empiricism remains important to research, positivism has not retained its pride of place, especially for the social sciences, where forms of knowledge making derived from the Western European Enlightenment and Scientific Revolution have had their monopoly on truth and rigorous inquiry challenged by a host of other perspectives from feminism to Indigenous research paradigms. Our various ways of knowing are never just about compiling random knowledge about the world; they shape and are shaped by how we interact with that world and what we want to get out of it. Maps, of whatever variety, are never made simply for the sake of it; they are made for the purposes of identification and navigation. But to what ends and in whose interests?

Both sociology and anthropology came into being as fields of study in the nineteenth century and have come to be considered foundational to the practice of social science more broadly. We can, of course, trace the roots of what could be broadly described as attempts to explore society back centuries and even millennia and to a diverse array of societies, but what we recognize as social science is of much more recent origin. In a sense, these academic disciplines are quintessentially modern, not only in their approach to inquiry and knowledge production but in the way they approach the process of making sense of the world and the issues and problems they seek to engage. If industrialization, the nation-state, imperialism, colonialism, capitalism, rationality, secularity, and progress were all pillars of modernity as a world-making project, they would similarly inform the academic disciplines that emerged from a central modern institution like the university.

Traditionally, anthropologists were concerned with the study of people outside the modern, capitalist, and industrializing North and West, while sociologists concerned themselves primarily with the study of complex societies within this space. Anthropology could be said to have been bound up with projects of imperial and colonial expansion and domination, studying "the other" in order to render them intelligible and so controllable to elites back home. Sociology, similarly, could be figured as a domestic form of inquiry focused on social order and control. It is incorrect and decidedly hyperbolic to regard either discipline simply as a tool of domination in the service of elite interests, but there is no escaping the entwinement between important institutions, authorized forms of knowledge, and dominant interests either then or now (see Asch 2015).

The capitalist element is also central here. The relationships between relations of production and consumption and the types of knowledge deemed useful to them are hardly incidental. What kinds of knowledge were most useful to dominant classes in the context of industrializing, mass, capitalist societies with imperial and colonial relations to other societies in other parts of the world? As social theorist Michel Foucault (1995) returned to time and again in his work, and as Marxist-feminist scholars such as Silvia Federici (2003) and Maria Mies (1986) and radical historians such as Peter Linebaugh and Marcus Rediker (2000) also emphasize, the rise of the modern world also marks the rise of a new kind of power and ways of exercising it.

If under feudalism nobles held the power of death over commoners who violated the king's law, the modern state is concerned with the way life is lived and social life is shaped. While feudalism was a system of exploitation and domination whereby elites lived off the labour of commoners in every sense, it was not terribly concerned with the nature of daily life. Peasant communities in feudal Europe were free of daily interference by nobles and their proxies, although they were totally subject to their power and absolutely had to provide wealth and labour to satisfy their obligations to their liege lords.

Modernity and the political rights and freedoms associated with it free people from feudalism's unaccountable and total power — the tyranny of the divine right of kings to rule as God's representatives on Earth — only to offer up a new, impersonal, and pervasive system of social control. Laws criminalizing vagrancy and joblessness were put into force even as peasants were driven off their communal land through a sweeping and violent process of enclosing and privatizing land to turn it into a source of profit-taking (Linebaugh and Rediker 2000). These poor laws were meant to secure a reliable, disciplined pool of exploitable labour. They were a critical tool in turning a communal peasantry into the new working class needed to build the infrastructure of the modern world, everything from ports to cities, factories to prisons.

This transition is about much more than what kind of work people are compelled to do to survive; it's also about the very nature of the work itself and the way it's organized. Under capitalism, owners no longer simply take a portion of what is produced by those labouring; they intervene in the labour process itself by buying a worker's ability to labour for a wage and bringing labour and capital together at a specific place and time to produce commodities and ultimately generate profit. Beyond the production process, this also has implications for how workers are trained, sustained, and disciplined. This implies a totally different context for organizing work and selling the commodities it produces. It also means that work and the capitalist's search for profit are taking place in a society very different than the feudal one.

Industrialization, urbanization, and mass societies organized as nation-states require different kinds of knowledge about the population inhabiting a certain territory than does feudalism. The dynamics of mass societies are fundamentally different from those that preceded them. Industrialization and urbanization give rise to social relations and, ultimately, to social problems that simply don't exist in societies of different natures and scales. Population management becomes central to the work of the modern state. No longer is power mainly about death. In the modern capitalist state, power over people and social life is manifested as control over the way life itself is lived and reproduced. To achieve this kind of pervasive, impersonal control also requires different kinds of knowledge about subject populations and the worlds they inhabit than do other forms of control.

So, what does this all mean for the development of anthropology and sociology? In the nineteenth century, both these disciplines emerge as something akin to an attempt to practise a science of society, to explain the forces, structures, and relations that produce the social in a decidedly empirical and positivist vein. Dividing their labour between the colonies (anthropologists) and the colonial-imperial centre (sociologists), the founders of these sister disciplines exhibited common interests in large-scale forces and processes shaping society.

For example, Karl Marx (1818–1883) focused on a dialectical understanding of society in which struggle between opposing interests and the classes they belong to is the motor of social change. Marx saw history progressing through this decidedly material struggle as new social relations emerge out of class struggle that is fundamentally about who controls society's productive capacities, who labours, and what the nature and ends of these relations of production are. Marx's contributions are incredibly wide and varied, but for our purposes what is important is that Marx's analytical perspective was vast, not narrow. He sought to advance a critical, comprehensive account of how human societies developed.

Similarly, early anthropologists, like Lewis Henry Morgan (1818–1881), sought to build explanatory models for how human societies grew and evolved over time, an evolution marked primarily by technological changes. Positing that all human societies developed along the same line stretching from savage to civilized, these *cultural evolutionists* attempted to articulate a single, comprehensive theory of human social progress. Their theories represented a significant advancement over previous ones that posited some human populations as fundamentally lower or less than others – or challenged their humanity entirely — since they conceived of all human populations as sharing the same developmental trajectory and potential. But if all humanity was conceived of as possessing a shared developmental capacity, what anthropologists would call the "psychic unity of humanity," human societies were still seen as occupying decidedly different points along this common trajectory. In other words, different human societies were seen by many early sociologists and anthropologists as potentially but not actually equally developed. This stagist developmental model retained the hierarchies and oppressive relations of the status quo, with Europeans posited as civilized, and racialized, colonized, and Indigenous people positioned as primitive (Asch 2015). This early social science challenged certain systemic prejudices while rationalizing others.

Another element binding this early science of society together was the conviction that society was more than the sum of individual interactions, that social phenomena had presence and significance beyond individuals' experiences of or roles in producing them. This may seem like a basic point, but it marked a significant step beyond an earlier focus on re-reading and synthesizing the accounts of explorers, travellers, missionaries, and merchants and formulating grand theories about other people and a diversity of social institutions and practices. The notion of exploring society as a thing in itself, produced by but not simply reducible to an amalgamation of human activity and consciousness, and with a logic and structure that could be rigorously explored and described, was a central element of this modern science of society. This broad perspective did not mean that its practitioners approached their object of study in the same way or with the same interests. Both Karl Marx and Max Weber (1864–1920) were interested in economics, social stratification, and inequality, but they approached their studies from different perspectives. While Weber was interested in the cultural and symbolic factors that sustained social phenomena and gave considerable weight to the meanings individuals attached to their own actions, Marx emphasized the centrality of the way societies organized their productive capacities and the relations of production that structured people's lived realities.

Marx's theories and careful empirical research were revolutionary in nature, and Weber's and the cultural evolutionists were not, yet the promise of a single, comprehensive, coherent account of human society is a root they shared and characterized much of the early work in both disciplines. In a similar vein Émile Durkheim (1858–1917) focused his own inquiries on the question of social solidarity in modern, mass societies. If so-called "simple" societies maintained their structure and integrity through "mechanical" processes such as kinship and traditions that give people a purpose and place in the social order, Durkheim argued that in modern, mass societies solidarity was an "organic" process driven by complex, large-scale institutions and diverse, impersonal social roles. In these modern societies, social cohesion was not a product of kin relations or tradition but an outcome of people's compulsory, anonymous reliance upon one another in an increasingly large-scale social system.

Durkheim was a proponent of the theory of *structural functionalism*, a perspective that would prove profoundly influential for both sociologists and anthropologists through the early part of the twentieth century. Structural functionalism approached society as an organism whose basic purpose was the achievement of equilibrium, a steady state of balance. In this view, every social institution has a role to play in maintaining this equilibrium, and understanding that function is a key objective of social research. Structural functionalism was a profoundly influential theoretical perspective for early anthropologists and sociologists, resonating with the modernist conviction that the world could be rigorously explored and its logic and structure exposed and held up to critical investigation.

At the same time, this theoretical perspective betrayed the interests and assumptions at the heart of these authorized knowledge-making projects. If every institution in every society had a function in maintaining the steady state of the status quo, that status quo came to be seen as the natural and legitimate state of society. Ethical and empirical questions about who a given order serves, who it benefits, and who pays the costs were entirely swept from view. On top of this, any social institution, no matter how problematic or odious, came to be seen as tacitly legitimate since from a structural functionalist perspective every institution had a critical, if not always obvious, role to play in reproducing the social order. Aside from these questions of who wins and who loses in any given social order, structural functionalism also could not account for social change. If the natural state of every social order was equilibrium or balance and if every institution played a critical role in maintaining this balance, then how does change happen? Since societies obviously were not locked in a single configuration, this was more than a minor problem for structural functionalism.

Cultural evolutionism and structural functionalism would not remain unchallenged as theoretical perspectives for long. Franz Boas (1858–1942) began his academic career in physics but was converted to anthropology after a research trip to northern Canada and an encounter with the Indigenous people there. Boas would go on to become one of the most important founding figures in North American anthropology and, perhaps even more importantly, would push the discipline and its practitioners to consider pressing social, political, and ethical questions. Unlike the cultural evolutionists and structural functionalists, who imposed sweeping, generalizing explanatory paradigms on diverse social realities, Boas discounted the relevance of such grand narrative explanations of human society and behaviour. His analytical perspective, known as *historical particularism,* insisted on the necessity of understanding every society in its unique historical context rather than seeking a universal schema for human social development.

Not only did Boas advance the four-field approach to anthropology (combining cultural, physical, linguistic, and archaeological sub-fields) that has become a defining feature of the discipline in North America, he also was a strong proponent of cultural relativism, participant observation, and the responsibility of scientists to speak truth to power. Unlike the evolutionists, who accepted the status quo and the civilizational standard set by Western Europe and its settler colonial fragments as the apogee of human progress, *cultural relativism* insisted that every society was a legitimate experiment in human collective life and as such needed to be understood on its own terms rather than being judged by external standards. Not only was this principle a vital response to the implicitly supremacist thinking in which so much early social science was steeped, it was also important methodologically since it emphasized understanding social practices, beliefs, and institutions in the context of their particular circumstances rather than imagining the world and all of its diversity on a trajectory defined by Western Europe. Boas was also among the first social scientists to take aim at theories of *scientific racism*, challenging racist theories of the evolutionary superiority of whites, based on shoddy anatomical supposition, with rigorous empirical evidence that demonstrated the faulty bases of these arguments. At a time in North America when many social scientists were propping up relations of domination and exploitation, however unintentionally, by positing theories of human social development that uncritically accepted Euro-American, settler-colonial, capitalist, industrial civilization as the height of progress, Boas and his students were practising an ethically and politically progressive research orientation that was methodologically rigorous as well. While in the minority, they were certainly not alone in this.

In the nineteenth century, Harriet Martineau (1802–1876) would become the first sociologist working from a woman-centred (if not yet explicitly feminist) perspective ("Early Social Research and Martineau" 2021). Martineau wrote extensively and often about topics concerning the status of women, race issues, and economics. Martineau's work is part of a tradition of critical, rigorous investigation into our social worlds in pursuit of greater social justice that has deep if often underappreciated roots in disciplinary histories.

In 1903 William Edward Burghardt (W.E.B.) Du Bois (1868–1963), the first Black person to graduate with a doctorate from Harvard University, published *The Souls of Black Folk*, his pathbreaking collection of essays about race, racism, and "the problem of the color line" (2017, 21) as the defining issue of the twentieth century. Du Bois's scholarship did more than address the problem of racism in the United States; it revealed racial inequality and injustice as a constitutive feature of the modern world. Considering the experience of being Black in America in the wake of legal emancipation from slavery, Du Bois asks, "Between me and the other world there is ever an unasked question: ... How does it feel to be a problem?" (2017, 7). Du Bois isn't suggesting that Black people are a problem; he is critically exploring what it means to be identified as a problem by dominant society. Du Bois wrestles with the problem of being Black and American, a state he describes as "double consciousness" since it means constantly seeing one's self through the eyes of dominant, white supremacist society rather than as an authentic, complex, and unique human being among others (9). Du Bois locates this tacit racial hierarchy at the heart of the modern world, what he calls "the problem of the color line" between "the darker to the lighter races" on a global scale (21). This critical, grounded interrogation of racism at the heart of modernity continues to be one of the most important objects of critical social science research. Du Bois's contributions to sociology, the civil rights movement, and advocacy of the Pan-African resistance to colonialism would set the stage for generations of scholars and activists invested in the struggle for racial justice.

Anthropology and sociology have produced a vast ocean of information about the human condition, and it is impossible to do justice to the breadth and depth of it here. That's a roundabout way of saying that the brief history I offer here isn't exhaustive. Through the twentieth century, and particularly in the aftermath of World War II, both disciplines have been marked by a turning away from the search for grand narratives explaining human and social development and toward an array of specific social problems and phenomena. One reason for this is that the more social research was done, the less convincing grand explanatory paradigms became.

As in so many fields, the more knowledge generated, the more practitioners became aware of the limits of this knowledge. The complexity, diversity, and richness of human experience deeply troubled explanatory paradigms positing single forces or causes driving society. But these grand narratives were also challenged by other factors. By the 1960s, universities were opening their doors to those formerly excluded, including women, racialized and ethnic minorities, and middle- and working-class folks. This was partly because of social struggles for equality, justice, and inclusion, and partly because of the university's increasingly important role as a training ground for workers. In this changing context, disciplines like anthropology and sociology were also challenged to address their blind spots and complicity in the status quo by people who did not see their experiences or concerns addressed.

Feminist and racialized perspectives challenged institutions and disciplines that had never critically considered their patriarchal, white supremacist, and class-privileged foundations. Indigenous students and scholars challenged the settler-colonial nature of the university and its academic disciplines. Queer perspectives would hold up the heterosexist assumptions of the institution to scrutiny and open up whole fields of experience for critical inquiry. Radicals from a variety of political perspectives would challenge the conservativism and status quo orthodoxy of their disciplines and institutions, bringing to light a wealth of alternative political perspectives, possibilities, and histories of struggle for social justice. To be clear, it is not that these perspectives, issues, and subjects did not exist before, but they had been marginalized and excluded from the university as an institution and from the craft of authorized knowledge production. As prevailing power relations were challenged on a global scale during the 1960s and '70s by well-organized and radicalized movements for social change, researchers of various stripes also expanded their fields of inquiry to consider a wider range of social issues.

The case of social movements as objects of study is exemplary. Social movements are most simply understood as collectives of people organizing for a common political goal but outside of formal channels of political participation like elections and political parties. Social movements can be conservative or revolutionary, right or left wing, radical or reformist, and utilize a huge range of strategies and tactics to effect change. We explore social movements and social change more fully in Chapter 8. For now, suffice it to say that social movements have been key engines of social change for a long time and in many different places.

While we are accustomed to learning about history as if it is a story of great people (usually men, usually white) doing great things, history is actually made by the masses of ordinary people whose lives and labour literally make the world. Until the 1960s, sociologists and other social researchers almost totally ignored social movements as a legitimate object of scholarly study. When they did consider them, they did so by reference to collective behaviour theory, which they borrowed from psychology, and essentially held that mass movements were little more than mobs without genuine political significance or intentionality. They were made up of ordinary people and not elites, and hence social researchers dismissed them as escape valves for the unwashed masses when the stresses of life became too much to bear — collective catharsis, nothing more.

Social movements exploded across the globe but especially across the Global North in the 1950s, '60s, and '70s, demonstrating such impressive strategic, tactical, and communicative innovation that they simply could not be ignored anymore. In addition to the opening of the university to people who would have previously been excluded from it, this coincidence proved significant. From civil rights to women's liberation, anti-war to student, mass movements of people threw themselves into struggles against dominant power relations and the glaring injustices to which they gave rise. These movements produced incredible social and political change, though many fell short of achieving their explicitly revolutionary aspirations and simply compelled power-holders and academics alike to take them seriously. The responses varied wildly of course, and we explore how the state deals with challenges to its supremacy in Chapter 8.

The response of social researchers, particularly sociologists and anthropologists, was to delve deeply and enthusiastically into social movement research. This produced a variety of consequences, but the story bears telling here because it shows how perception is never neutral. It isn't that in the 1960s social movements suddenly changed and became society-shaping forces deserving of being taken seriously by policymakers and researchers alike. The movements did demonstrate tactical and strategic innovation at the time, but that isn't the reason they suddenly became a legitimate object of study for social researchers and, eventually, a whole field of study unto itself.

Because social research requires such personal involvement with the research process and participants on the part of the researcher, the social position we hold and the privileges we possess (or don't) dramatically affect how and what we perceive. Scholars and researchers in the first half of the twentieth century didn't see social movements as legitimately political, intentional, and organized because they were not what politics looked like to them given their social position — their racialized, gendered, and classed position in the social order. Politics, like teaching and research for so many of these academics, simply did not belong to common people, who were presumed to lack the intellectual capacity to engage in such weighty discussions. In all research, but perhaps especially in research committed to investigating the social world, what we are able to see depends a great deal on who we are. This doesn't mean we are not individually capable of exploring or coming to understand social realities and experiences unlike our own. If that were true, human communication across difference would be impossible. But it does mean that, especially for those of us who don't live our lives up against the cutting edges of structural violence, we can never assume our own experience is the baseline for everyone else's.

RIGOROUSLY AND INTENTIONALLY EXPLORING THE WORLD

There are as many ways of doing social research as there are social phenomena to explore. There is no one-size-fits-all approach to exploring the complexities of collective social life. For example, studying how, why, and with what consequences young white men are being drawn to ethno-nationalist movements online calls for a different research project design than studying kinship systems in the highlands of southern Mexico. The methodological and ethical issues a researcher has to consider and the choices they have to make are always contextual. That doesn't mean there aren't better principles and practices to follow in the course of doing research with people, some of which we explore here.

In comparison to a controlled and sterile lab environment, social research by its very nature tends to be messy. It happens out in the world, in the midst of all kinds of other activity; its unpredictability stymies attempts to impose control over the phenomenon in question and to neatly isolate variables for consideration. This does not mean that rigour and validity are not possible in social research, but it does mean that building a research process that is rigorous, valid, and ethical requires a deep understanding of the *field* that the researcher is about to enter.

Conducting rigorous research about a social phenomenon – whether body image, police brutality, poverty, or the social impacts of climate change – is different from offering anecdotal opinions about it. We live in an age where social media and a globalizing digital infrastructure (the Internet) has seemingly generalized the ability to communicate with people in a way largely inconceivable just a few decades ago. More importantly, we live in a *neoliberal* age, where capitalism has alienated us from each other and built up a culture of hyper-individualism marked by the commodification of nearly every aspect of our social lives. In this context, superficially witty and brashly performed opinion now seems to have been elevated to an art form and cultural industry.

It would be wrong to suggest that in the past people engaged in reasoned public debate, and now everything is "fake news" and brand-building. But we forget at our peril that there is a great distance between statements that *seem* authoritative and correct because they are confidently and cleverly performed and statements that ought to carry some weight because they are based on careful, rigorous research. Just because I live in a society doesn't mean I'm fully conscious of how it operates, how I'm placed within it, and how my subjectivity (my experience of my place in the world) is shaped by it. In fact, being socialized and enculturated within a given social order makes it more likely that we will not be able to fully unpack that order without significant work given that the very purpose of socialization and enculturation is to integrate us into a social order, to make it seem natural to us, to give us a home within it.

Critical social research is never casually anecdotal; to be research it has to be systematic and empirically grounded. Social research is always theoretical in two important ways. First, it's shaped by the researcher's theories about the world and the way it works, theories that are themselves the work of other people exploring and thinking about the world. Second, research is theoretical because when we try to make sense of different things in the world (what's the relationship between health and poverty? How and under what conditions does a revolution happen?), we're theorizing about it, not just putting facts that speak for themselves together like a jigsaw puzzle. But just because research – and not just social research – is theoretical doesn't mean it can happen only in our heads. We can't just make up theories about the world based on our casual, everyday experience of it and call it research or argue that it tells us anything bigger about social life.

For theories about what's going on in the world to matter, they need to make effective arguments that use the best available evidence. What that evidence might be and how we might get at it varies hugely across contexts. It all depends on what we're doing and what we're looking for. Evidence-based arguments grounded in a method that the researcher can show others and invite them to repeat or experiment with is critical to research as a practice. We cannot pretend to understand what people think at any particular moment or how this aggregates, moment-to-moment, to make society happen. Happily, we don't need to be able to read minds to investigate society and its problems and possibilities. What we can aim for are better accounts of social life, especially social problems, that allow us to identify the causes of a host of social inequalities and injustices and address them at their roots. The question of how to do this is what we turn to next.

METHODOLOGICAL CHOICES

Research is made up of both a methodology and methods. What's the difference and why is it important? *Methodology* refers to the systematic study of the methods belonging to a specific field of study. It is the theoretical examination of the reasoning for and practice of a particular way of exploring the world. *Methods* are the tools of research itself, the specific techniques used to gather information out in the world about the thing we want to figure out. Every research project has an organizing methodology and a set of methods it puts into action to investigate something. Methodologies and specific methods can look very different and vary widely in their ontological (what's real?), epistemological (what can we know?), and political (in whose interests? With what consequences?) positioning.

If methods are the tools, methodology is the toolbox, one that a good practitioner is always intentionally and thoughtfully packing and unpacking. Aside from being a practical way of transporting tools, the toolbox represents how and what we think about the problem or task in front of us and what we think might be useful for exploring and, ultimately, intervening in it. The choice of actual tools someone has in their toolbox might appear to be just common sense. People who know how to fix things also know what tools to carry around. But that only seems commonsensical because we rarely stop to think about the infrastructure of our world and how it came to be. It isn't inevitable that people live and work in the environments that we do; those are the outcome of complex social, political, economic, ecological, and cultural factors. So too the technology humans have developed over millennia are not preordained steps on some irresistible conveyor belt of progress but rather the outcomes of creativity, culture, context, necessity, and accident, often in some combination. Our early human ancestors were not somehow destined for traffic jams, self-checkout aisles, and cute cat videos.

We can think about our social research toolbox (methodology) and the tools (methods) it carries in precisely the same way. The ways we rigorously and intentionally explore the world and seek to make sense out of it are not bias free, value neutral, objective, or inevitable. They can be robust, accurate, and effective, but they come from somewhere, they operate with their own assumptions about what is true and real, and they are vested with interest. We must never forget to consciously pack and unpack our methodological toolboxes, to think about what they and the tools they carry can and can't do, what they can and can't show us, how they encourage us to think and act. Critically and intentionally reflecting on methodology and methods is a critical step in developing better ways of doing research in any discipline. We discuss research and ethics later in this chapter, but from the outset it's important to recognize that choices about methods in research are always also questions about ethics.

So, what are some of the methods social researchers use to explore the world? Broadly speaking, social research methods can be divided into two approaches: qualitative and quantitative. A third possibility mixes qualitative and quantitative approaches. As the names imply, qualitative approaches to social research emphasize the experience and meaning of social phenomena, while quantitative approaches explore their significance using statistical methods. Table 2-1 highlights the differences in approach, data generated, what we learn, and what we miss when using each method. These methods are not in competition with one another; the question of which approach is best can't be fairly answered outside of a specific context. What's the nature of the phenomenon the researcher wants to explore? Is it well understood and defined or is it more ambiguous and in need of further mapping? Is the objective of the research to find out how often something is happening and what its scope is, or is it to discover the experience of that thing? Is the aim to measure the thing in question, or is it to figure out what it means? Qualitative research methods give us insight into the social world as a lived experience. They explore social phenomena in an in-depth way that seeks to understand their significance in terms of what they mean to those living them. Quantitative methods give us insight into the frequency and scope of a defined social phenomenon, allowing us to offer a numerical account of a given phenomenon and to explore its social significance by measuring how often it occurs and what other things it correlates with.

Table 2-1 Method Approaches

	Qualitative methods	Quantitative methods	Mixed methods
Approach	• Interpretive	• Statistical	• Combined
Data generated	• Subjective • In-depth • Longer term • Depth over breadth	• Numerical • Survey • Breadth over depth	• Quantitative and qualitative (depending on emphasis and research design)
What do we learn?	• Complexities and nuances of lived realities • Social significance • Unexpected	• Overview of the phenomenon • Population data • Quantification of a defined phenomenon	• Potentially a "best of both worlds" approach, potentially vulnerable to incompatibility issues and the blind spots of both methods
What do we miss?	• Big picture	• Details • What we don't already know	• Dependent on the issues above

Take the example of poverty. A researcher exploring poverty from a qualitative perspective would learn about the experience of those living in poverty, what their lives are like, what they do to survive, what challenges they face. A researcher exploring poverty from a quantitative perspective might count how many people live in poverty and what other demographic variables (racialized identity, gender, education background, disability, age, marital and family status, etc.) correlate with it. The qualitative approach would be relatively longer term and in more depth. It prioritizes understanding poverty from the perspective of those living through it and requires that the researcher come to understand that reality through immersion in the social context. This could involve interviews with those living in poverty and others involved in their lives, such as social workers, government bureaucrats, police, activists, and outreach workers. It often involves the researcher spending considerable time in the social contexts of poor people in order to get a direct, lived sense of their day-to-day lives. Qualitative research provides depth of insight into what something means but little breadth in terms of how widespread the experience is. The quantitative approach is shorter term and broader in scope. It prioritizes surveying the frequency of a given phenomenon and the other social categories (or variables) it is associated with. The researcher's goal is to assemble and analyze datasets that allow for tests of statistical significance in order to understand the scope and larger-scale dynamics and dimensions of the thing being studied. Quantitative research offers considerable breadth in terms of surveying the prevalence of something but only superficial insight into its meaning.

RESEARCH AS METHOD

How do researchers get at the information that allows them to make sense of a given social phenomenon? While there is a wide range of methods, they derive from a set of fairly basic ones. For qualitative researchers, *fieldwork* is often essential to research. Fieldwork simply refers to a researcher going out into the world – to the field, wherever the thing they are seeking to explore lives – and situating their methods there. Depending on the research subject, the field could be a rural village on the other side of the world, social media platforms like Facebook or Twitter, a public housing district, a neighbourhood park, an activist or artistic scene, or anywhere else that people come together to make social life. Getting access to the field and building trust and rapport with those inhabiting it are crucial steps without which qualitative research cannot happen. Gaining access and building trust and rapport can be more or less difficult depending on a variety of factors, including the researcher's familiarity with the context, the perceived risks and rewards of the research for potential participants, and the conditions of daily life.

Entering the field is also fraught with ethical considerations. If people's lives are already difficult, dangerous, or hard and their community under stress, why should they bother to take the time and energy to take part in a research project? Is the researcher an outsider? If so, what's the benefit and risk to letting them in? This isn't to suggest that research should be narrowly instrumental or only be conducted when it appropriately rewards those who participate. Much research – social and not – is carried out without specific beneficial outcomes in mind and has yielded vital insights. What knowledge might we cut ourselves off from if we restrict ourselves only to research promising specific, tangible outcomes and immediate benefits? How do we know what we don't know? This doesn't mean that anything goes, justified under the banner of untethered curiosity and free inquiry. Codes of ethics pertaining to all kinds of research exist today precisely because horrors have been visited on people and other living creatures using all manner of deeply flawed but lofty-sounding justifications. But there is more to the ethics of research than simply avoiding harm.

Particularly in social research that involves a researcher getting to know those participating, it is hard not to see the importance of conducting research that meaningfully contributes to the community and context in question. How to do this and what opportunities and challenges it poses is something we consider shortly.

All research begins with a question. Many people associate research with testing a hypothesis, where a researcher postulates a theory about something and then designs an experiment to test it. Social research rarely employs hypothesis-testing, particularly when it is qualitative in approach. More commonly, we notice something in the world that draws our attention and defies a ready answer and so further investigation is required. The goal is not to prove or disprove a theory. At this level, research is animated by some basic questions: What's going on? Where do we find it? Who's involved? What are its effects? Why does it matter? These types of questions underpin any good social research project, and every researcher needs to articulate them as clearly as possible as they develop their research plan. Once these central questions have been settled upon, at least in a basic sense, researchers review the existing knowledge in the area of interest, often called a *literature review.* It would be wasteful for people to be asking and answering the same questions, so reviewing the existing body of research is essential to not reinventing the wheel. More than this, the review allows researchers to build on the work of others who have come before and work alongside them.

While the research plan or proposal is being formulated, researchers also must figure out how they are going to fund the project. All research involves costs, even if it's just the time spent by the researcher carrying the project out, and most research involves significantly more than this. Travel, housing, equipment, research assistants and other specialized personnel, honoraria and other supports for participants, and much more all need to be paid for. Identifying a source of funding is necessary for most research, and the process of applying for research funds is always competitive. In Canada, much university-based research is supported by public money through one of the three main research agencies: the Canadian Institutes of Health Research (CIHR), the Natural Sciences and Engineering Research Council of Canada (NSERCC), and the Social Sciences and Humanities Research Council of Canada (SSHRCC). Other levels of government from municipal to provincial also offer grants that researchers may be able to tap into depending on their focus and whether it aligns with government goals. Non-governmental sources of funding include charities and non-profit organizations as well as for-profit corporations.

For researchers interested in questions of social justice and social problems, private funding sources tend to be less significant because this research does not lend itself to commodification, profit-making, or market-ready solutions. Of course, funding is always tied to the interests of those providing it. Just because something is public does not mean it isn't beholden to a set of interests. Indeed, as we explore in Chapter 8, the state structure itself isn't an inevitable or rational way of organizing large masses of people; it is a way of organizing them in the interests of the class of people who wield the most power and influence. When politicians talk about the "national interest," they have not solicited opinions from the majority of people living in the state they represent. They are referring to the interests of the people who have the most power to make themselves heard by politicians and bureaucrats. This doesn't mean all research just ends up serving powerful and monied interests, far from it, but it does mean that we need to be clear about the expectations and outcomes attached to funding and the way it shapes what gets researched, how, and in whose interests.

Research methods are central to any research project. We can think of them as the next step in the process of building a research project, but the reality is that researchers come to their question trained in a methodology and corresponding set of methods. This training affects and reflects the way researchers think about and engage with the world, and so questions of methodology and methods can never be treated as purely technical. How we imagine exploring a problem or a question says a great deal about the way we think about the world, what counts as important, what research can and should accomplish, and what we are capable of knowing and doing.

Quantitative researchers often engage in survey-based research that gathers data relating to specifically formulated questions across a broad population. The responses are then aggregated and statistically analyzed to provide a big picture of the phenomenon. Quantitative researchers might also work with already established datasets, such as those generated by a government census, with the intention of tracing the contours of this bigger, population-level picture of the questions at the centre of the project. This kind of research is ideal for answering questions that are looking for a lot of breadth but not a great deal of depth, such as how many people are un- or under-employed at a specific point in time. How many people have experienced food insecurity within a defined period? How many people have been subject to sexual harassment in the workplace? Answers to these questions can also be correlated through statistical analysis with other criteria gathered through pre-existing datasets or survey questionnaires. So, for example, how do any of the above phenomena relate to race, class, gender, age, disability, education level, or marital status? We can learn a great deal about the extent and shape of a social issue through this kind of research.

But if we want to explore the lived experience of un- or under-employment, food insecurity, or sexual harassment, other methods are called for. This deep exploration of a specific problem or issue is what qualitative research methods excel at. Qualitative researchers might use any combination of interviews, *focus groups, field observation, participant observation, discourse analysis,* and more to find out what it means for people to live through the social phenomenon being studied. Rather than a broad snapshot, qualitative research provides a lot of depth. Rather than correlation between variables, researchers are interested in the nature, quality, and meaning of social phenomena and how they come into being.

As anyone who has ever completed a survey knows, the information gathered only allows for narrow answers to specific questions, so a lot rides on how the researcher frames the questions. Qualitative research, on the other hand, emphasizes an open-ended, exploratory approach to information gathering and brings the researcher into contact with people whose lives are impacted by the issue at the heart of the research. A *mixed method* approach combines these two method sets. As with any combination, the mix reflects the framing of the problem or issue under examination and the underlying training, assumptions, and expectations of the researcher or the team directing the project. No methodological approach can do all things, so choices always have to be made and, depending on what they are, they can reveal or obscure critical information.

Raw data, however gathered, never simply speaks for itself. Once a researcher has completed the active research phase, the task is to make sense out of the data. There's no one way to do this, nor is there only one analytical framework, or paradigm, a researcher can use to interpret the information they have gathered. Depending on the nature of the data, different analytical paradigms can be brought to bear, but the basic interpretation falls along the qualitative/quantitative divide.

While qualitative researchers can differ in a variety of ways in terms of how they approach research and its outcomes, all analysis of qualitative data is inherently oriented toward understanding social meaning and significance. That is, it requires the researcher to comb through the data (field notes, interview and focus group transcripts, documents, and more) and find the thematic threads – the deep social meanings — that connect them. Quantitative researchers can similarly differ widely in their orientations but, essentially, all quantitative interpretation is rooted in measures of statistical significance. That is, statistical formulae are applied to the raw data in order to tease out a phenomenon's significance and the correlation, or relationship, between variables. As always, the best way to see how researchers do research and how they make sense of the information they gather is in the context of concrete examples. In the following intervention, Gary Kinsman explores a particularly interesting example of qualitative social research that aimed not only to explore and understand the world but to contribute to efforts to make it a more socially just place.

POLITICAL ACTIVIST ETHNOGRAPHY – *GARY KINSMAN*

POLITICAL ACTIVIST ETHNOGRAPHY (PAE) brings together social movement activism and organizing with activist research to produce knowledge for movements for social transformation both outside of and within universities. This approach is not an external or neutral study of social movements nor a type of social movement theory classifying social movements. PAE relates to the broad realm of the political as it impacts people's daily lives and not just narrowly to official politics (politicians and Parliament), and it tries to facilitate the varied activist ways that people defend and advance their rights, improve their living standards, establish more democratic control over their lives and communities, and protect the environment through the formation of social movements and campaigns. Ethnography is an important qualitative method for producing knowledge used in anthropology, sociology, and other ways of producing knowledge about the social worlds people live in. Its focus is on how people's cultures and social worlds are organized. For instance, anthropologists are supposed to go into other cultures without preconceived notions and to learn from people in that culture through observation and discussion the methods that people use to produce their cultures. Sociologists have used ethnography to produce rich descriptions of youth or street cultures in our society, including interactions with the police, to see how these cultures are socially organized.

PAE grows more specifically out of the research and writing of feminist sociologist Dorothy Smith on institutional ethnography (IE). This is a method and theoretical perspective for doing sociology very differently than "objective" mainstream forms of research and theorizing that produces knowledge that assists in organizing the marginalization and oppression of many groups. IE turns the powers of investigation within ethnography against ruling institutions in our own society to produce knowledge for those who are oppressed within these relations. One example would be to describe how the daily experiences of people living in poverty are organized through state policies including social assistance policies and regulations. Central contributions of this approach (and continuing to use this example) are a critical analysis of institutional ideologies (often organized through documents and other texts, including those of social welfare policies) through which people living in poverty are portrayed as less deserving than other people and as requiring restrictions to receive benefits that are not imposed on other people. This also involves a broader notion of work drawn from the feminist domestic labour debates that view unpaid reproductive and domestic labour as crucial work even if it receives no wage. In relation to people living in poverty this makes visible all the important unpaid labour they engage in — often raising children and doing lots of hooking up work to access and maintain their social assistance status so they do not get cut off benefits. Finally, this approach links this investigation of the social organization of poverty with the broader social relations (including capitalism) that organize poverty in many people's lives. Institutional ethnographic analysis leads to mapping the institutional relations that organize poverty in people's lives so that they can be understood.

George Smith (1935–1994), who developed PAE was a gay and AIDS activist. He was an important organizer in the Right to Privacy Committee, which defended men arrested in the bath raids in Toronto in the early 1980s and in AIDS ACTION NOW! in the late 1980s and early 1990s expanding treatment access for people living with AIDS/HIV. It was out of these organizing experiences that his work on PAE pushed institutional ethnographic inquiry further by taking up the social standpoints of activists in order to produce knowledge that is useful for activists in their movements. The test for whether or not this research is successful is the extent to which it enables people to transform the world. This is a much higher test for research and theorizing about the world since it needs to produce knowledge that activists can rely on in their struggles. It is also based on a practice-theory-practice relation that produces knowledge as part of changing the world.

Activists in social movements (like the Ontario Coalition Against Poverty) are already engaging in researching and theorizing about the social world as an everyday part of their organizing. The work of PAE is to make this research and theorizing more visible, critical and developed in both activist and more scholarly contexts. Reflecting on organizing experiences and figuring out what to do next in a social movement is also about research and producing knowledge. Even planning an occupation of a politician's office is about doing social research. In movement organizing, moments of political confrontation with state institutions can be seen as important learning and knowledge-creation opportunities. Through confrontation with ruling regimes (governments, the police, corporations), activists are able to uncover aspects of their social organization. Through an analysis of the institutional relations movements are up against, more effective forms of activism can be developed.

Social movements can be seen as often engaging in breaching experiments where social order is disrupted to see what can be learned from this disruption. This is similar to an approach within sociology called ethnomethodology (the study of people's methods), which describes the social methods that people use to produce their social worlds. One research strategy is called a breaching experiment, where researchers intentionally disrupt social order to see what can be learned. Harold Garfinkel, the initiator of ethnomethodology, would ask his students to go home and breach social order by acting like they were boarders at home. This challenge to social order created havoc, with some students being threatened with being thrown out of their homes. This demonstrated the fragility of social order and how it rests on socially shared practices that when violated causes problems. Social movements through their rallies, demonstrations, civil disobedience, and other actions are constantly disrupting social order in a collective fashion and seeing what can be learned from it.

Rather than relying on the speculative or ideological (ungrounded) approaches that can sometimes dominate in social movements (like homophobia in LGBTQ+ movements or AIDSphobia in AIDS organizing), PAE tries to analyze the social roots of the problems movements are up against so that the best knowledge can be produced for movement activists to rely on. For instance, in response to police repression, George Smith insightfully pointed out that mass arrests of gay men were not actually organized through the individual homophobia of police officers (their phobia against gay men) but were actually organized through the heterosexist provisions of the Criminal Code that in the 1980s directed the police against gay sex in so-called "public" places like bars and bathhouses. Rather than a focus on public education and consultations with the police, this led to an approach to repeal the laws the police were able to use to criminalize sex between men. Problems for people living with AIDS/HIV were not simply caused by the AIDSphobia of government officials or doctors but through the lack of social organization of treatment access to get treatments into the bodies of people who need them. The task of AIDS activists, George argued, was to begin to put this needed infrastructure for treatment access in place.

PAE is based on the view that how we know about the social world (epistemology) is through a process of reflexive and mutual social determination. We learn more about the social world as we interact with other people and learn from them about how their lives are put together. And how these social worlds are put together (ontology) has to do with the social practices and relations produced by people ourselves. If our social worlds are produced by people, they can also be transformed by people.

My specific contribution to PAE has been to stress the importance of mapping social relations of struggle so that as activists we can locate ourselves within the web of relations we are engaged in and use this mapping to strategize how best to move forward in winning the goals of social movements. Mapping relations of struggle involves not only investigating or mapping ruling relations (which IE does) that our movements are organizing against, including how these relations can contain our resistance, but also inquiring into the composition of struggle that movements can mobilize in challenging and transforming these relations. Mapping relations of struggle is not neutral, but rather a politically engaged process of capturing the relational contestations and connections between ruling relations and social movement struggles. Mapping relations of struggle also involves explicating movement capacities and strengths, including possible allies and strategies and tactics, and identifying weak points and contradictions where we can best disrupt ruling relations. This produces knowledge that assists social movement organizing.

ETHICS

All of our engagements with the world are in some way ethical ones. We make choices, consciously and not, about how we're going to act in the world and in relation to those with whom we share it. These choices are shaped not only by our own sense of right and wrong, what we might call a "moral compass," but also by the social norms and values we've been socialized into and the power and privilege we exercise as social agents. In an age where "ethical consumption" has become a small but significant lifestyle niche, marketing campaigns encourage us to buy commodities from coffee to cars that we are told have been produced under better conditions and/or yield fewer damaging consequences to people, other life, and the planet than conventional ones. But ethics extends beyond individual consumption choices and our personal identities; they underwrite the way we live together and what constitutes acceptable social relations.

Ethics are, of course, directly implicated in research. The kinds of questions we can and should be asking, the ways we should investigate them, how we ought to treat people involved in the research, and what we owe to our participants, other researchers, and society broadly are all vital ethical dimensions of research. Unlike the law, ethical codes are not concerned with enforcing narrow, specific rules governing our social life, the violation of which carry punishments and consequences. *Ethics* refer to the principles that guide our decision-making and behaviour with an orientation toward establishing or maintaining the social good. How the social good is defined is an open-ended question and can vary widely, so we can never assume to know what "good" is out of context. That is not to say that researchers aren't subject to a variety of laws while doing research. Legislation relating to privacy, confidentiality, human rights, and intellectual property all carry implications for researchers and consequences if they are found to be in violation. But research ethics are not like criminal or civil law. They are more like a code of conduct that requires researchers to think through how to apply principles in diverse contexts rather than narrowly adhering to specific rules as if they can be universally applied.

There is no one code of ethics that governs all social research. Many professional scholarly associations, such as the American Anthropological Association and the Canadian Sociological Association, have developed their own statements on research ethics to provide discipline-specific guidelines for their practitioners. These statements are a set of principles meant to guide researchers toward more ethical research practices. In the Canadian context, university-based research is governed by a statement issued by the three federal funding agencies mentioned above, which collectively are known as the "Tri-council."

The *Tri-Council Policy Statement: Ethical Conduct for Research Involving Humans* (TCPS) was first issued in 1998 and is a living document in that it is subject to reconsideration and revision as new issues arise. For researchers who receive funding through any of the three federal agencies, compliance with the policy is mandatory and universities are charged with ensuring that occurs. Violations of the policy can result in researchers being denied access to funding for research. The key orientation to the statement is that "respect for human dignity requires that research involving humans be conducted in a manner that is sensitive to the inherent worth of all human beings and the respect and consideration that they are due" (Canadian Institutes of Health Research, Natural Sciences and Engineering Research Council of Canada, and Social Sciences and Humananities Research Council of Canada 2018, Ch.1, B. Core Principles). The principles guiding the TCPS are respect for persons, concern for welfare, and justice. Significantly, respect for persons includes not only the duty to acknowledge people's autonomy – their right to govern themselves – but the responsibility of the researcher to "protect those with developing, impaired or diminished autonomy." Concern for welfare "is the quality of [a] person's experience of life in all its aspects," from their physical, emotional, and mental health to their socio-economic circumstances. Part of a researcher's ethical obligations include protecting and, if possible, contributing to the welfare of people involved in research. Justice is the "obligation to treat people fairly and equitably." Fairness means "treating all people with equal respect and concern," while equity involves "distributing the benefits and burdens of research participation in such a way that no segment of the population is unduly burdened by the harms of research or denied the benefits of the knowledge generated from it." The TCPS is a lengthy document which develops these principles and their specific applications comprehensively. Nevertheless, this overview conveys the spirit of ethical social research.

Universities have their own research ethics boards (REBs), which provide ethical clearance for faculty and student researchers and feedback and guidance on research processes. Even if a researcher has not received funding through one of the three federal agencies, ethics clearance from their own institution is a necessary step in conducting research with people. But neither REBs nor the TCPS are the last word on ethics in social research. As Gary Kinsman illustrates, social research can aim to do more than meet the minimum ethical standard of respecting people and contributing in some general way to society. Drawing on rich legacies of social justice–oriented research, some social researchers today understand their work as directly contributing to broader struggles for social change and collective liberation.

In recent years there has been a flowering of what might be called an orientation toward *scholar activism*. This kind of research aims not merely to describe society or a specific problem or phenomenon but to contribute to grassroots struggles to build liberated societies. In part, it builds on the legacy of feminist and participatory action research. These practices advanced the notion that research should do more than take seriously people's lived experiences; it should also work to empower them and contribute to their struggles to change their own worlds. Research conducted from a scholar-activist orientation often involves researchers sharing resources and helping communities build skills, not just parachuting in to collect data and then dashing away. Scholar activism is hardly a cure-all for the social problems confronting us or the power imbalances between those who study and those who are studied. As a methodological and ethical orientation, it at least acknowledges that coming to know about the state of the world implies a responsibility to do something about it. How this looks needs to be worked out in each context; there is no one-size-fits-all program to follow as a researcher wishing to work in this vein.

How can research remain rigorous and critical while offering something useful to grassroots struggles for social change? How does a researcher ethically navigate power imbalances within a given social space? Are there lines between research, activism, and advocacy and, if so, are they important to maintain? If researchers work with communities and struggles they personally identify with, what do they risk missing? What are the ethical responsibilities engaged researchers need to keep in mind in relation to participants, the public, the scholarly community, students, funders, and more? How do we know we are actually contributing to struggles for social justice and not just deluding ourselves that we're "on the right side" while perpetuating the status quo? These questions are critical for anyone claiming the label of scholar activist but they elude easy answers. They are beyond the scope of this book to answer but they are vitally important to raise as students take their first steps into the theory and practice of social research.

CONCLUSION

Social research is the intentional, systematic, rigorous, and critical practice of exploring our social worlds in all their richness and complexity. As a practice carried out by people, research is, of course, never free from the dominant interests and power relations at work in society. The ways we seek to figure out the world and its problems, issues, and possibilities are deeply wrapped up in relations of power that tell us what's real, important, and knowable. No research – social, physical, or theoretical – is free of values and vested interests. That doesn't mean everything we do is hopelessly compromised and we should just give up trying to understand anything. Actually, it means the opposite.

Given the weight of dominant interests and the force of prevailing power relations, we should never take common-sense explanations for social phenomena at face value. What passes for "common sense" is often a reflection of those interests and institutions that benefit most from the established order. Understanding what's really going on requires us to be more intentional, more systematic, more rigorous, and more critical than we are socialized to be in our daily lives. While people may see qualitative social research as subjective and biased because it focuses on people's lived experiences and accounts, there is no form of human knowledge making that isn't shaped by power, values, and biases. Even quantum physicists exploring the most fundamental levels of the universe have discovered that the act of observation changes the behaviour of particles. This doesn't mean we can't know anything or that all truth is fundamentally relative, but it does mean that no act of exploration is neutral or objective. Part of doing good research is accounting for the way we approach the phenomena we are investigating and being honest about our position and assumptions, particularly in relation to dominant power relations. Who gets to research and who and what get researched are never neutral or natural decisions. If we fail to ask hard questions about them, we reproduce the status quo, a social order that is a manifestation of particular interests, values, norms, and power relations. We can and must do better than this.

While some people view social research and the knowledge produced from it as a competition between qualitative and quantitative approaches, I've tried to push past such pointless and circular paradigm wars. The question of how best to explore a social phenomenon, or any phenomenon for that matter, never rests in some perfect technique but in selecting the right methods for the context. Again, this doesn't mean that anything goes in research or that anecdotes and casual observations are the same as systematic inquiry. This is why it's vital to have an expansive understanding of what it means to conduct ethical research in social contexts. More than just avoiding doing harm to our research participants, ethical research demands that researchers explicitly account for themselves and their projects.

Social researchers are situated in a web of responsibilities to their participants, their academic communities, the public, students, funders, and perhaps more. These responsibilities are not merely technical issues, boxes to be checked, but rather, they are living relationships that change across time and space. As Gary Kinsman illustrates, some researchers go beyond conventional research ethics to take up the question of how and on what terms research can contribute to struggles for social change and collective liberation. As we explore in the chapters to come, the knowledge produced by social research often presents us with difficult questions about the state of the world and why it is the way it is. For some, that knowledge demands we do more than comment on the world and accept the challenge of using research as a process to meaningfully engage and assist in changing it.

KEY CONCEPTS

anthropology: the study of humanity.

axiology: a theory of value and morals, what it means to be right and ethical.

cultural evolutionism: an anthropological paradigm from the late nineteenth and early twentieth centuries positing that all human societies developed along the same developmental trajectory and potential stretching from savage to civilized.

cultural relativism: an analytical and ethical perspective first advanced by anthropologist Franz Boas in the early twentieth century that understands every society as a legitimate experiment in human collective life that needs to be understood on its own terms rather than being judged by external standards.

discourse analysis: a research method in which the researcher strives to understand language use in specific contexts. Unlike linguistics, which involves the technical study of grammar, syntax, and semantics, discourse analysis focuses on language use in social contexts with a focus on how meaning is made.

empirical: based on observation of and experience in the world.

epistemology: a theory about what we can know, what knowledge is, and how we can gain access to it.

ethics: principles that are meant to guide our decision-making and behaviour with an orientation toward establishing or maintaining the social good.

European Enlightenment: a social transformation spanning the seventeenth and eighteenth centuries in Western Europe that extended and deepened many of the core principles animating the European Scientific Revolution. The European Scientific Revolution and Enlightenment mark the threshold onto what many consider to be the modern world.

feudalism: the social, political, and economic order that held sway in Europe between the ninth and fifteenth centuries whose core economic relationship was the ability to hold or access land in exchange for labour.

field: the social world where social research is situated, where the phenomena under study exist.

field observation: a research method where the researcher strives to observe an individual or group in their social environment.

fieldwork: the process of data collection, especially in qualitative research. It refers to a researcher going out to wherever the thing they are seeking to explore lives and situating their methods there.

focus group: a qualitative research method involving the researcher facilitating a discussion between a small group of research participants. The point of the method is to get participants to talk together about the research focus with the intention of garnering rich insights.

historical particularism: anthropological framework advanced by Franz Boas in the early twentieth century that insisted on understanding every society in its own unique historical context rather than seeking a universal schema for human social development.

imperialism: the process of expanding the power of one people to rule over other peoples and places. It involves the extension of economic, political, and social domination of one group over another using tools from diplomacy to military force.

literature review: a review, commonly presented as a written narrative, of the existing knowledge in an area of research interest.

methodology: the systematic study of the methods belonging to a specific field of study.

methods: the tools of research, the specific techniques used to gather information out in the world about the thing the researcher wants to figure out.

mixed methods: a combination of qualitative and quantitative approaches to social research.

modern: the historical age ushered in by the European Enlightenment, characterized by belief in reason, progress, and individualism as well as the rise of the nation-state and capitalism and the political institutions broadly associated with them.

neoliberalism: a particular form of capitalism that emerged in the 1970s. Economically, it emphasizes deregulation of markets and the shrinking of public institutions and interventions to the greatest degree possible. Socially, neoliberalism promotes the privatization of public space and services and strives to limit to the greatest extent possible democratic oversight of capital's operation. Neoliberalism holds the market up to be the best arbiter of possible outcomes, not just economically but socially and politically.

ontology: a theory about what is real, what the nature of being is, and what makes up reality.

paradigm: a framework for making sense of phenomena.

participant observation: a qualitative research method that involves the researcher immersing themselves in the social context and day-to-day activities of the study participants.

positivism: the belief that truth and verifiable knowledge exist in the world as a consequence of natural and social laws and can be uncovered through empirical investigation and logical reasoning.

qualitative approaches: social research methods that emphasize the experience and meaning of social phenomena. Qualitative research methods explore social phenomena in an in-depth way that seeks to understand their social significance in terms of what they mean to the individuals and collectives living through them.

quantitative approaches: social research methods that explore social phenomena using statistical methods. Quantitative methods give us insight into the frequency and scope of a defined social phenomenon, allowing us explore its social significance through measuring how often it occurs and what other things it might correlate with in a given population.

scholar-activism: an approach to research that aims not merely to describe society or a specific problem or phenomenon but to contribute to grassroots struggles to build liberated societies. This research orientation often also includes skill-building and resource-sharing with communities of concern.

scientific racism: a pseudoscientific perspective that attempts to justify racism and theories of racial inferiority/superiority through supposedly empirical evidence.

sociology: the study of the development, organization, and functioning of human society.

structural functionalism: a social scientific paradigm popular in the late nineteenth and early twentieth centuries that conceived of society as an organism whose basic purpose was the achievement of equilibrium, a steady state of balance.

3

MAKING SOCIETY

Bringing the World into Being

What is this thing we call society? Is it a thing or it is more like a big, collective activity we are all doing together? What is the relationship between individuals and society? Where do a society's values, norms, and institutions come from? How do we come to know them? Whose interests do they serve? Like the air we breathe, the social order can seem so natural and inevitable that we take it for granted. The human capacity for sociality is deeply ingrained in us as a species; we couldn't have survived without it. But it would be a mistake to believe that just because humans are an innately and intensely social species that our experiments in society are natural, neutral, or interest free. The common-sense story about civilization is a good example of what gets lost when we assume social development is a neutral and linear process.

The familiar version of this story is that around 10,000 years ago people in what today is known as the Middle East developed agriculture, allowing for the production of surplus food. This surplus meant that people could live in more or less permanent settlements and innovate many of the things we understand today as part of modern social life: the state, markets, law, writing, and other civilizational hallmarks. Agriculture provided food security and allowed people to leave behind the mobile, egalitarian, hunter-gatherer lifeway to embark on the road to hierarchical, ordered civilization. Or so the story has been told.

It's interesting to think about the assumptions reflected in this narrative. Food security is a lynchpin here, but so also are hierarchy, authority, and order. In this story, people essentially trade an egalitarian way of life for a much less free one, all in the name of security and, eventually, progress. But why would they do that? The evidence strongly suggests that mobile, egalitarian, hunter-gatherer ways of life were not less secure than sedentary ones (Scott 2017). In fact, because these people relied on diverse food webs rather than on a single food source, they were more likely to be food secure. Because they were not living in larger settlements alongside domesticated animals, they were less likely to encounter new and deadly pathogens for whom such conditions are ideal breeding grounds. Indeed, from the archaeological record we can discern that people may have made use of a variety of food production methods, including limited forms of cultivation, for thousands of years without turning to sedentism and the state. What sedentism did afford was an opportunity for would-be elites to control people's labour and hoard the wealth produced by it (Scott 2017). Sedentism and proto-state formations had to be coerced into existence; they didn't just spring up spontaneously as a more evolved form of social life. Warfare and the taking of prisoners was one of the primary mechanisms for securing labourers and compelling them to work.

This is not just a matter of setting the record straight. These stories tell us much about what values we are being told to embrace and what vision of society we are being told to commit to. We may like, tolerate, detest, or think very little about any given social order, but we should never mistake our individual feelings about society for its actual nature, particularly when one of the key functions of the social order is to bind people to it. Part of the role of good, critical social research is to unsettle this feeling of the naturalness or inevitability of the way we live. Only when we effectively disrupt the sensibility that the way we live is "normal" can we begin to understand the way that society works, what effects it produces, and what its costs are. This kind of critical, rigorous investigation and knowledge production is a necessary step in learning to act in our world.

HUMANS AS BIOCULTURAL ORGANISMS

As we explore in Chapter 1, while it's easy to fall into the trap of imagining humanity as above and beyond other life on this planet, as a species we are decidedly a part of this biological universe. Our biology certainly doesn't define us individually or collectively, but it carries huge implications for our social lives together. At the same time, humanity's capacity for complex, symbolic thought and communication pushes our diverse forms of sociality into territory not seen in other animal populations. Taken together our biological needs and our facility for culture-making and self-awareness make us *biocultural organisms*, beings who are reducible to neither biological characteristics nor cultural-symbolic dimensions but are a complex amalgamation of both. Why is this important and what does it mean for society? As we discuss in Chapter 1, the foundation for humanity's survival, global reach, and world-shaping capacity is due not only to some important evolutionary traits (large and complex brain, dexterous hands, bipedalism) but to the bedrock of sociality and cooperation to which they are intimately connected. By ourselves, humans are not very impressive physical specimens, but our capacity to work together has literally re-made the world in a way that no other species can or has (for good and bad).

Over the course of our time on this planet, *Homo sapiens* and our ancestors have had to develop ways of working together to survive. This is what society is in its most elemental form. From child rearing to food production to security, it is impossible to understand humanity's persistence on this planet without considering it as a collective rather than individual phenomenon. Society is the name for our efforts to sustain life collectively. But while society is a way for humans to attempt to satisfy fundamental physical needs (food, shelter, security, reproduction), it is not merely a machine built to meet them. Lines of analysis that attempt to reduce complex phenomena to single causes are always flawed and incomplete.

While human social life arises in part to meet the necessities of existence, we cannot reduce every social phenomenon to these needs. Just because humans require food as energy to survive and have to engage in reproductive sex to propagate the species doesn't mean that factory farming and Internet porn are inevitable. We can't understand human societies by retreating to some imagined primordial source, and it is equally wrong to see society as nothing more than the sum of interactions between individuals. While biologically deterministic arguments about society threaten to send us down rabbit holes of (imagined, inaccurate) biological imperatives, accounts that posit micro-level interactions as the source of society reduce everything to an effect of interpersonal relationships, as if society is nothing more than the sum of these exchanges. While it is undoubtedly true that for what we call society to exist people must enact it, literally live it into being, we do not do so as perfectly free, autonomous, and equal individuals. We are shaped individually and collectively by power relations, dominant institutions, and systems of ideas about the world and our place in it. Our lived experiences and the way we see the world are not uniform, random, or timeless. They are wrapped up in systems of ideas that are deeply connected to specific ways of organizing social life that have direct, material consequences. While we navigate the world as individuals, our experiences of it are profoundly shaped by these systemic forces, ideas, and relationships.

ENCULTURATION AND SOCIALIZATION

You probably don't wake up every morning and deliberate about whether or not you're going to participate in society. While you might have a hard time deciding what to wear, you probably don't actively consider whether or not to put on clothes before leaving your home. While the people you encounter may please or annoy you, you probably don't actively make individual decisions about whether or not to physically assault them. While you may love, hate, or be indifferent to the activities that you do as part of your daily life (for example, waged work, school, care work for children, elders, or the infirm), you probably don't make the decision to renew your commitment to any or all of them on a day-to-day basis. And this is to say nothing of all the thousands of smaller decisions we make almost automatically all the time. How close is too close when it comes to standing next to someone you don't know well? Why not eat the family companion animal? Why not just take things that you want from other people ?

We are encouraged to think of ourselves as individuals who make our own choices, but there is a remarkable consistency to collective social life in terms of the routines and conventions that characterize society. *Norms* are the often-unspoken social conventions that implicitly guide our social behaviour. Social norms, dominant values, and roles are all critical to understanding our place in the social order, and none of them are with us from birth; they are products of the processes of enculturation and socialization. *Enculturation* is the process of acquiring culture, and *socialization* is the process of learning and becoming a part of the social system. While anthropologists tend to talk about enculturation and sociologists about socialization, the terms are most fruitfully understood by combining them and thinking about them as pointing to the sometimes formal but often informal process of coming to know about the norms, values, and roles that define the social order of which we are a part.

As anyone who has spent time around babies understands all too well, human beings do not come into the world pre-programmed with the skills and information necessary to keep themselves alive let alone navigate our complex social environments. The prolonged period of children's dependency on their caregivers that is unique to humans is a time not only of physiological but also of social development. Knowledge about language, what is good to eat, when and how to sleep, basic social cues, and so much more is acquired by children as they learn about the world they inhabit and where they fit. One way to think about this period is as the time when children become social beings, a process of becoming that is separate from physiological growth.

Much of this learning takes place informally in the context of daily life. It isn't conveyed by formal lessons or in institutions like school; it happens through the social interactions we observe and take part in, the stories we are told, the lessons passed on to us, and the reinforcement or censure we receive for our behaviour from family, peers, and the wider society. It happens intergenerationally between adults and children but also in peer groups as young people grow into the world and socialize each other. Of course, given the penetration of the fabric of daily life by capitalist relations in so much of the world, the role of waged care workers (migrant and domestic) and institutions like daycares and other places charged with providing early childhood education has become increasingly central in socialization. In fact, one of the roots of the modern education system from early childhood to postsecondary is to accustom young people to the hierarchical, disciplinary structure and competitive logic of the waged workplace (see Haworth and Elmore 2017). It is no accident that the school day mirrors the classic industrial workday or that the reward and disciplinary systems instituted in schools are often linked explicitly to how people will be expected to behave for a boss.

Nevertheless, much socialization still happens in largely informal ways — first, through caregivers and family, then through peer groups and other social institutions such as popular media, organized sports and social activities, and simply navigating society and interacting with other social beings. Adults go through these processes too, of course, as anyone who has ever spent time in a significantly different socio-cultural context can attest. Whether living in another country or simply exploring an unfamiliar social space closer to home, most people can identify with that feeling of being out of place. Anthropologists describe this feeling of being out of place in another socio-cultural context as *culture shock,* that sensation of uncertainty and strangeness that accompanies being somewhere very different from what is familiar. These feelings tend to dissipate with the passage of time as people figure out the basic features of the new context – the language, rhythms of daily life, norms, values, and social protocols. In other words, culture shock tends to fade as we learn our place in a new social space.

Socialization and enculturation are universal processes, but they are hardly uniform either in process or outcome. If socialization and enculturation worked the same way for everyone, people would be much like cars rolling off an assembly line, but no society looks like that. Like all social phenomena, how and what we learn about our place in the world have a great deal to do with where we are structurally located within that world, and that is not at all random. Factors such as socioeconomic class, racialized identity, gender, sexuality, and ability all have profound consequences for what we are taught to expect out of society and what kinds of life circumstances we face. Capitalism and liberalism celebrate the idea of the individual as an entrepreneurial free agent capable of making magic in the world with enough gumption, creativity, and ambition. Time and again, social research bears out that achieving "success" or "failure" in life has little to do with the individual and their choices, let alone how hard they try to "pull themselves up by their bootstraps." It has much more to do with where they are located in a society's matrix of power relations based on the kinds of categories listed above.

While socialization and enculturation are universal processes in the sense that no society can exist without integrating people as social beings, as processes they always and only belong to the context of their particular social order. In other words, socialization and enculturation bear all the marks of the relations of power prevailing in a given society. Unsurprisingly, these power relations are replicated, reproduced, and reflected in society's dominant institutions. *Social institutions* refers to the basic rules of order and behaviour in the society. This includes enduring and enforced norms, roles, values, and organizations, which can be formal or informal. Examples of social institutions are dominant mores and taboos, the family, peer groups, legal and political systems, religion and other systems of belief, media, education, the nation-state, and many more. The primary purpose of social institutions is the maintenance and reproduction of the established order. That doesn't mean social institutions are bad or inherently tools of domination, though they certainly can be. All societies need social institutions, and people create and require them to navigate social life and meet the needs of life (food, shelter, safety). The question is what kinds of social institutions can and should we create and to what ends should they be directed?

Examples drawn from liberal-democratic capitalist societies show the different effects of socialization at work. Whether we look at official government policies or the broad ideas that serve as a society's bedrock, we encounter predictable calls for people to be active and engaged citizens, contributing members of society, and happy, healthy, and fulfilled members of the social order. But as soon as we examine the way people experience the social order, differences in opportunities and outcomes are readily apparent. To focus on the narrow category of socioeconomic class, it's fairly easy to see that the expectations of someone growing up in a middle-class household (meaningful and usually professional work, home ownership, yearly vacations, eventual retirement) are a reflection of that context. We'll unpack the slippery language of the "working," "middle," and "upper" class in a bit, but for now let's take it at face value that these are points on a spectrum moving from poor to rich.

No one would expect a child raised in a working-class household to experience the same kind of material and social conditions as a child raised in a wealthy household. The working-class kid isn't going to horse-riding lessons and the family country home for the weekend. More importantly, working-class kids aren't taught to expect to be a member of their society's *ruling class*. From the dwelling you live in to the food you eat to the car(s) your parents drive to the places you go to school and to socialize, every meaningful coordinate of social and lived experience is dramatically affected by class in a capitalist society.

While it's easy to see how people with more money enjoy greater material comforts, French sociologist Pierre Bourdieu took this analysis further and identified "social" and "cultural" capital alongside of the economic capital (money, material wealth) that we are used to talking about. *Social capital* refers to the resources a person gains access to because of their social networks. *Cultural capital* refers to the non-economic assets a person can mobilize to make their way up the hierarchy in a stratified society: things like knowledge, manners, style of speech and dress, and other forms of cultural competency appropriate to a given context. We're really talking about social networks and ways of presenting ourselves. The process of acquiring and cultivating these forms of capital is precisely what elite socialization is supposed to achieve. Through private schools, country clubs, and ivy league universities to exclusive forms of art (the opera, for example), activities (polo, for example), and sociality (fraternities and sororities, for example), a stratified society's ruling class is not born but made. It is this social networking and learning the cultural codes associated with it that demonstrate authentic belonging to this privileged world and the considerable entitlements (wealth, power, access) that come with it.

How people come to know about their society and their place in it has been a long-standing preoccupation of anthropology and sociology. The world around us often seems so normal, natural, and inevitable, even if we don't particularly like or agree with it, that we rarely stop to think about how each of us takes part in reproducing that society on a daily basis. Through our social activity we bring relationships and institutions to life. What is a university, for example, without the faculty, students, and staff who bring it into being by teaching, learning, and taking care of it? That's to say nothing of the vast variety of other things that go on at institutions like universities and make them what they are.

Where does our social imagination come from? The fact that people have lived in all kinds of different societies over the last 10,000 years or so is evidence that we are not preprogrammed to follow some narrow social template. Where do we get our ideas about what kind of society we could and should live in? Family certainly plays a role, especially given the long period of growth and development during which human children are intensely dependent on their caregivers. Religion and other systems of belief also factor as central orienting stories about who we are, where we come from, and what our purpose is. We might also mention things like formal education and media (any communication form or tool used for storing and delivering information). Looking at these elements might tell us how ideas about society are spread, but none of them really address the human capacity to imagine and then act society into being. Nor do they tell us anything about how our imagination is shaped and directed. Without suggesting that society is simply a belief or collective hallucination, we can't create anything together without imagining it first.

The *imagination* as a collective, social force that plays a huge role in driving our activity as social beings has been studied extensively by social researchers (see Anderson 2006; Appadurai 1996; Castoriadis 1987; Haiven and Khasnabish 2014; Kelley 2002; Taylor 2004). Some argue that the imagination is a fundamental aspect of modern social life without which many of our social institutions, practices, and identities would not be possible (Taylor 2004). It doesn't require much of a leap in thinking to understand ourselves as members of kin groups, given our dependency on our closest social connections for basic survival. Imagination certainly comes into play when we identify as citizens of nation-states, given the scale and highly abstract quality of this form of community (Anderson 2006).

Similarly, we don't have to think too hard to understand the necessity of the work required to sustain ourselves and those who depend on us on a day-to-day basis, whether that's cooking, cleaning, maintaining our shelter, or tending to the sick, old, and very young. But there is a great deal more imaginative work required to think about our own place in the collective sphere of work and wealth production that we call the "economy" (see Patel 2009). Providing the necessities of life for ourselves and our loved ones seems like a fairly concrete, immediate activity, but the sphere of human activity that we shorthand as "economics" in modern societies is not just different in scale, it's different because it seems to have a life of its own. The economy, particularly under capitalism, is seen as an entity unto itself, a thing with its own needs, demands, and capacities that must be served lest it fail or be otherwise compromised and throw social life into chaos. But the economy isn't independent of us, nor is it an entity with its own consciousness and desires. We are taught to think of it in these terms and our imagination allows us to invest in and bring this concept to life in a way that simply doesn't match the facts on the ground.

Much of modern social life demands a great deal of imaginative work. Think, for example, about the symbols and spectacles associated with national identities, the regimes of work to which we're supposed to devote our lives, or our notions of what life could or should be like (sold to us by those with the wealth and power to control the media, through which our modern imagination is so frequently fed). At the risk of oversimplification, we can get a sense of the work of the imagination in modern, large-scale societies by comparing them to life in small-scale ones. Small-scale societies of a few hundred people connected primarily through kin relations allow people to have direct experience of the whole social order and to know their place in it in a lived, material way. In large-scale societies, which are geographically vast and whose members number in the millions or even billions, an unmediated experience of the social whole is impossible.

Take an example like justice. In a small-scale society, individuals might settle grievances with each other directly or through appealing to the decision-making power of the chief or elders. In large-scale societies, justice might be thought of both as an abstract principle connected to philosophical traditions and as something codified in laws, delivered (or not) by institutions like courts, police, and prisons, and attached to other sets of codified principles like constitutions. In the first case, justice is grounded, immediate, and experienced. This does not mean it is perfect; it only means it is not abstract or removed from people's experiences of it. In the second case, justice is both abstract and elaborately codified, and it is most certainly removed from the sphere of daily lived realities in the sense that it doesn't seem to belong to people and their relationships but to institutions and their artifacts.

Exploring the roots of nationalism, Benedict Anderson (2006) famously argued that modern nations are "imagined communities," collective identities that people are encouraged to imagine themselves into. This may sound strange since so many of us take the system of nation-states that divides up the world today for granted, but if we stop to consider the nature of nationalism, the imaginariness of the phenomenon becomes clear. What does it mean to think of belonging to a nation (Canada, France, Mexico, Japan, South Africa, etc.) when you will never meet most of its other members? How can we be said to be naturally part of national communities when our nationalist identities are things we learn about through official holidays, government propaganda, authorized histories, anthems, school curricula, state-sponsored sports and arts, and more? Without being entirely cynical about it, this sounds more like indoctrination than organic identification with a real, living community.

Part of the problem with the use and abuse of the notion of "culture" is how it has become intertwined with nationalism, leading to static, chauvinistic, xenophobic, and top-down visions of the nation, including who is allowed to belong to it and on what terms. Nationalism, in this sense, is the experience of people coming to identify themselves as belonging to a community that they can never really touch but that has powerful disciplining effects. More significantly, it is the experience of identifying as belonging to a community that is shaped in every sense by those with the power to do so. Nationalism can never be divorced from the agenda of those with the greatest power to shape it.

Other scholars have explored the imagination as a collective, social force in different ways. These explorations include tracing the relationship between imagination and globalized movement of goods, ideas, and people (Appadurai 1996); popular media and people's sense of socio-political alternatives (Fawaz 2016); social movements and social change (Castoriadis 1997; Haiven and Khasnabish 2014; Kelley 2002); new ways of working and creating value (Haiven 2014; Hardt and Negri 2000), and much more. This collective ability to envision that which does not yet exist is strongly linked to people's ability to act in the world. All this is to say that the way we experience being in the world, our subjectivity, is not simply a natural, inevitable expression of our humanity. There is no one right way to be in the world; there are many possibilities, and often what decides between them is the way power relations work and the agenda behind them.

POWER

Few examinations of what society is and how it works can avoid questions of power. Power relations structure our daily lived realities, shape our understanding of what is possible, right, and good, and seep into every aspect of our social lives together.

We don't need to retreat to conspiracy theories to explain how the world works, but we must never forget that the world as we know it has been worked over by power relations and there is no such thing as a neutral, natural, or inevitable social order.

So, what is *power*? Most commonly, power is thought of as the ability to exert force or control over others, to exercise one's will regardless of opposition or resistance. In this sense, power is something one has or doesn't. But is this really all it is? For example, as a professor I have considerable power in my courses and in my dealings with students. I have the power to establish what the course looks like, what students have to accomplish in order to get the credit, and ultimately to evaluate students and fail them if necessary. But is that power really mine? A closer look reveals that not only is that power not total but, more importantly, it doesn't actually belong to me. My power as professor isn't absolute because there are university regulations, codes of conduct, and academic policies that set limits on what faculty can do in courses and what recourse students have when they feel they have been treated unfairly. Professorial power doesn't belong to me because there is nothing about me as an individual that gives me this power in my classes at my university. Instead, it is my role (professor) in an institution (university) that gives me this power in specific settings (my classes) and not in others (for example, the cafeteria, the campus pub, the parking lot, another professor's class). But if power is a thing that I either have or don't, how does this make sense?

Let's consider another example. A boss in a workplace is, like a professor in a classroom, considered a powerful person in relation to their workers. The boss sets the work schedule, apportions tasks, hires and fires, sets and enforces workplace policies, and generally has considerable control over the nature of the work experience on a day-to-day basis. Do people become bosses because they are powerful and so rise into those positions, or do they become bosses and acquire access to the power that comes with that role? Perhaps a better question to ask is how powerful a boss would be if their workers were to collectively decide to no longer obey their orders?

Let's say that a group of workers at a given workplace are fed up with the abuse they suffer at the whims of the boss and refuse to carry out their orders. Maybe they even refuse to show up for work at all. What happens? Certainly, there is the possibility that the workers will be punished for this act of resistance, perhaps even fired. But what happens at the workplace? In the absence of workers, the work comes to a grinding halt. From a capitalist perspective, no profit is made because no one can buy anything. So, who has the power here? Obviously, the boss exercises power as a result of their role in the enterprise, but the workers clearly have power as well since it is they who actually enact whatever the business is about. They do the work. Complex, hierarchical, and unequal social systems often mask the relations of power that undergird them precisely because those with greater access to power, privilege, and material resources have a clear and vested interest in maintaining the appearance of the righteousness and naturalness of the status quo.

Under capitalism, CEOs and bosses often appear powerful while workers don't. In modern nation-states, political and economic elites appear to be the shot-callers while the rest of us are forced to play by their rules. However, bosses without workers cannot accomplish the goal of the business, both in terms of producing the good or service it's dedicated to or, critically, generating the profit that is the core reason for its existence. Similarly, without the acquiescence and obedience (however grudging) of common people, rulers have no one to rule. This is precisely why such systems develop frightening and spectacular ways of punishing those who openly express disobedience to them. Without the compliance of the governed, there are no rulers, only increasingly precarious oppressors and exploiters. This is why it's far less useful to talk about power as a thing and much more useful to talk about it as a relationship.

Another way we can think through the conundrum of power is to consider the differences between what some social theorists call "power-to" and "power-over" (Holloway 2002). In this formulation, "power-to" is the capacity people wield when they work individually or collectively to create something in the world, whether that creation is a work of art, a scientific discovery, a piece of furniture, or a nurturing relationship. "Power-over," on the other hand, is what happens when this innate power to create, reproduce ourselves and society, and collaborate is enclosed, captured, and redirected by another. Power is a relationship between multiple subjects through which force is exerted in the world and on us. The costs and consequences of the exercise of power come back to the way these relations are organized and the context in which they occur.

We exercise power when we come together for common, consensual projects just as much as we do when we find ourselves compelled to direct our energies at the behest of someone else. We have the ability to act on and in the world individually, and this ability to do something (anything, really) is also power. Building a deck, caring for each other, organizing a free school, or preventing racists from recruiting and harassing people in our neighbourhoods are just as much an exercise of power as when we submit to authority and carry out its desires. Critically, this view of power allows us to see its collective rather than individualistic nature. It is possible to exercise power individually, but its effects are greatly amplified when it becomes a collective effort, which is why so many of our modern examples of power (armies, corporations, nation-states, social movements) are collective rather than individual.

IDEOLOGY

How do we make sense of the world around us? A recurring theme in this book is that society doesn't just spring into existence fully formed but that humans create it together. We don't engage in these acts of creation spontaneously or individually though. It isn't as if we are all at work in our own little corners of reality cobbling together some piece of the social order that we then add, LEGO-like, to other people's pieces. Where do we get our ideas about the world and how it ought to be?

As we've already explored, socialization and enculturation are power-laden processes fundamental to bringing us into the social order, and dominant institutions in society are central to reproducing it. We've also explored the way that imagination operates as a collective, social force that underpins sociality and modern life. But what about those ideas that tell us about the world, why it is the way it is, and how it ought to be? *Ideology* is the name for these systems of ideas that are shared among a group of people and that allow them to make sense of the social world. If imagination is the collective capacity to envision that which does not yet exist, ideology is something much more fixed, structured, and vested with interest.

No ideology is a neutral description of the world; it is a set of ideas that tell us why the world is the way it is and how we fit into it. But an ideology isn't just a collection of all the ideas that benefit a society's ruling class, nor are these ideas the force that drives history. An ideology is deeply linked to the human social and productive relations that dominate in any particular moment (Bannerji 2016). In a sense, ideologies are a kind of storytelling that offer a rationale for the way the world is and tell us how we might fit into it.

Ideologies are not only the possession of a society's ruling class. A variety of ideologies can and do exist among groups who do not have their hands on the levers of power. When a group of people advances a vision of society different than the one we live in now, they are advancing a different ideology. Collective struggles for social change are animated by ideas that oppose those embodied by the established order. If they weren't, there would be no social conflict. Ideologies can fall anywhere along the political spectrum from collective liberation to fascism. Again, these ideas don't exist in some kind of free-floating, disembodied way; they emerge and develop as people work together for the social change they want to see.

Let's look at examples of ideology at work. As we explore in Chapter 2, ideas about who counts as human and who doesn't didn't simply fall from the sky into people's heads or spring up spontaneously because they were "superstitious" or "backward." Such ideas were developed in step with new relations of exploitation as feudalism gave way to capitalism. As the chapters to come discuss, ideas about race developed, expanded, and became weaponized alongside the rise of modern systems of science, social control, economics, and politics. It's not that the ideas about structured inequality came into being and then people started living them out, nor is it that people started acting out some essential human nature and then developed rationalizations for their behaviour. Thinking and doing are intertwined. Elaborate, and sometimes monstrous, ideas about the world and those with whom we share it are cobbled together as people make their way through it, often propelled into motion by systems not of their own making.

In the process of making the modern world, Western European empires competed for control of other people's labour, territory, and resources. As these things became increasingly central to the emerging capitalist order, ideas about who and what mattered grew up in the swirl of imperial and colonial expansion. Francis Bacon's theories of monstrousness and just war against those "unavowed by God" found fertile soil in this context. The Valladolid debate about whether "Indians" had souls and assertions of the civilizing mission of colonial domination and exploitation also only really made sense within this imperial-colonial matrix of power. Ideologies and material practices exist in a feedback loop with each informing the other, all subsumed by the ruling-class interests of the day.

What of oppositional ideologies? Whether in struggles to abolish slavery, win the right to vote for women, end child labour, oppose war, secure reproductive freedom for all, or build a non-exploitative economy, ideas and action develop as people try to move toward the world they want and oppose that which they do not. It's often easiest to see ideology and why it matters when we take a step back and look at the big picture of what people are trying to achieve. While social struggles are always made up of specific demands, tactics, and strategies, it's easy to get lost in these particularities instead of understanding that ideology is about the way we see the world and how it works.

For example, the struggle to abolish slavery was not simply about changing the laws that allowed Black people to be owned by whites. It was also a grassroots struggle for human dignity and freedom that connected with other liberation struggles, particularly those of white workers and women, and offered an expansive vision of what it might mean to live in a just, democratic, and free society (Roediger 2017). In other words, it was a struggle for a different world. The actual practice of working out what the struggle would look like and how relations of solidarity with others were going to be built and maintained was difficult, uncertain, and often less than equal to the liberatory aspirations animating it. Solidarity breaks down, powerholders push back, movements are repressed or co-opted, the established order is more resistant or adaptive than anticipated, or members of the broader public prove difficult to engage. Alternatively, victories achieved, alliances built and maintained, and momentum gained can expand struggles on the ground and amplify alternative ideologies, circulating them through society and creating opportunities for change, often in unexpected ways.

CONSENT AND COERCION

All societies have some kind of order. Even anarchic societies and collectives, while without rulers, have an order to them that allows members to engage each other in reliable and predictable ways. Chaos isn't the same as anarchy (societies without hierarchies and without rulers), and most people, understandably, do not want to live amidst chaos. But that does not mean that social order is necessarily good or desirable or that the ways social order is maintained are neutral or natural. This points to one of the classical sociological formulations for understanding how social control is maintained: formally and informally.

Informal social controls are often exercised inter-personally. They take such forms as gossip, ridicule, shame, and discipline at home, and they are meant to encourage compliance with social norms by those perceived to be deviating from it. *Formal social controls* are carried out by authorized agents who apply specific punishments for deviance from the norm. Such agents include bosses, teachers, doctors, social workers, police, and administrators. Obviously, in the course of daily life there is considerable overlap between formal and informal social controls. Think, for example, about an office workplace; workers can face formal discipline from bosses for a variety of infractions, real or imagined, while also dealing with workplace gossip, shame, and ridicule tied to what other workers have internalized about how the office should work.

It would be wrong to think of one type of control as good and the other bad. The point is not whether social control is exercised formally or informally (almost always, particularly in large-scale societies, it is a combination of both) but to what ends it is committed. This is where paying attention to the means we employ to get to our desired ends is particularly important. Liberated, just, and peaceful societies cannot be arrived at through forms of social control that are oppressive, coercive, or subjugating. In a society like our own, marked by so many punitive and dominating forms of social control, from prisons and police to gossip and public ridicule, it should really be no surprise when we encounter consequences that are also oppressive, degrading, and violent.

In many small-scale societies, the kinds that humans have lived in for the vast majority of our time on this planet, order is exercised through influence, common agreement, competence, and social bonds (Scott 2017). If you were to live in a group of a hundred or so other people, your social obligations, responsibilities, and freedoms would probably be fairly clear and they would largely be enforced through common agreement and practice. This does not mean that such societies were or are utopias without conflict, inequalities, or abuses. However, such societies tend to maintain order and settle disputes in ways that are inherently non-coercive and largely non-hierarchical. Without formal, punitive measures like police and prisons to maintain order and the hierarchy of dominant interests, communities are compelled to address problems between members in ways that emphasize negotiation, compromise, and moral influence. On the other hand, in large-scale societies like nation-states, order and authority are maintained through an elaborate system of institutions, roles, and relationships that are fundamentally impersonal, forceful, and rigidly codified. The law is a perfect example. No code of law in a modern society is based on convincing people intellectually or ethically to abide by it. No one cajoles or convinces us to obey the law or other forms of authority. In fact, we are expected to abide by these social conventions without much explanation at all. So where does the force and legitimacy of law and political authority come from? In modern, large-scale, state-based societies, how do we know who and what to obey?

Unlike fascist social orders, where obedience is compelled through the use or threat of violence, a cult of personality and infallibility surrounding the leader, and a celebration of jingoistic and xenophobic nationalism, liberal democratic orders rely on the consent of the governed for their legitimacy and authority (Finchelstein 2017). In modern liberal democratic states, it is not governments or the state bureaucracy that are sovereign but "the people" who are the source of all political power and authority. But who are "the people" and how do they exercise this power? It isn't all of us who create laws, for example, or set government policy or decide where and under what conditions to deploy the armed forces. While liberal democratic sovereignty is rooted in "the people" as a collective political actor and force, practicalities are very different from political myth-making.

In practice, elections are among the few ways that most people participate in political life. Most people rarely have any influence over political decision-making or social and economic policies. So, while "the people" are invoked by politicians as the source of authority and legitimacy, in practice the sphere of political power remains fairly exclusive, with citizens only engaged during election cycles, when they are asked to pick their favourite from a small field of challengers. The rest of the time decisions are made and courses charted by political and economic elites and their functionaries, who often share worldviews, interests, and expectations based on their education and location within the matrix of relations of ruling. Later in this book we'll take up the question of political organization and alternatives to the status quo. For now, I consider what realities like this tell us about the way that social control is established and exercised. More importantly, I focus on the interests vested in any given social order and ask the question: who wins and who loses?

As we've already discussed, there is no such thing as a single "human nature." While there's a certain kind of baseline set by our evolutionary journey as a species, who we are and what we are capable of remains highly contextual. We may reproduce sexually, require food for energy, and bear the marks of a highly social, cooperative species of big brained, upright, two-legged walkers, but other than that there's an incredible range of possibility in terms of how we arrange and comport ourselves. So, whenever catchall theories positing a specific and narrow vision of who we are as a species are advanced, we should not only be skeptical of them from a scientific perspective but ask the vital question of who they benefit. What story are they trying to tell about people and society and who stands to gain from it?

One story common to capitalist societies is essentially about how the world is a dangerous place and that people need an array of modern institutions to protect us from each other. Indeed, a whole subsection of the culture industry produces slick myths for our media consumption about how we should fear each other and how the police, prisons, judges, and courts are the "thin blue line" separating civilization from barbarism. The notion that humans exist in a natural state of war of "all against all" and that without the state and the social contract it embodies and enforces, life would be nothing but "solitary, poor, nasty, brutish, and short" was famously described by English philosopher Thomas Hobbes at the turn of the modern era in Europe. Writing in the seventeenth century, Hobbes and other European philosophers were fashioning the intellectual architecture for a new social order that was emerging to replace feudalism.

The Western European Scientific Revolution and Enlightenment were not just about the development of new ways of thinking about and exploring the world; they also marked a move away from established forms of authority and social hierarchy and the development of new ones. Instead of royalty being seen as the manifestation of divine will on Earth while all others are condemned to toil and be ruled over, modern institutions like parliaments promised some measure of accountability, representation, and legitimacy derived from popular will. This is, essentially, the basis for political philosophies like liberalism and the origins of the modern state. Of course, none of this meant that the new elites were any less hostile to common people than the old ones were. As one way of organizing and exploiting the world (feudalism) gave way to another (capitalism), new forms of social order also emerged commensurate with this new regime of socio-political organization and economic exploitation.

This "transition" from feudalism to capitalism didn't equal the levelling of social hierarchies or the liberatory redistribution of power and wealth. Far from it. Indeed, the transition to capitalism marks the moment in Western European history where the state in its modern form comes into being as an instrument of class rule. While common folk are freed from the rigid hierarchies and obligations they had to live under feudalism, relations of ruling merely take on a new form in step with the new productive basis of society and those who control it. It is during this long period that many of the institutions we now associate with modern life under capitalism come into being. Not only does this include factories but also prisons, poor houses, asylums, and other forms of social regulation.

Social theorist Michel Foucault called this period the birth of *biopolitics* since it is the era in which relations and institutions of social control become invested in the way that social life is lived. While under feudalism nobles certainly exploited the labour of peasants (demanding a portion of their crops or goods, enlisting them as combatants when they needed to raise an army, even demanding sexual access to women), as a system it had very little interest in their day-to-day affairs at the level of village life. This switches dramatically under capitalism. First, peasants living a collective, grounded, village-centred life need to be "pulled up by the roots" in order to be turned into waged workers so they can't simply rely on each other or their collective life on the land to sustain themselves but must sell their labour for a wage (Federici 2003; Linebaugh 2008). Second, the kinds of discipline necessary to secure wealth accumulation under capitalism, where workers' time and activity needs to be monitored, directed, and controlled, require very different forms of social control than feudal ones (Linebaugh and Rediker 2000).

The transition from feudalism to capitalism in Western Europe is the period during which we see a proliferation of new laws criminalizing poverty, joblessness, and homelessness. While population management was not a serious concern for nobles under feudalism, under capitalism workers and their labour are targeted directly for exploitation, turning population management into a central matter of state concern. Eventually this leads to modern institutions like public schools, organized, not coincidentally, to mirror forms of discipline, reward, and punishment found in factories (Haworth and Elmore 2017). Even current debates over women's control of their own reproductive function date back to this period as elites moved to make sure they would have enough workers to gainfully exploit (Federici 2003; 2012).

Of course, modern institutions like schools, parliaments, hospitals, and more have positive functions in society. But replacing the punitive, life-or-death model of absolute rule that existed under feudalism did not simply usher in a world of rational order and individual liberties. In fact, one of the key consequences of this transition was not to do away with the dynamics of the few ruling the many but to sink those dynamics into the institutions and relations making up everyday life. This has the effect of naturalizing relations of ruling in such a way that makes their oppressive and exploitative nature more difficult to perceive.

The institutions and relationships that serve this purpose shift across time and social location. While religious institutions and patriarchal family relations might have once been key sources of social order and control, today precarious work and ubiquitous culture industries discipline us and our imaginations of what is possible by crafting myths of happiness through conspicuous consumption, nightmares of precariousness and catastrophe, and social media echo chambers that nurture narcissism and limitless self-promotion. Italian Communist, anti-fascist, and political theorist Antonio Gramsci (1985) called this process of ideological domination by one class over others *hegemony*. Conventional institutions provide the essentials of socialization in a large-scale society as well as offering the ruling class recourse to the force necessary to preserve the status quo when more subtle methods of coercing compliance fail or when the targets of control and repression are socially, politically, and economically marginalized.

Fear of downward economic mobility and precarious work are regularly invoked to keep white, middle-class youth docile and compliant, while prisons, the police, and a mushrooming apparatus of state repression are brought to bear against racialized, gendered, and sexual minorities, Indigenous Peoples, political dissidents, and the poor. As we see in the intervention by Ardath Whynacht, notions of justice and how to achieve it are never free of the wider social, political, and historical context. While it's understandable for those of us not up against the cutting edges of structural violence to imagine our world as a fundamentally just one, we would do well to question where we get the coordinates by which we navigate society and what the stories we accept about it tell us. Control mythologies are stories that circulate through a variety of media telling us to believe, obey, and trust in the status quo and the powers that be (Reinsborough and Canning 2010). When combined with low-intensity social war against society's marginalized and downtrodden, this matrix has proven to be a remarkably effective and durable way of maintaining capitalist relations of ruling in liberal democratic societies. However, no order is stable indefinitely, and a perfect storm of a globe-spanning pandemic, climate crisis, widening inequality, austerity, and unending war threatens the existing capitalist order as never before. The question now is what will replace it.

"JUSTICE" AND THE CYCLE OF VIOLENCE
IN SETTLER COLONIALISM — *ARDATH WHYNACHT*

EVERY YEAR ON CANADA Day, red and white flags are waved with enthusiasm and pride, but fireworks and cheerful backyard barbeques can't erase a history of bloodshed and colonial occupation. Traditional narratives of statehood in settler colonialism position the act of colonization as a "civilizing" move to bring stability and peace, yet history books tell us of scalping bounties and residential schools. Our social institutions emerged from this troubling history, and our medical, legal and education systems perpetuate colonizing injustices today.

Taiaiake Alfred (2016) reminds us that "Canada is built on the assumption of a perpetual re-colonization of people and land that allows settler society to enjoy the privileges and the prosperity that are the inheritance of conquest." How, then, can state-based responses to violence be effective when the state itself is a manifestation of colonial violence?

Prisons as a Symptom of Violence

American scholar and activist Angela Davis (2003) argues that prisons are obsolete for this very reason. She demonstrates how the prison system in the United States is a modern reincarnation of slavery and makes links between state military violence and gender-based violence in the home. Prison abolitionist scholars and organizations like Critical Resistance, in the United States, advocate for a world without prisons because policing and incarceration are not effective in preventing violence (Davis 2003; Richie 2012). Indeed, a racist prison system often works to teach violence rather than to heal or rehabilitate. Moreover, Michel Foucault (1995) points out that we live in a disciplinary society, where the logic of discipline and punishment structure all our social relations along what he calls the "carceral continuum." In a carceral society that is founded and maintained by violence, the logic of punishment eclipses "healing," "prevention," and "rehabilitation." The prison is kept alive in our all our relations when discipline and punishment become widespread tools of social control. In a neoliberal society, individuals are made responsible for problems that are collectively produced and maintained. In a society that teaches violence through military action, heavy-handed policing (Maynard 2017), and rape culture, it hardly seems fitting to blame individual perpetrators for a deeply embedded social problem. In this way, the criminal justice system can be seen as a symptom of the cycle of violence rather than a solution to it.

Violence in Canada

Violence is a complex and persistent social problem that impacts us all. Violence disproportionately impacts those who are made the most vulnerable within a settler colonial society that was founded on patriarchal, white-supremacist ideologies that devalue women and Indigenous and racialized people. A woman is killed by an intimate partner approximately every six days in Canada (Canadian Women's Foundation n.d.). Indigenous, Inuit, and Metis women are six times more likely to be killed than white women. Young women, racialized, and immigrant women also face higher rates of victimization and are taken less seriously by police. Those living with disabilities are also among the most vulnerable. Lesbian, bisexual, and transgender women also face higher rates of intimate partner violence than their heterosexual counterparts. Children who grow up in homes where there is physical, sexual, or emotional abuse face increased risks for suicide, substance use, or mental illness. Although rates of reported violent crime have been steadily dropping in Canada since the 1970s (Statistics Canada 2017a), the prevalence of interpersonal violence is much higher than what is reported to police. Some studies reveal that natural disasters, recessions, and rising unemployment rates cause an increase in intimate partner and family violence (Graveland 2016). Furthermore, reported sexual assault rates have not declined in Canada since 1999, and, in fact, rates of reported sexual assault in intimate relationships increased between 2009 and 2013 (Canadian Women's Foundation n.d.). Social and economic investment in prisons and policing have not broken the cycle of violence in our homes and communities.

Blurring the Line Between "Victim" and "Perpetrator"

The criminal justice system is often concerned with drawing a hard and fast line between "victim" and "perpetrator." Deliberations on guilt and innocence are made according to these dualistic ways of thinking about violence. But many perpetrators are also victims. Research demonstrates that an overwhelming majority of those living in prisons have traumatic life histories, characterized by family abuse, sexual violence, and abuse at the hands of others (Government of Canada 2020; CBC News 2015). Approximately 80 percent of federally sentenced women have histories of physical or sexual abuse prior to incarceration, and for Indigenous women who are living in federal prisons, the number increases to 91 percent. Men who are living in prison also show disproportionately higher rates of victimization through sexual and physical abuse (Miller and Najavits 2012). Where trauma treatment programs are not available in provincial health-care systems and where poverty and social ideologies work to frame our suffering as an "individual failure" rather than a collective problem, those who have been harmed by violence often find themselves at risk for addiction, unstable employment and housing, and subsequent arrest and incarceration. Few resources are available to those who have experienced this harm, and, as a result, they become more vulnerable to violence within the prison system, where institutional violence, overcrowding, and bullying compromise any possible "rehabilitation" the prison seeks to provide (Government of Canada 2020). Further complicating the cycle of violence is the effect of the prison system on family members of those who are incarcerated. A major study in the US shows that the incarceration of a family member constitutes an adverse childhood experience that can impact the physical, emotional, and psychological health of a child well into adulthood (Centers for Disease Control and Prevention 2021). In this way, the prison system feeds into a cycle of violence and trauma.

Trauma-Informed and Transformative Justice?

If the state cannot effectively break the cycle of violence through the criminal justice system, what could "justice" look like in settler colonialism? Trauma-informed, or "transformative," justice is a movement that expands the scope of traditional restorative justice practices in favour of transforming communities, healing from violence, and re-patterning our relations with each other (Morris 1999, 2000; Nocella 2011). This approach takes up notions of Indigenous justice that pre-date our current criminal justice system (Vancouver Aboriginal Transformative Justice Services Society n.d.). Transformative justice seeks to transform our world by refusing the logic of the "carceral continuum" and resisting the ways that the state, and our broader social world, teach us to control, punish, and harm each other. If the state began as a project of imperialism and violence, then perhaps "justice" might mean resisting all forms of violence in favour of creating grassroots resources for healing from trauma, holding space for community dialogue on the social problem of violence, and working on collective rather than individual strategies of rehabilitation. Groups such as the Third Eye Collective in Montreal (2017), the Gatehouse in Toronto, and Circles of Support and Accountability (several sites in Canada) advocate for healing and form stronger community relations as a means of resisting the cycle of violence.

CHALLENGING AND CHANGING SOCIAL RELATIONS

Knowledge about the world is never free of the interests and perspectives of those who produce it. At the turn of the twentieth century, structural functionalism and other dominant theories about society and how it works stressed the naturalness of the established order and the equilibrium of the status quo. Sociologists and other social scientists studying social order and change right through the mid-twentieth century consistently dismissed any suggestion that social change could be driven by people who were not elites operating from within society's dominant institutions. Drawing on psychological collective behaviour theories, these academics saw people organizing and mobilizing outside of established channels of political control and representation as little more than unwashed, unconscious mobs who were simply blowing off steam and venting frustrations before returning to their roles within the status quo (Staggenborg 2012). Similarly, conventional histories of the world's "great revolutions" include the American and French Revolutions but have consistently excluded the Haitian Revolution despite the fact that the Haitian Revolution was pathbreaking as the lone example of a revolution successfully carried out by enslaved people and constituted the first free Black republic in the Western hemisphere (James 1989).

Mainly white, mainly male historians have also systematically minimized the depth and extent of the European witch hunts during the Middle Ages, dismissing a systematic, widespread, brutal collusion between church and state that led to the torture and murder of hundreds of thousands of women (Federici 2003; Mies 1986). Feminist scholars have excavated a very different history, demonstrating the intentional role played by the witch hunts in destroying women's social power, facilitating a process of primitive accumulation, and pulling up grassroots resistance by the roots. Indeed, the Inquisition in Europe would be the proving ground for the techniques deployed by colonizers in the so-called New World as they sought to subjugate or, failing that, exterminate Indigenous Peoples (Federici 2003). Other radical historians have also shed light on pirates, enslaved people, rebels, outlaws, common folk, and many more who resisted the relations of subjugation and exploitation elites sought to impose upon them (Linebaugh 2008; Linebaugh and Rediker 2000; Rediker 2004; 2007). Not only did the labour of these people literally build the modern world, but their struggles to defend their dignity and autonomy while seeking alternatives to the designs of the powerful have indelibly shaped the world.

So why are these histories so little known and why did they take so long to come to light? Simply put, many academics — privileged in classed, gendered, and racialized terms and invested in the systems committed to maintaining those privileges — could not believe that common folk were capable of being world-shaping forces. For them, all change came from the creativity, enlightenment, innovation, and benevolence of the ruling class. For academics studying social movements, it would not be until the 1960s that people's attempts at grassroots organization outside the halls of power would be taken seriously as a form of politics rather than simply "mob behaviour" (McCarthy and Zald 1977; Zald and McCarthy 1979; Piven and Cloward 1977).

This conceptual and analytical awakening was due to the intentionality, organization, and commitment of movements themselves. These movements, including civil rights, women's liberation, student activism, anti-war, and much more, were so well organized, communicated with wider society so clearly, and mobilized for social change so consciously and effectively that they simply could no longer be written off as the masses blowing off steam. Academics were compelled to think and write differently about them, a process that within sociology and anthropology gave birth to the field of social movement studies. The significance of this is not so much in the scholarly acknowledgement of social movements as genuinely political and worthy of attention as in the recognition that ordinary people are capable of coming together to exercise their collective power and change their world. While elites frequently claim that they have everyone's best interests at heart and are progressively improving society, even a cursory glance at the maldistribution of power, wealth, and resources between those with the most and the vast majority of humanity tells a very different story. From the right not to be arbitrarily detained to the emancipation of enslaved people to the eight-hour workday to basic public services, many of the key elements of modern democratic life that we take for granted were won by people organized collectively in struggle. They were not given by elites; these victories were extracted from them by people's movements. Indeed, this is what a social movement essentially is: a group of people coming together for a common cause who organize themselves to exercise collective power in pursuit of that cause.

Social change is, of course, a complicated and dynamic process. Just as it is not simply the province of elites, neither can social movements lay unique claim to it. No one can predict with any reliability when openings and opportunities emerge for those ready to lay hold of them, nor is there ever any guarantee that change will be progressive or social-justice oriented. However, by studying periods of significant socio-political change and those marked by upsurges in social movement activity, we can begin to understand the balance of forces, institutions, and actors at work and the ways people have organized with others to affect their lifeworlds. This doesn't mean we can create a roadmap or toolbox for changing the world since contexts are constantly developing and actors and institutions of all kinds learn lessons and adapt over time. It does mean that we can learn to be more effective in our efforts to create a more just, dignified, and peaceful world. We can also appreciate just how much of what we currently take for granted is due not to the benevolence of the ruling class but to the creativity, passion, and commitment of those common folk who, like you and me, are sometimes willing to risk everything for a chance at a better world.

CONCLUSION

What is society and how does it come into being? In this chapter, we briefly explore and debunk arguments that suggest that society is either a ready-made, ever present structure into which we are slotted like machine parts or the sum of everyone's individual personality and experience. Social order is a complex amalgamation of material practices, relationships, institutions, and ideologies. In a very real sense, each of us makes society every day by acting it into being, by continuing to believe in it, and by investing in it emotionally, intellectually, and physically. We also explore the idea that society exists to serve our individual and collective needs as human beings and social subjects. While it's true that humans are biocultural organisms constituted by a complex interplay between biological and socio-cultural forces, we miss a great deal when we fail to ask in whose interests a given social order works.

For most people, the social world into which we were born seems normal, even natural. We are not born into the world as fully formed members of society. The whole reason for processes like enculturation and socialization is that new people need to be trained into the social world they are becoming a part of. If social order was simply natural none of this would be necessary. Beyond this, we explore how social order and its related processes and dynamics are fundamentally power-laden in nature. That is, society, from social values and norms to institutions and relationships, is not a neutral outcome of an inevitable development process but the product of vested interests and power relations. While we all live in societies of one kind or another, we are far from equal in terms of where any one of us might find ourselves located in terms of opportunities, resources, access, and authority.

Following this insight, we critically examine power not as something that people possess but as a relationship that is shared amongst them. Understood in this way, power is a terrain of possibility, not just a weapon to be wielded for or against something or someone. Our capacity to do is what power is at its root. It is when this capacity to do is collectively exercised that it is at its most impressive and world-shaping. But who decides to what uses our collective power-to ought to be put? Just as we all live in society without being equally placed with respect to its matrix of privilege, our collective power-to is channelled and shaped in ways that often do not benefit people equally.

In addressing this, we turn our critical gaze on ideology, a system of ideas about the world and our place in it. We explore how our ideas about the world, what it is, why it is the way it is, and what is possible or not are deeply shaped by the stories we tell (and are told) about the world. These stories are fundamentally linked to the interests of those with the greatest ability to shape and disseminate them and are connected to the material and productive basis of society.

Finally, we consider the dynamics of social control and social change. To do this effectively, we must begin by calling into question the naturalness of the social order we are investigating, particularly if it's the one we've been socialized into. It then becomes possible to examine the dynamics of social order and control from the perspective of who they serve and in whose interests they act rather than fuzzy ideas about "good" versus "bad" social orders that always end up trapped in whatever ideology they are invested. We cannot forget that social orders, their dominant institutions, and the relations of ruling that sustain and reproduce them are first and foremost beholden to those with their hands on the levers of social power. That does not mean we have to be either total cynics about society or resigned to being acted upon by the powerful. Instead, it means that to understand and act effectively in our social order and in pursuit of a better, more just, more peaceful, and more dignified one, we must never shy away from asking hard questions about who wins, who loses, and what tools — or weapons — are used in the maintenance of the status quo.

KEY CONCEPTS

biocultural organism: a term denoting humanity's existence at the intersection of our biological needs and our facility for culture-making and self-awareness. As a species and individuals, we are not reducible to either biological characteristics or cultural-symbolic dimensions but a complex amalgamation of both.

biopolitics: coined by social theorist Michel Foucault, it refers to a form of social organization in which relations and institutions of social control become invested in the management of populations and the way that life is lived.

cultural capital: the personal assets a person can mobilize to make their way up the hierarchy in a stratified society. These assets refer to things like knowledge, manners, style of speech and dress, and other forms of cultural competency.

culture shock: the sensation of uncertainty, out-of-placedness, and strangeness that accompanies finding oneself somewhere very different from what is familiar in terms of social and cultural context.

enculturation: the process of acquiring culture.

hegemony: coined by Italian Communist, anti-fascist, and political theorist Antonio Gramsci to refer to the process of ideological domination by one class over others.

ideology: a system of ideas shared among a group of people that allows them to make sense of the social world. No ideology is a neutral description of the world; it is a set of ideas that tells us why the world is the way it is and how we fit into it.

imagination: the collective capacity to envision with others that which does not yet exist, a key aspect of people's ability to act in the world.

norms: the often-unspoken social conventions that implicitly guide our social behaviour.

power: most superficially, the ability to exert force or control over others, to exercise one's will regardless of opposition or resistance. It is less useful to talk about power as a thing one either has or doesn't and much more useful to talk about it as a relationship. In this sense, power is a relationship between multiple subjects through which force is exerted in the world and on us. We exercise power when we come together for common, consensual projects just as much as we do when we find ourselves compelled to direct our energies at the behest of someone else.

ruling class: refers broadly to the strata of individuals in a society who exercise the greatest power over others. Under capitalism, the ruling class are the owners of the means of production.

social capital: the resources to which one gains access as a result of the social networks of which one is a part.

social controls (formal and informal): the mechanisms used to maintain a given social order. Informal social controls are often exercised inter-personally, are meant to encourage compliance with social norms, and take such forms as gossip, ridicule, shame, and discipline at home. Formal social controls are carried out by authorized agents who apply specific punishments for deviance from the norm. Such agents include bosses, teachers, doctors, social workers, police, and administrators.

social institutions: the basic rules of order and behaviour in a society. It refers to enduring and enforced norms, roles, values, and organizations that can be formal or informal. The primary purpose of social institutions is the maintenance and reproduction of the established order.

socialization: the process of learning and becoming a part of the social system.

4

WHO ARE WE?

Identity and Intersections

Who are you? Instead of jumping in to answer the question with all the social facts we're trained to respond with (name and age, residence, gender, nationality, likes and dislikes, school/work status, and so on), stop for a moment and really think about it. Who are you and how did you come to know about where and how you fit in the world? Perhaps more importantly, what shapes your experiences as you move through the world? Do you worry about interacting with police or other state authorities? Do you feel safe walking home after dark? Do you easily take up space in public?

As we explore in Chapter 3, enculturation and socialization are the processes of acquiring knowledge of the socio-cultural codes that we need to figure out and fit into a given social order. While these processes are universal in the sense that every society does them to ensure its reproduction, they are experienced differently depending on our location in the wider web of power relations that structure social life. For example, formal education is a critical dimension of socialization and enculturation, but there is a world of difference between the experience and outcomes of formal learning in exclusive private schools and the under-resourced, overcrowded public system. More than a question of resources, this is also bound up in the social position and expectations of students before they even enter the doors of their respective institutions.

In this chapter we dig into the power-laden process of identification as a collective rather than individual phenomenon. How we come to know who we are is central to a society's relations of ruling — the way a society's ruling class advances their ideological and material interests over, above, and at the expense of others. That does not mean identity is merely a ruling-class straitjacket into which we are all compelled to fit in order to go work in the social factory. Like culture, identity is contested and dynamic, and all kinds of creative work goes into making social identities at the grassroots that actively seek to rework, create anew, or resist ruling-class impositions. Making sense of this complex intersection of power, feeling, history, and collective identities is our task in this chapter.

SOCIAL CONSTRUCTIONS, MATERIAL REALITIES

Let's get something out of the way at the outset: all identities are social in nature. There is no such thing as an identity that is pre-social or rooted in something other than our social world. This goes beyond the understanding that the words we use to identify social status or life stage are arbitrary and socially constructed. More basically, it refers to the fact that taken-for-granted categories like "race," gender, sexuality, age, and ability, to name only a few, are products of the social work of meaning-making that we are constantly doing together, not objective biological facts. It is no more natural or factual to see gender as dividing the entirety of the human species into two categories (man and woman) than it is to understand gender as a fluid spectrum of many possible expressions. Given the incredible diversity of human social life, the idea that gender could be divided into two discrete and fixed categories seems rather silly. The same could be said of racialized categories; in a very real sense, there are no "white" or "Black" people. Of course, melanin concentration leads to different hues of skin tone and these categories have powerful social significance. But "white" and "Black" people as distinct and fixed groups do not exist biologically; rather, they are brought into existence by powerful social institutions and processes that make them real. In this case, the animating forces are the legacy of slavery, colonialism, imperialism, and capitalism.

The notion of the social contract is often invoked in discussions about the need to balance individual rights and freedoms with collective security and social order. This idea, which emerged out of the Western European Enlightenment, posits that modern, liberal democratic governance depends on the consent of the governed. People willingly submit to the authority of the state and sacrifice unfettered freedoms in exchange for the state's defence of other rights and a stable social order. The social contract is thus seen as the basis for rational, enlightened, and modern rule. From this perspective, social problems like racism, classism, and misogyny are aberrations, irrational holdovers from previous times that are bound to disappear with time and progress. But what if they are not aberrations but rather are consequences of these modern forms of rule and, in particular, modern relations of oppression and exploitation?

Eminent philosopher Charles Mills (1997) argues that the basis for modern, liberal democratic rule isn't a social contract but a racial contract. Think back to our explorations of who counted as human as the modern world was being ruthlessly cobbled together under colonial, imperial, and capitalist rubrics. Surveying the fruits of modern liberal philosophy and democracy, Mills shows us that you can express grand sentiments in defence of dignity, rationality, and individual autonomy and participate in a regime that denies these things to huge swaths of humanity precisely because many people are excluded from being considered fully human. The social contract can apply but only to those who are seen as worthy. This exclusion isn't accidental; it's a function of those relations of exploitation that are integral to the way wealth is accumulated and power exercised.

Our modern ideas about gender and race can be traced to ruling-class attempts to accumulate wealth through the exploitation of other people's lives and labour, not to some set of primordial or ancient beliefs about essential human difference. People were not "Black" or "white," "settler" or "Indigenous" before social relations of oppression and exploitation rendered them so. They were simply different people in all their unique socio-historical specificity. The rigid policing of racialized borders only came into being once colonialism and colour-coded slavery were set in motion as forms of wealth-taking. The policing of gendered boundaries became a matter of prime concern once social reproduction (the everyday reproduction of people and their ability to work) became central to wealth production.

As Marxist-feminist scholar Silvia Federici points out, the Marxist concept of *primitive accumulation* does not refer only to the necessary precursor stage to capitalism where workers and capital are concentrated and accumulated by those prepared to exploit them. It also speaks to the "accumulation of differences and divisions within the working class, whereby hierarchies built upon gender, as well as 'race' and age, became constitutive of class rule and the formation of the modern proletariat" (2003, 63–64). This doesn't mean that all oppressions come down to capitalist exploitation but rather that it is impossible to understand relations of exploitation and oppression without considering how they work together. Exploitation and oppression are a double-helix of relations of domination; they cannot be considered independently from one another if we are to understand and move beyond them.

In his pathbreaking work *The Wages of Whiteness*, David Roediger (2007) explores how whiteness as an identity became a vital form of currency for working people who could identify as such in the US in the nineteenth century. While racism was obviously a central pillar of the trans-Atlantic slave trade, whiteness became more important to "white" working people after the formal end of slavery in the US. It served as a way for white working people to distinguish themselves as free citizens of the nation over and against those cast as degraded and unworthy of freedom or security, namely, Black people. This became more important as white workers faced proliferating forms of unfreedom and exploitation. In this context, whiteness became a form of identification that acted as a psychological and social buffer for white workers who, if confronted with insecurity, at least could claim they were not as degraded as Black people. The "wage" paid by whiteness in this example is psychological and social in nature, comforting those who can claim it while allowing the system of exploitation to continue its business as usual.

IDENTITY AS PERFORMANCE

In June 2015 a news story broke in the United States about a woman by the name of Rachel Dolezal. She had recently resigned as president of the Spokane, Washington, chapter of the National Association for the Advancement of Colored People (NAACP) as rumours began to circulate publicly that she was not, as she claimed to be, a Black person. Dolezal had also worked as an instructor in the Africana Studies Program at Eastern Washington University. Dolezal appeared to be a light-skinned Black person or, at the very least, someone of African American heritage. As the controversy deepened, Dolezal's parents, both of whom identify as white, came forward to state that their daughter had been trying to "disguise herself" as African American but that she was, in fact, white (Mosendz 2015).

Eventually Dolezal admitted that she was not African American but continued to assert that she identified as Black. Claiming that her identity was "transracial," Dolezal's public line was that she saw race as a social construct, not a biological reality, and that she identified with Black culture and experience (Ellison 2017). The curious case of Rachel Dolezal occupied media cycles for a short time, but the questions raised by it linger. On the face of it, there is something sensible and even liberatory about Dolezal's assertion of "transraciality," which she and others obviously linked to transgender. Race is indeed a social construct and it is vitally important to assert that these categories are flexible, not essential. On the other hand, as a white person, Dolezal had taken up space and resources in Black institutions, spoken on behalf of communities in which she had no roots, and claimed a different "race" in a way that most members of oppressed groups could never mimic. One commentator noted, "Black people could never be transracial the way she's attempting to be. Dolezal's whiteness provides the empty template for her to redesign. I am troubled by her version of transracial because it's something only white or light-skinned people can enact" (Ellison 2017). Given this, we might ask: is Dolezal's "transraciality" anti-racist or racist?

The case of Rachel Dolezal points to the importance of performance in relation to identity. Our social identities are like the roles actors play. They are not manifestations of some essential, unalterable nature but ways of being in the world that we learn to accept and inhabit. As philosopher and gender theorist Judith Butler famously argues, gender is an identity "instituted through a *stylized repetition of acts*" (1988, 519). What Butler means by this is that gender is an identity that's acted into being as people physically and socially embody it through "bodily movements, gestures, and enactments." There is no single, transhistorical, universal way of practising gender roles. The idea that there is a single correct set of gender roles is quite simply blown apart if we take even the most cursory tour of what gender roles look like in different times and places and even in the same times and places but among different communities.

A thought experiment is usually a good way to demonstrate the incoherence of the common-sense conviction that there is such a thing as "proper" gender roles. Make a list of the characteristics stereotypically associated with masculinity and femininity. Typically, this looks something like masculinity being associated with strength, a lack of emotionality, aggression, ambition, decisiveness, toughness, and being the breadwinner/provider. Femininity, conversely, is often associated with emotionality, nurturing, gentleness, submissiveness, domesticity, empathy, and vulnerability. Now think of all the self-identified men and women in your own life who do not conform to these stereotypical characteristics. Do you know people who identify as men who are gentle and caring people? Do you know people who identify as women who do not want to have children? Do you know people who identify as women but who freely express anger? Does it make my partner less feminine because she enjoys training in kickboxing and isn't afraid of an argument? Does it make me less masculine if I enjoy caring for my children and recognize housework as important and part of my shared responsibilities?

When I run this little experiment in class and ask students to raise their hands if they know someone who identifies as one gender but does not conform to any or many of the traits conventionally associated with it, there is rarely a hand that doesn't go up. Like all broad identity categories, gender can seem contained and coherent in our minds and much more fuzzy, complicated, and messy when played out in real life. If we reflect carefully and honestly, most of us would agree that our own experience of gender isn't neatly bounded. While it's common for people to understand that social roles like gender change over time, it's at least as important to understand that gender is diversely experienced and enacted at any specific point in time. In other words, we are not only seeing change over time but diversity as a fundamental characteristic of lived experience. Understandings of what it means to be a man or woman, to take only two points on a much longer spectrum, differ across lines of generation, class, racialized identity, ethnic background, and much more.

To get a sense of changing gendered expectations and norms, just look at popular representations in the mainstream media of what it means to be a proper man or woman (from Hollywood blockbusters to local folk tales) from any time period. We can see gender roles changing because gender is, like all identity categories, a public, social expression that we perform for ourselves and each other. From the way we dress to the way we speak and take up space to our expectations of life, gender roles and relations are things we literally live into being. If we expand that survey to the world, we encounter an incredible range of what it means to express gender identity across the scope of human experience. This is why the controversy around transgender marshalled by conservatives, the far right, and feminist-appropriating radical transphobes is so telling and so absurd. There is nothing fixed, fundamental, or unalterable about gender. If it were so, the incredible work that goes into socializing people into and policing so-called "traditional" gender roles would be entirely unnecessary because we would just enact them like any other autonomic response.

I love that argument!

When people express anger and anxiety over transgender or other issues of gender justice, they are really expressing anxiety over a perceived challenge to the way they understand the world, and more importantly, to their own power and entitlements. Bemoaning the loss of traditional gender roles is therefore little more than a complaint about challenges to institutionalized forms of power by those whose unearned privileges are threatened by struggles for greater diversity and justice. Social and collective identities are always implicated in relations of power; what is at stake when we seem to be arguing about identity is really a struggle over power and who gets to exercise it.

This notion of identity as performed and embodied can also be extended to ways of being in the world beyond gender. As we've already seen, social class is profoundly performative. Which fork do I use for which course of the meal? What's the difference between enthusiastically supporting my team at a hockey game and knowing how to appreciate opera or ballet? Do I have the kind of job that expects I shower before the workday or at the end of it? This idea of performance extends to all forms of identity. Think about any national holiday. How do people demonstrate patriotic feeling? They engage in a variety of elaborately staged and ritualized mass events, dress in ways that celebrate nationalist symbols, and take part in activities linked to a stereotyped national identity. They perform national belonging. What about the admonishment to "act your age"? The practice of socializing the young into the social order is, at heart, all about them learning how to conform to dominant expectations and standards of behaviour, particularly in public.

Let's return to the example of Rachel Dolezal to explore this idea of identity as performance a little more deeply. Is Dolezal's claim to "transracialism" anti-racist? By taking on the role of a Black woman in a white supremacist society, isn't she demonstrating the socially constructed nature of race and how grouping people according to arbitrary characteristics like skin colour is just an elaborate fiction? While the issue is complicated, I think it's safe to answer "no." While Dolezal's case helps us see race as a socially constructed identity that's not essentially "true," it also exposes how and why race as a power-laden category of identity matters. Social identity is not like an all-you-can-eat buffet where people are equally empowered to pick and choose the identity they want. Social identity is a phenomenon deeply linked to the prevailing power order.

For example, in Medieval Europe, peasant and noble were categories of identification and in that sense clearly constructed and "made up." But whether a person was a noble or peasant wasn't just a matter of identity; it also carried profound implications for the kind of power people wielded in society and the material wealth and security they enjoyed. In a settler-colonial state like Canada, one could argue that the categories of "settler" and "Indigenous" are also constructed identities, but they carry legal, social, political, and cultural consequences that deeply shape the life experiences of those who fall into them. So while Dolezal may be telling the truth when she says she's honouring her own truth by identifying as Black, as a white person she can opt in and out of that "Black identity," allowing her to either enjoy or escape the real life consequences with which that identity is freighted.

Struggles over Indigenous rights in the context of settler-colonial states highlight what is at stake when it comes to identity, belonging, and power. As sociologist Darryl Leroux explores in his research, there has been a veritable explosion of "Eastern métis" organizations in Ontario, Quebec, New Brunswick, Nova Scotia, and Maine since the early 2000s, all claiming rights as Indigenous Peoples. Under Canadian law, the Métis are recognized as an Indigenous people with constitutionally enshrined rights, but there are important distinctions between the Métis and other Indigenous nations. As a people, the Métis are not only the product of Indigenous women producing offspring with European fur traders in the eighteenth century in west central North America. They are recognized as a distinct people as a result of carving out their own social and political practices and institutions, cultural forms, and language in the context of "ongoing kinship relations with Cree, Saulteaux, Assiniboine and Dene peoples" (Leroux 2018). In other words, it isn't enough to claim a distant Indigenous ancestor to be able to identify as a member of the Métis Nation; what matters most are the kin relations, socio-political and cultural distinctiveness, and enduring connections to community and territory. In the words of Kim TallBear, "Indigenous peoples' 'ancestry' is not simply genetic ancestry evidenced in 'populations' but biological, cultural, and political groupings constituted in dynamic, long-standing relationships with each other and with living landscapes that define their people-specific identities and, more broadly, their indigeneity" (2013, 410).

Indigenous people are not simply born into indigeneity; they live it collectively as a consequence of their relationships to place and the other beings that inhabit it. Identity and belonging are inherently relational (Wilson 2009). This relationality of course extends to other groups as well. Settlers are only settlers because of their relationship to ongoing processes of settler-colonialism and the social and political relationships and institutions produced out of them. As Leroux details in his research, so-called "Eastern métis" organizations arose in recent decades in the context of conflicts over land, access, and resources between settlers and Indigenous Peoples across eastern Canada. Following a strategy of "self-indigenization," thousands of people across Ontario, Quebec, New Brunswick, and Nova Scotia who previously identified as white sought to lay claim to Métis belonging by claiming a distant sixteenth-century Indigenous ancestor. More than this, they quickly organized themselves into a variety of lobbying organizations to press the courts for the recognition of their rights and entitlements as Indigenous people.

As Leroux notes, according to census data, in 2016 more than 23,000 people claimed Métis identity in Nova Scotia (2.5 percent of the population) compared to only 860 (0.09 percent of the population) similarly identifying as such in the census in 1996. Seeking to leverage the courts in a struggle over land, resources, and other benefits, people who formerly identified as Euro-ancestry white people turned to claims of primordial indigeneity not because they had found themselves and their people but because such claims were politically and legally effective, or so they hoped. Working under a "métis" banner, these new organizations have attempted to leverage Indigenous identity claims in pursuit of two specific and troubling ends: first, to secure greater rights and entitlements for people who until very recently claimed Euro-ancestry identities; and second, to push back against Indigenous Peoples' struggles for self-determination and resurgence.

In the most audacious cases, Leroux explains, what we are witnessing is the weaponization of Indigenous identity claims in defence of a white-rights agenda. Some of these newly minted "métis" across eastern Canada have taken commercial DNA tests and mobilized the results (often as little as a single Indigenous ancestor who lived in the seventeenth century) to "prove" their Indigenous belonging, while others simply sign a sworn statement testifying to their ancestry. But even where a long-lost Indigenous ancestor can be confirmed, the courts have been unmoved by such shallow accountings of Indigenous belonging and have affirmed that enduring relations to culture, community, and territory are the real hallmarks of Indigenous identity, not the mere existence of a distant biological ancestor.

As the Dolezal and Eastern métis cases illustrate, claims to identity, particularly group identity, always have to be considered in light of their contexts and what is at stake in their affirmation or rejection. In both these cases, identity claims not recognized by the community at issue (African Americans in Dolezal's case, Métis and other Indigenous Peoples in the Eastern métis case) provide the basis for the appropriation of rights, entitlements, resources, and space by members of a more socially privileged group at the expense of those from marginalized and oppressed ones. What is at issue here is not just how we feel as individuals and how we wish to be recognized by others. This is an issue of material realities. Dolezal's appropriation of Black identity cannot be separated from the fact that her claim-making occurs in the context of white supremacy. Assertions of Eastern métis identity cannot be divorced from the ongoing realities of settler-colonialism in Canada and the unfinished work of justice and reconciliation.

It's clear that identity isn't just about truth in an objective, eternal sense. Following such a path, however well-intentioned, leads us quickly into "blood and soil" narratives that fascists have employed with murderous consequences since the 1920s. We should always be suspicious of assertions of "pure" identity wrapped in mystical notions of blood, destiny, and belonging. If certain people are bound for grand historical missions, the clear implication is that other people are not. The resistance and even mere existence of these others stand as a challenge to this group and the sacred mandate to which it is attached. Such a challenge cannot be tolerated; neither purity nor destiny allow for such accommodation and must be uprooted by whatever means necessary. This is, in short, a rationale for genocide.

Our social identities cannot be essential and immutable, and they are most certainly not rooted in our DNA. The American Society for Human Genetics (ASHG) states unequivocally, "Genetics demonstrates that humans cannot be divided into biologically distinct subcategories" (ASHG 2018). In the same statement, the ASHG denounces the misuse of scientific discourse in the service of white supremacy and other forms of racist thinking and practice. Humans are a diverse species, but as the ASHG points out, there is no genetic basis for the belief that humans can be divided into distinct and separate "races." In fact, genetic science shows us that there is "considerable genetic overlap" between members of supposedly distinct "racial" groups, and there is at least as much diversity genetically within supposedly discrete "racial" groups as there is between them (ASHG 2018; Prontzos 2019). The ASHG statement nicely sums it up, "Race ... is a social construct." By the ASHG's own admission, this is a particularly vital insight at a time when white supremacy, white nationalism, and other forms of racist thinking and practice are resurging. There is no genetic scientific basis for the belief in the superiority of one "racial" group over any other.

Of course, pseudo-scientific manipulations of genetics and racist ideologies have never been about good faith interpretations of the scientific evidence; they are about power. As people we belong to and are recognized by our communities; this is where social identity is formed and grounded. But we don't belong to homogenous, incommensurable groups in a mystical, eternal, or fundamental way. That line of thinking and action quickly leads us to fascism and the conviction that our "pure" community needs to be protected from pollution or degradation by others who do not and can never belong to our precious unity.

The productive tension in thinking critically about identity, about who "we" are, is to recognize that all identities are constructed, relational, dynamic, and situated within power relations. In the Dolezal example, what makes her claim problematic is that she appropriates Blackness without being legitimately recognized by other members of her desired community as being a part of it. She refuses to see this act of appropriation as an act of power; she enjoyed power as a white, middle-class person who was able to pass for what she wished to be seen as and even take up space and resources within Black organizations. This intersection of identity with power is what really matters.

RELATIONS OF RULING

Every system of power and order claims the right to tell its subjects who they are. The *relations of ruling* specific to each society are all about telling people who and what they are in the service of those who rule, whether they are kings and queens or CEOs and prime ministers. Beyond familiar concepts like power and the state, "ruling relations combine state, corporate, professional and bureaucratic agencies in a web of relations through which ruling comes to be organized" (Frampton et al. 2006, 37). For these relations of ruling, identity is a central site of struggle and power, and can, of course, also be a site of resistance and alternative building. It's worth thinking about the differences between identities that arise from common experiences and living together and those that are enshrined in the dominant order's institutions and relations and imposed upon people. While identity is central to human social experience, the way it is connected to and mobilized by the prevailing relations of ruling is critical to appreciating the work it does and in whose interests. Challenging the dominant, power-laden accounts of belonging and identity is the subject of the intervention by Eva Mackey. What happens when we look closely at the stories about who we are and the way they are connected to relations of power? What happens when we scrape the surface of our common-sense assumptions and are confronted by our collective implication in a web of relations of exploitation and oppression? Rather than seeing these moments only as indictments of who we are and turning to either anger or resignation, can we see these challenges as opportunities to imagine how we could live together in other ways?

UNSETTLING SETTLERS — *EVA MACKEY*

Since the final report of the Truth and Reconciliation Commission in 2015, terms such as "decolonization," "Indigenous," "racism," and "settler" are heard more often in the mainstream, and there seems to be more awareness of some of the horrors of Canada's relationship with Indigenous Peoples. Controversies over Indigenous land rights, missing and murdered Indigenous women and girls, the Trans-Mountain Pipeline, and Colten Boushie's murder remind us that Indigenous people have been resisting Canada's treatment for years. The tensions over Indigenous/non-Indigenous relations that began before Canada was founded have never stopped. It's clear that the foundational dilemma of the nation has not been settled. How can Canada justify building a nation on land that was not ceded by Indigenous Peoples? How can a nation be legitimate if it was founded, settled and developed on land taken illegitimately, an ongoing process, never recognized and accounted for?

In this context, why would someone in the twenty-first century want to identify themselves as a "settler"? It's not a term that invites admiration or pride. People say that the term settler makes them uncomfortable, even angry, because it's not how they see themselves. "Settlers were the ancestors of Canada," some say. "That's the past. It's over." "We aren't 'settlers' anymore," they say. "We are all Canadians."

Claiming the term "settler" means understanding Canada as a settler nation – a settler colony. Settler colonialism differs from other forms of colonialism because the colonizers don't return to their homelands; they stay and try to replace the societies that were there first with their own society and laws. Settlers differ from immigrants in that they do not adapt to the laws and society of where they go; they bring their laws with them. Replacement in Canada meant a violent process of taking the land and turning it into property for the nation and its citizens and includes violence, diseases, laws, reserves, residential schools and assimilation. Seeing Canada as a settler nation also means knowing that that colonialism is ongoing today, as Indigenous people have been saying for years. So, calling oneself a "settler" means one works to be aware of, and tries to challenge, the ongoing colonialism in Canada. For me it means listening carefully to what Indigenous people are saying and working to change the world. It means asking myself how diverse peoples, with complex and overlapping histories of injustice and collusion, might live together justly, when history, property and the division of lands, resources and power are so contested? What gets in the way of decolonizing these relationships *and* territorial spaces? How is it possible to even imagine a collective project of diverse people living together in a settler colony in a way that does not reproduce the brutal and subtle violence of ongoing colonialism and nation-building? How can we even begin to imagine what it might entail? I think a small beginning is thinking consciously about what it means to be a settler.

If identity is a performance, as this chapter suggests, then embracing the term "settler" for oneself is an uncomfortable, unsettling performance. It is therefore a different kind of identity claim than "queer" or "Black." Those resistant identities work by proudly claiming a previously silenced and oppressed identity to critique dominant society. Claiming "settler" is unsettling because it isn't about pride. It identifies oneself as the inheritor of unearned privileges. It is a mirror no one really wants to look into because it urges us to look at history and the way we live in the present in a different and uncomfortable way.

Everything around us tells us that Canada and its occupation of land and authority over us — and especially over Indigenous Peoples — is natural and normal and will continue forever. Using the term "settler" for myself shifts that sense of naturalness and entitlement. It makes me question the legitimacy of what has been built – how it was built and how it might be changed. It unsettles my certainty that settlers are entitled to all the benefits we tend to see as natural and just the way life is. We start to ask: How did it get to be this way? How did Indigenous land become the property of the nation? How did my back yard and my home become something I could "own" and pass on to my children or sell on the market? How did Canada become my "home" when Indigenous people never consented to the way the territory was taken or the way it has turned out?

We tend to think that racism is about individual bad actions or thoughts – about individual attitudes. Using the term "settler" helps me think about racism and inequality — and the complicated relationship between history and the present — in a different way. It helps to direct my attention to the social and political structures that exist today, structures built on racial ideology and unjust laws and policies, structures that reinforce and reproduce racism and inequality. Whether we have bad attitudes or not, these are the structures of inequality we have inherited and that allow so many privileges to some of us. The term "settler" then, unsettles the idea of us (settlers) as either "good" or "bad" individual citizens who may or may not have "racist" attitudes. It reminds me of the collective land theft that is the foundational structure of our nations and citizenships, and that is ongoing. It's not about guilt for the past, but about acting responsibly and with deep awareness of power in the present. It means taking care of relationships with the world around us. It allows me to begin to open my mind and heart to listen, to see the world differently, and to imagine other possibilities of how we might live together justly and responsibly in this territory. Unsettling myself as a settler is a first step to beginning that process.

As Mackey urges us to consider, some identities are tied to power in a way that others are not. This isn't about creating a list of good identities versus bad ones. But it should encourage us to think about who we are and how some ways of being serve powerful interests much more than others. Nationalism is a particularly potent example of this, so let's explore it. That sense of belonging to a vast community that stretches across physical distance and time clearly isn't something we're simply born with; it's something we learn. As we explore in Chapter 2, the modern nation-state is a kind of "imagined community," an idea of belonging to something much bigger than the individual and the lived relationships that make up our daily existence. The notion of being a part of a people with a distinct, essential identity corresponding to the lines on political maps is a relatively recent invention.

The imagined community of the modern nation really only became possible in the last few hundred years with the advent of forms of media, socialization, and governance that allow (or compel) people's participation in collective, idealized, and ritualized forms of imagining belonging to something together (Anderson 2006). Standardized national languages, mass media technology like the printing press, and the development of a whole symbolic economy (flags, anthems, food, pastimes, dance, dress, and much more) are some of the initial ways people came to see themselves as members of a temporally and territorially vast community. Today, the specific forms used to communicate and consume national identity have been updated but their basic purpose remains the same: to get people to invest in a form of collective identity that binds them together, usually against or above others, and to obscure other important power relations in society. In this sense, nationalism is a modern society's origin myth in that it tells us a highly selective, idealized, and value-laden tale about who we are and what we are here to do.

Nationalism often depicts the people of the nation as the bearers of a special destiny, unique subjects who are the inheritors of values and a mission that sets them apart from others. This destiny or mission is often cast as a sacred trust, and protecting the nation is a paramount duty for the people. It's no coincidence that nationalism as a form of collective identity emerged at the same time as older forms of ideology and social control were ebbing. As feudalism in Europe was giving way to capitalism, the Western European Scientific Revolution and Enlightenment were undermining belief systems like the great chain of being and the divine right of kings. A land-based, self-sufficient peasantry was being transformed into a waged, urbanized working class. This radical change required new forms of ideological control.

Particularly as Western European inter-imperial competition for new territories heated up through the sixteenth century and beyond, it became ever more essential for elites to find a way to bind common folk to their interests and get them to disregard the profound inequalities and injustices defining their own lives and societies. This is the formative period for modern nationalisms, prior to which people would have found it unthinkable to consider themselves belonging to a historically and territorially expansive group with a pure, primordial identity. The incredible labour required to transform the feudal world into a capitalist one, including the work of out-competing other imperialist powers, necessitated a new kind of rationalization for new forms of work, discipline, control, authority, and sacrifice.

Nationalism is highly ritualized. Anthems, flags, sports, art, and leisure activities all show how specific social practices can be bound to national identity. Publicly participating in them is a kind of patriotic duty. The fact that many people fervently express patriotic feeling for their country and nation doesn't mean nationalism is any less constructed in the interests animating it. Of course, nationalism and patriotism also serve to sanitize the less admirable aspects of a given country. Nationalism in settler-colonial countries, like Canada and the United States, conspicuously avoids recognizing that the genocide of Indigenous Peoples was a core aspect of the founding of the nation-state. Canadian nationalism also trades in the fiction that settler-colonialism in these territories was benign and benevolent, not violent and genocidal like in the United States. It sustains this fiction by studiously avoiding mentioning practices of forced displacement and dispossession, cultural genocide, residential schooling, and much more (Daschuk 2013).

Entrenched injustices and inequalities within the national community are obscured, ignored, or naturalized. Canadian nationalism, for example, is replete with these conventions while conspicuously avoiding the belligerent jingoism often associated with the United States. Canadian nationalist myth-making portrays Canada as the end of the Underground Railroad for people seeking to liberate themselves from slavery without acknowledging that Black people were enslaved in Canada well into the nineteenth century (Maynard 2017).

Nationalism often glorifies the military adventurism of the country's armed forces with such activities depicted as necessary, noble, self-sacrificing, and civilizing. Canadian nationalism regularly trades in the trope that Canada's military is committed to peacekeeping and humanitarian intervention while never breathing a word about Canada's imperialistic interventions in a host of countries around the world, often in defence of the interests of Canadian capital (Engler 2009). Nationalism is a little like looking at a reflection in a fun house mirror. Not all the elements are wrong, but the overall picture is incredibly out of proportion with reality. Like the fun house, the experience of it is supposed to be pleasurable, which makes the distortion even more compelling.

Perhaps most importantly, nationalism is a way of obscuring the real power relations at work in society. Rather than looking at how power and wealth are distributed in society, nationalist ideologies and patriotism encourage us to see ourselves as members of one big national family who share common concerns, interests, values, and purpose. This dynamic is particularly obvious in times of crisis as people are not only encouraged to make sacrifices but to identify culprits responsible for their predicament. For example, in the face of industrial restructuring, job losses, and fiscal austerity, workers are told we all have to "tighten our belts" in the national interest even as wealth continues to be accumulated by the owning class. If blame is apportioned, it is often even more vulnerable groups who are identified as responsible for suffering. These include immigrants, the poor, working people in poorer countries, and whatever other marginalized group can be tarred as "unproductive" or an unreasonable drain on the social order.

The reality is far different. In 2015, the average pay for the top hundred CEOs in Canada was 193 times that of the average worker (Mackenzie 2017, 8). Put another way, it took until noon on the first working day of the new year for those CEOs to make what the average Canadian worker makes in a year. This trend has only increased over time and in spite of crises like the Great Recession of 2007–08, when one would have expected to see across-the-board cuts to remuneration. It's all the more striking given the speculative and reckless practices of the world's largest financial institutions, which actually precipitated the Great Recession. But as always, those with the power not only got to declare the crisis but the solutions to it (Roitman 2013). Some argue that this kind of inequality simply reflects the important work done by those at the upper echelons; however, if austerity, belt-tightening, and bootstrap-pulling are necessary for the benefit of the nation, why are all of us not expected to participate? In times of crisis, shouldn't it be those at the top who set the example for the rest of us? It's telling that this is not the case, and it's worth reflecting on how the construction of a collective "we" through nationalism serves to cover over these contradictions.

IDENTITY POLITICS AND OPPRESSION

The term "identity politics" has recently moved from academic and political circles of discussion and debate to the mainstream. By and large, this mainstream usage has come into fashion as something of a slur. Across a variety of media, pundits of various stripes denounce "identity politics," making it a caricature depicting members of some group (women, queer folks, Indigenous people, racialized people, and more) who are accused of weaponizing their identity in order to claim grievance against the established order and demand redress. Disparaged as a form of shrill, tribalistic, moralistic, and inaccurate political discourse, playing "identity politics" is something no one wants to be accused of. But is this what identity politics is? And, as we've already explored, aren't our social identities wrapped up in the way power operates and relations of ruling?

The term "identity politics" entered radical political discourse in North America in the 1970s when a group of radical, socialist, Black lesbian feminists organized as the Combahee River Collective and sought to describe their political orientation and how it differed from other feminist politics. In their statement, members of the collective described "identity politics" and its importance in the following way:

This focusing upon our own oppression is embodied in the concept of identity politics. We believe that the most profound and potentially most radical politics come directly out of our own identity, as opposed to working to end somebody else's oppression. In the case of Black women this is a particularly repugnant, dangerous, threatening, and therefore revolutionary concept because it is obvious from looking at all the political movements that have preceded us that anyone is more worthy of liberation than ourselves. We reject pedestals, queenhood, and walking ten paces behind. To be recognized as human, levelly human, is enough.

Far from claiming a privileged position and special status, the Combahee River Collective's statement reminds us of the importance of understanding the lived, material realities of oppression. Locating our experiences of oppression socially, collectively, and in the midst of the relations of ruling that structure our lived realities is essential work.

Oppression is the act of one group exercising power over another in order to maintain structured injustice and inequality at the expense of the latter and to the benefit of the former (Bishop 2002, 51). Oppression is not about conflict, disagreements, or even interpersonal abuse. It needs to be understood as a collective social phenomenon that is the degradation and debasement of a group of people by others that is aimed at maintaining structured inequality and injustice. It results in lived and material benefits for the oppressors and lived and material costs for the oppressed. It is impossible to understand the way oppression works without taking social identities seriously as sites of power, possibility, and struggle. While people obviously experience oppression at the level of their individual lives, oppression is fundamentally a structured, collective phenomenon. In other words, oppression is something experienced by groups of people and exercised by groups of people.

Any identity category can be an *axis of oppression*, a way of organizing power and privilege in society dividing those who are in from those cast out. Some of the most common ways of dividing people into seemingly distinct groups include but are not limited to gender, sexuality, class, race, age, ability, and nationality. There are, unfortunately, many ways of organizing oppressive relations within society. For example, *patriarchy*, literally meaning "rule of the father," is an oppressive social organization in which men hold power, dominate roles of political leadership, exert moral authority, and exercise disproportionate privilege and control of property. *Racism* is an oppressive social relation rooted in the spurious conviction that humanity is divided into distinct and unequal groups based on arbitrary observable characteristics like skin colour, with implications for who counts as fully human and who doesn't. *Classism* is an oppressive social relation that asserts that social hierarchies based on wealth and power correspond with who gets to rule and be ruled. *Heterosexism* is an oppressive social relation based on the conviction that there are only two distinct and complementary genders (man and woman) with corresponding "natural" social roles. In this view, gender, sex, and sexuality are all aligned and the only legitimate intimate relationships are between "born" men and women, with all others considered aberrations.

It is often the case that oppression isn't organized only along a single identity axis. When several identity categories are weaponized to facilitate domination, they become axes of oppression. For example, in a white supremacist society, a non-white person is a target of oppression, but they may also face oppression because of their gender, sexuality, class position, ability, and more. Oppression is often multidimensional and experienced differently by members of an oppressed group. A queer person is oppressed in a heterosexist society but being a member of the professional class and identified as white advantages them in other ways. Indigenous men might face considerable racist oppression in a settler-colonial society but as men they are less disadvantaged than Indigenous women, who also confront structured male supremacy and misogyny. This way of looking at oppression that considers its multidimensional aspects is called *intersectionality* (Crenshaw 1989).

When a group of people are identified according to some shared characteristic as being less worthy of living dignified lives than others, that's an important sign that oppression is at work. Sometimes oppression is glaringly obvious. Think, for example, about the Nazi Holocaust and the systematic labelling, harassment, demonization, imprisonment, and mass murder of groups of "enemies," including Jews, the Roma, homosexuals, communists, the mentally and physically ill, and more (Snyder 2016). The use of publicly recognizable symbols to identify these groups, their imprisonment in ghettos and concentration and death camps, and the constant rhetoric from Nazi leaders emphasizing the sub- or inhuman nature of these groups are all glaring examples of systematic oppression. Similarly, the Canadian state's policy of dispossession and disenfranchisement directed at Indigenous Peoples is a long-standing example of oppression. Broken treaties, forced resettlement on remote reserve lands, stripping Indigenous women and their children of Indigenous identity, the forced removal of Indigenous children from their families to send them to be assimilated and brutalized at residential schools, and the systematic whitewashing of the epidemic of violence experienced by all Indigenous people but most particularly by women and girls are all manifestations of these oppressive relations (Coulthard 2014; Daschuk 2013; Paul 2006).

These two examples are striking but, importantly, they also show that oppression is often organized legally through the state and its laws, so legality should never be mistaken for justice. Another instance of this is the control of women's reproductive function through laws criminalizing or restricting access to contraception and abortion. However one feels individually about abortion is not the issue; rather, what is at stake is the fact that women's bodies are legislated, surveilled, and policed in ways that men's bodies never are. Again, in this circumstance there is no evil mastermind orchestrating these relations; they appear impersonal, institutional, and diffuse. The point is that there is nothing primordial, normal, or natural about identity and its weaponization through oppression. In fact, the dehumanization of specific groups of people always needs to be understood in light of the power relations it makes possible and the ends they yield. El Jones's intervention explores the intersection of identity with oppression and the way one specific form of oppression, anti-Black racism, overlaps and interacts with others.

ANTI-BLACK RACISM – *EL JONES*

EARLIER IN THIS TEXT, you learned about racism. We understand racism as an ideology that systematically denies people their full humanity, dignity, and autonomy along arbitrary physical, biological, and cultural lines in order to appropriate their lives, labour, and wealth. The term anti-Black racism refers to the specific histories, experiences, and structures of racism that impact African people. It is important to recognize that there is not one universal Black experience and that Black people across the diaspora and on the African continent have a diversity of cultures, backgrounds, religions, social class, gender identities, and other experiences which shape their lives. However, histories of colonialism and enslavement have created particular stereotypes, images, and social, cultural, and political narratives about Black people in order to control and repress them.

Anti-Black racism is embedded in all structures and institutions in our society. You may experience this ideology overtly – for example, in specific policies directed at Black people, in white supremacist marches or groups, or in things like racist graffiti. Anti-Black racism is also covert, meaning that it is unconsciously present in how we think about Black people, the images and stories about Black people we consume, the limited representation of Black people in the media, or in ideas of Black people as "lazy," "loud," "angry," "ghetto," etc. that are present and absorbed throughout our society and culture.

Examples of anti-Black racism you may be familiar with are police shootings and mass incarceration of Black people. In the documentary *13th*, director Ava Duvernay explains how after the end of slavery, the image of Black people as criminals was created in order to continue to subject Black people to white control. Policing and prisons are institutions that disproportionately profile, surveil, and incarcerate Black people. Black Lives Matter and the broader Movement for Black Lives formed in response to police and state violence against Black people.

In her book *Black Feminist Thought*, scholar Patricia Hill Collins identifies the following four controlling images of Black women: the Mammy, who nurtures white children and families at the expense of her own needs; the Matriarch, the controlling, aggressive, cold Black woman who emasculates men; the Jezebel, the sexualized Black woman that justified the rape of enslaved Black women; and Sapphire, the angry Black woman with attitude. Hill Collins shows how these images, used to enact violence on Black women's bodies during slavery, are still active today. For example, images of the Welfare Mother justify the disproportionate number of Black children placed in the child welfare system under the belief that Black women, particularly single mothers, are not capable of raising their own children. These images are an example of how narratives of anti-Black racism intersect with gender.

Anti-Black racism also intersects with transphobia and homophobia. Historically, Black women were seen as unnatural, not feminine, and incapable of feeling. Unlike white women, therefore, Black women could labour in the fields or have their children stolen from them without feeling any physical or emotional pain. Seeing Black women as not "real" women is one example of ongoing homophobic and transphobic concepts of Black people. Black trans women are subject to disproportionate amounts of violence. Black Lives Matter was formed by queer Black people and recognizes that the liberation struggles for Black people must also include how racism and capitalism intersect with gender-based oppression.

In Canada, one feature of anti-Black racism is the mythology that it only exists in the United States. Histories of enslavement in Canada, for example, are commonly not taught, and many Canadians are not aware that slavery existed in Canada for over two hundred years. Robyn Maynard's book *Policing Black Lives* (2017) examines the history of state violence against Black people in Canada. Some of the ways anti-Black racism has been enacted in Canada include immigration laws that deliberately excluded Black people from the country, segregation in schools in Nova Scotia, the ongoing discrimination against Black people in education and employment, and the overrepresentation of Black people in prisons, the youth justice system, and child welfare.

An example of how anti-Black racism works that you may be very familiar with is the issue of cultural appropriation. While Black people face ongoing violence and exclusion from the state, Black cultural products like music, fashion, language, dances, food, etc. are adopted by the majority, without credit or compensation. Just as during enslavement, Black people are expected to work for free; Black creative work is still seen as the property of white society.

Black Canadian legal scholar Anthony Morgan argues that Black people are still not considered full human beings. That can be seen in the ways white juries view Black defendants as more guilty and less capable of remorse, or in the image of the "angry Black woman," who isn't vulnerable and doesn't have the same feelings as white women. Across society and throughout institutions, Black people have been stripped of humanity, and those reverberations are felt in all parts of society today.

As El Jones shows us, the effects of oppressive relations like anti-Black racism are expansive rather than limited. Identity is not just a pathway to domination. As we've already learned, the work of making culture and forging collective meaning and the identities that go with it are a fundamental aspect of human experience. It also makes a good deal of sense to distinguish roles, responsibilities, entitlements, and privileges based on commonly agreed upon social identities and statuses. But these social identities and the roles, responsibilities, entitlements, and privileges to which they are attached can never be taken to be inevitable, natural, or eternal. We do not have to look very far back in history to witness times when women, racialized people, those with different mental and physical abilities, and children were regarded as something less than fully human. These views, often entrenched in the laws of the day, had direct, lived, material consequences for those relegated to less-than-fully-human status, whether that meant being treated as property, subjected to arbitrary violence, denied social and political standing, or an array of other degrading and dehumanizing behaviours. It's important to acknowledge that despite many of these forms of entrenched, institutionalized oppression having come to an end, the pernicious forms of injustice and inequality to which they are connected have simply morphed into new relations that are often cast as normal, natural, or traditional in the context of contemporary society.

While these oppressive relations are always at work, there are times when they come to the fore. Much like fascism arose in the 1910s and 1920s in Italy and Germany as they experienced social, political, and economic crises that the established liberal democratic orders proved unable to solve, our current moment bears witness not only to crisis but to the resurgence of a range of far right and explicitly fascist ideologies. Across the overdeveloped north and west of the world, white supremacy and white nationalism have been on the march for years. *White nationalism* is a political ideology that views white people as a distinct group and calls for the creation of whites-only ethno-states through the purging or expulsion of non-white people. Sometimes this purging is characterized as "peaceful ethnic cleansing," but more often it is implicitly and explicitly violent. As we've already seen, *white supremacy* is the belief that white people not only constitute a distinct people in racial and ethnic terms but that they are superior to non-white people. The sentiment underlying the resurgence of far-right politics and open white supremacy has been described by sociologist Michael Kimmel as "aggrieved entitlement" (2015, 21). In the context of not insignificant gains toward equality made by women, racialized minorities, immigrants and others who "had been successfully excluded for decades," as well as the deepening of capitalist precarity, alienation, and austerity, white men in particular have experienced these changes and challenges as theft of what is "rightfully" theirs. As Kimmel explains, this is "the anger of the entitled: we are entitled to those jobs, those positions of unchallenged dominance. And when we are told we are not going to get them, we get angry" (2015, 21).

The aggrieved entitlement expressed by white men in the context of white supremacist and patriarchal societies like the US and Canada shares remarkable similarities with fascism. Robert Paxton defines fascism as

> a form of political behavior marked by obsessive preoccupation with community decline, humiliation, or victimhood and by compensatory cults of unity, energy, and purity, in which a mass-based party of committed nationalist militants, working in uneasy but effective collaboration with traditional elites, abandons democratic liberties and pursues with redemptive violence and without ethical or legal restraints goals of internal cleansing and external expansion. (2004, 218)

Dominant identities (masculinity and ethnic nationalism) are weaponized and become a lightning rod for reactionary anger and, ultimately, the mechanism by which that anger is violently directed at a host of vulnerable groups in an effort to reclaim what is perceived as a degraded or fallen status. As Kimmel notes, the anger of aggrieved entitlement is "real" in that "it is experienced deeply and sincerely," but it is not "true" as it does not "provide an accurate analysis of their situation" (2015, 9). At no point do those moved by such sentiments recognize that their losses, real or perceived, are due to a web of power relations that could be challenged and changed for the collective benefit of all. Instead, weaned on privilege and power, those whose material and symbolic entitlements are tied to dominant identity categories seek to reclaim what is lost or under threat by targeting those who have already been suffering under those very same relations.

The realness of the anger of dominant groups has significant lived consequences for everyone else, regardless of the truth of the rationale driving it. In Canada, hate crimes, criminal acts motivated by hatred toward an identifiable group, rose 47 percent between 2016 and 2017, with Muslims, Jews, and Black people the most frequent targets of such attacks (Reuters 2018). In the United States, hate crimes reached an all-time high in 2017 after years of increases (Barrouquere 2018). "Incels," men who identify themselves as "involuntarily celibate" and blame women and feminism for their sexual failures, have become a bloody and explosive social phenomenon in recent years (*CBC News* 2019). Incel culture mirrors other forms of extremist and terrorist organizing and violence as atomized individuals connect and become radicalized through online forums like 4chan and Reddit and then take their misogynistic rage out in public, targeting women and other people.

Trans-excluding radical feminists (TERFs) or, perhaps more appropriately, feminist-appropriating radical transphobes (FARTs), are women who, under the banner of "feminism" and "women's rights," publicly vilify, dehumanize, and degrade transgender people, claiming that they are defending "real" or "born" women. Tellingly, FARTs often end up in alliance with other far right movements with xenophobic, white supremacist, and nativist and ethno-nationalist reactionary politics. The point to these examples is that dominant forms of identity, tied intimately to prevailing relations of ruling, become organizing nodes for oppressive and even fascistic politics when the status quo is perceived to be in unresolvable crisis. White people are not inherently racist, men are not inherently misogynistic, people are not inherently ageist, cisgender people are not inherently transphobic. To repeat, this is not about some identities being bad and others good. What matters is the way some ways of being in the world are tied to the operation of power at specific times and places and in specific configurations. Germans and Italians were not fated to become Nazis and Fascists in the 1920s and 1930s, and it would be a fool's errand to look for the primordial seeds of fascism in specific national cultures. To understand how and why some people become oppressors and others oppressed, we have to attend to the social, political, and economic context within which such shifts occur and the socio-cultural repertoires upon which they draw.

CONCLUSION

How do we know who we are? What is "identity," and how and why do we come to share it with other people? What's the relationship between certain kinds of identity and power relations in society? In this chapter we explore these questions and more. Fundamentally, all forms of social identity are public performances. This does not mean they are unreal or fake; it simply means that none of the forms of identity we are accustomed to (race, class, gender, sexuality, age, ability, and more) are natural or immutable. It also means that, just like we learned about society in Chapter 3, we act our identities into being and, in so doing, reproduce, challenge, and change them. We fight publicly and privately over what our social identities mean and how they are tied to power and ruling relations in society at large. Even though our personal sense of who we are is often very powerfully felt, just like we learned about social norms and roles, we should never mistake this sense of naturalness for reality.

At the same time, social identities are not something we can simply adopt or consume at will. As we discuss in this chapter, particularly through the cases of the so-called "Eastern métis" and Rachel Dolezal, claiming identity isn't an innocent or individual proposition, particularly when people who occupy dominant positions in society seek to claim membership in marginalized or oppressed communities. This is because social identities are always located in the web of power relations that make up society. Those power relations, as we've seen in previous chapters, are never natural or inevitable and always benefit particular interests. This serves as a vital reminder that identity is always a symbolic and material practice embedded in social relations. Identities neither live exclusively in our heads, nor are they simply products of dominant social practices and institutions; they are both at once. What makes the identity appropriation engaged in by Dolezal and Eastern métis groups so problematic is that such identification is directly tied to their claiming of resources, status, rights, and entitlements that oppressed groups have struggled for, only to have them reappropriated by members of dominant social groups.

We can believe identity matters while simultaneously accepting that it's socially constructed. Race is a biological fiction in the sense that there is no genetic basis for the division of humanity into distinct and separate racial groups. But race is also a social fact in that many people believe in it, and, more importantly, it is tied intimately and intentionally to relations of ruling in society. All forms of identity are rooted in their social context and can only be understood in that context. This turns us away from pointless and circular debates about "authentic" identities and instead encourages us to understand identity as socially and collectively produced. From gender and race to sexuality and class, our identities are complex public expressions that are always in the process of being made and re-made. Despite reactionary rhetoric to the contrary, there is no one, true, real way of being a man, a white person, or a working-class person. If we look across time and space it's easy to see how expectations about specific social identities shift or how whole categories of personhood come into being, often as a result of people challenging dominant social relations that systematically deny them dignity and autonomy.

Social identities are not just implicated in oppression; they are also vital to our individual and collective sense of meaning and belonging in the world. No identity is automatically oppressive or oppressed; this is only determined by the prevailing relations of ruling in a given social context. While it's common for us to imagine that people have always understood themselves in ways and in terms that would be sensible to us, the examples we explore in this chapter show that the truth is quite different. Before the end of slavery in the British Commonwealth and the United States, it would have seemed strange to most settlers in the territory now known as North America to think of themselves as "white people." This identity category only acquired meaning and social power in a context where poor whites found themselves in competition with formerly enslaved Black people for waged work and, more importantly, where these white people were mobilized by elites as a bulwark to keep Black people "in their place" and maintain prevailing power relations.

Few forms of identification demonstrate this performed, power-laden nature of identity as much as nationalism. As feudal ruling-class power gave way to modern forms of social control, the idea of the nation and its authorized ways of demonstrating belonging became essential tools in the arsenal of class rule, dividing people who should have found common cause with one another and pitting them against each other in the interests of the ruling class. Every form of oppressive social relation (sexism, racism, classism, ageism, ableism, heterosexism, homo- and transphobia, etc.) essentially weaponizes social identity in the service of dominant actors and their vested interests. This isn't personal, even though the consequences are experienced at the level of lived experience; it's a social and collective experience. What matters is not the specific way social identities are elaborated — the possibilities are myriad — but the way identities are tied to power and privilege and so become tools either for liberation and relational autonomy or oppression and social violence.

KEY CONCEPTS

axis of oppression: a way of organizing power and privilege in society dividing those who are "in" from those cast "out." Some of the most common ways of dividing people into seemingly distinct groups include but are not limited to gender, sexuality, class, race, age, ability, and nationality.

classism: an oppressive social relation that asserts that social hierarchies based on wealth and power correspond with who gets to rule and be ruled.

heterosexism: an oppressive social relation based on the conviction that there are only two distinct and complementary genders (man and woman) with corresponding "natural" social roles. In this view, gender, sex, and sexuality are all aligned, and the only legitimate intimate relationships are between "born" men and women.

intersectionality: a term coined by Kimberle Crenshaw referring to the overlapping, mutually constitutive nature of our social identity categories, such as race, class, gender, sexuality, age, and ability, and how they work together to sustain structured social relations of privilege and oppression.

oppression: a collective social phenomenon that is about the debasement of a group of people carried out by another group that aims to maintain structured inequality that has tangible, lived, and material benefits for the oppressors and tangible, lived, and material costs for the oppressed.

patriarchy: literally meaning "rule of the father," it is a form of oppressive social organization in which men hold power, dominate roles of political leadership, exert moral authority, and exercise disproportionate privilege and control of property.

primitive accumulation: a Marxist concept referring to the necessary precursor stage to capitalism where workers and capital are concentrated and accumulated by those prepared to exploit them. Marxist-feminists further develop this concept to include the work of pitting the working class against itself in order to better exploit it by building social hierarchies based on gender, race, age, ability, and more.

racism: a system of oppressive social relations rooted in the spurious conviction that humanity can be divided into distinct and unequal groups based on arbitrary observable characteristics like skin colour, with implications for who counts as fully human and who doesn't.

relations of ruling: the combination of state, corporate, professional, and bureaucratic agencies in a web of relations through which ruling comes to be organized in the interests of those with the most wealth, power, and prestige.

white nationalism: a political ideology that views white people as a distinct group and calls for the creation of whites-only ethno-states through the expulsion of non-white people, often through violent means.

white supremacy: the belief that white people not only constitute a distinct people in racial and ethnic terms but that they are superior to non-white people.

5

LIVING TOGETHER

Family, Kinship, and Social Bonds

Family matters. Few other concepts carry as much weight in terms of signifying relations of mutual obligation, enduring connections, and emotional complexity. We often refer to our closest friends using the terminology of family. My best friend is "like a brother to me." A cherished mentor might be described as a "surrogate parent." A close family friend might be known by a kin term like "aunt" or "uncle." We also often commiserate with each other over the challenges of family life and the often-complicated relationships we have with our kin. Popular media is filled with stories about the beauty, pain, hilarity, violence, absurdity, and abuse that so often characterize family life. Some of us have no contact with our family at all, choosing instead to form families of choice on our own terms and outside the regular rules of kinship. For some of us, our family relations link us to social systems of power and privilege, while for others these relations transmit trauma and impoverishment intergenerationally. Family relations are also about the life-sustaining work that goes on at a day-to-day level, from making food to caring for the young, old, and sick, and just making sure we can get out of bed to help bring our social worlds back into being. The focus of this chapter is family and kinship, and critical is this central question: What is kinship and why does it matter?

↳ parents

ALL OUR RELATIONS

For many of us who live in large-scale, industrialized, capitalist societies, family and the kinship relations that produce it occupy an in-between place in terms of how we relate to and organize our social worlds. Family relations are freighted with all kinds of meaning and significance. At the same time, family is probably not the way most of us survive or navigate the social world, although it's certainly an important element. We're constantly told family should matter to us, and yet almost everything about our social lives under capitalism encourages us to find success as individual free agents. What are we to make of this?

At the end of the nineteenth century, sociologist Émile Durkheim drew his now-famous distinction between what he termed "organic" and "mechanical" solidarity in societies. Mechanical solidarity, Durkheim asserted, referred to societies where integration and cohesion came from a small group of closely related, culturally homogenous people living and working together. In such societies, relations of responsibility and obligation were often delineated through kinship, and social structures were reproduced against this small-scale, homogenous background. As an example, a band of hunter-gatherers living in a community of a couple of hundred people have an intimate understanding of who they are responsible for and to whom they bear obligations. These responsibilities and obligations are lived out daily in the context of a community where people regularly encounter one another, share common frames of socio-cultural reference, and organize themselves through kin networks rather than large and impersonal institutions.

In contrast, "organic solidarity" emerges out of the job specialization and social diversification present in modern, large-scale, industrial, capitalist societies. In such societies, people live and work with many others without ever coming to know or find affinity with most of them. Cohesion and integration are produced in societies like this, Durkheim argued, through the necessary interdependence of people who rely on each other without knowing each other and certainly without any formal system spelling out relationality like kinship. As an example, I'm a professor in a society like this. I rely on a sprawling and complex web of relations to sustain my daily existence. While I teach students, do research, and write books, someone else is growing the food I eat, producing the electricity that powers my computer and lights, and caring for my children. Most of these people I will never know, and I will probably have a fairly superficial relationship with the few that I do know. But knowing each other or not, we are dependent on each other as we move through our social lives.

Durkheim's distinction between mechanical and organic solidarity tends to pit small-scale societies based seemingly on sameness against modern, large-scale societies based on diversification and interdependence. Remember that sociology and anthropology are academic disciplines produced by the Western European Enlightenment tradition and out of the institution of the university and so are thoroughly "modern" in this regard. As we've seen in Chapter 2, ways of understanding and exploring the world are never innocent of the contexts and interests from which they spring. In this respect, it's a typically modern conceit that posits organic solidarity as a deeper, more robust form of social integration than mechanical solidarity, which is seen as superficial and homogenous. Small-scale societies are "simple" while mass societies are "complex." Mechanical solidarity is formulaic, conservative, and limited, while organic solidarity is dynamic, innovative, and expansive. Durkheim's ideal types don't overlap, even though in reality they could. Particularly in large-scale societies, people could practise mechanical solidarity at the everyday level of their neighbourhood or community, while also being part of a context where organic solidarity characterizes social relations more broadly.

There's also the issue of what's being identified and how it is being conceptualized. Rather than characterizing the anonymous, enforced dependency mostly on strangers in large-scale societies as "organic solidarity," what if we instead employed the Marxist notion of capitalist alienation? Alienation is not just the experience of being disaffected, isolated, or lonely; it is the necessary precondition of the capitalist wage relation. For people to be turned into waged workers who must sell their labour in exchange for the money to buy the things we need to survive under capitalism, these people first have to pulled away from non-market, independent means of survival.

As radical scholars Silvia Federici (2003) and Peter Linebaugh and Marcus Rediker (2000) so richly demonstrate, the necessary precondition to the transition to capitalism was the destruction of peasant life and its forms of collective sociality. Pulled apart from and pitted against each other, ripped from the land and village life that had previously sustained them, and denied access to the means of production, which are now held privately by capitalists, these new proletarians were compelled to turn to capitalist market relations to meet their needs. It is true that that capitalism exists parasitically on top of a web of social relations of cooperation and collaboration, but to describe this situation as "organic solidarity" misses the fundamental role played by the violent processes of dispossession and alienation. As a result of the destruction of communal forms of social life, proletarianized individuals have no choice but to rely on a sprawling web of social relations to sustain them, if they are able to sell their labour for a wage. But this interdependence is produced through exploitation and dispossession in the first instance, not through diversification or specialization.

This is not to romanticize small-scale or non-capitalist societies. All kinds of social formations can produce outcomes both desirable and not. Instead, this unpacking is a reminder not to take the mythology of any particular social context, institution, or social relation at face value. The "organic solidarity" of large-scale, industrialized, capitalist societies relies fundamentally on a social logic that encourages us not to know anything about the conditions of life of those whose labour we depend on. My labour as a teacher, researcher, and writer is made possible by a web of social relationships that capitalism keeps intentionally concealed from me by the money relationship. I don't see the army of people who have built the computer I work on, dug the raw materials it is made of from the earth, or maintain the electrical grid and telecommunications network that I rely on to do research and communicate with others. Instead, I pay money to faceless corporate entities so these products can be available to me. To call that "solidarity" is a profound perversion of that word.

Under such conditions, it's often in my interest to ensure I don't know anything about the lives and circumstances of the people who make my life and work possible. After all, I'm paid a wage by the institution I sell my labour to, and since that wage is limited, it's to my benefit to make sure I pay as little as possible for the things I need and want. So, the less other people are paid, the more exploitative their conditions of work, the better my own circumstances are in terms of the money I have available. Of course, other people feel the same about me, so this exploitative and alienating dynamic circulates and accelerates. This is precisely the dynamic when one group of workers in society is told to resent another group because of their privileges (a decent wage, pensions, health benefits, control over working conditions).

KINSHIP

At this point, you might be asking, "But what does all this have to do with kin or family?" The simple answer is that exploring how we live together is not exclusively about our kin relations; it's about a broad set of social relationships that make up our daily realities. Kinship is the term anthropologists have used since the late nineteenth century to refer to those social systems that tell us about who our relations are and what our obligations to each other are in the context of those relationships. A common way of thinking about kinship is as a systematic way of determining who is related to whom and what the nature of the relationship is that flows from that relationality.

While many of us think about kinship and family as primarily constituted by *consanguinity* ("blood" or bio-genetic descent) and *affinity* (marriage), even a brief survey of how people identify their relations shows this to be only two components of a much more expansive and dynamic human practice. Anthropologists, sociologists, and other social scientists who spend their time studying kinship have long recognized fictive kin as an important category referring to those who are like family despite not being related by blood or marriage. In fact, in spite of our deeply socialized feelings to the contrary, it's important to understand that even the scientific facts of biology and shared bio-genetic substance should be understood as symbolically significant rather than unmediated markers of kinship neutrally describing the actual state of affairs.

As David Schneider (2004) notes in his classic study of American kinship, while shared bio-genetic substance is commonly assumed to be the bedrock of kinship in this part of the world, when people talk about how they figure their kin, blood and biology are only part of that accounting. For example, people talk about others to whom they are related by shared bio-genetic substance as close, distant, or even non-relations depending on a host of other factors, such as physical proximity, shared experiences, affinity, family histories, and more. If many of us have friends who are as close as siblings, we also have "blood" family members who don't count as kin because we don't feel that way about them for any number of reasons. This is in part why Schneider famously argued that there are good reasons to see kinship as a "non-subject," that is, as something that exists in the minds of social scientists as an analytical category but not something that exists in the culture itself (Schneider 2004, 269).

Schneider's influential challenge to conventional kinship studies doesn't argue that there's no such thing as family or kin relations. A cursory glance at any society would disprove that. Schneider's point is that there is no such thing as kinship as a cultural category or discrete social system that people identify and use. As we go about our daily lives, we don't move through distinct areas of activity with their own neat, exclusive labels. That doesn't mean we don't act differently in different contexts or around different groups of people. It means that our social worlds aren't divided into the categories we use as convenient tools to make sense of them. No one moves through the world thinking, "I'm at my place of work doing economy," "I'm at a public protest doing politics," or "Now I'm at home taking care of my children doing kinship." Reality is much messier, alive, and dynamic.

My kin relations and the obligations that flow from them bear on every significant decision I make in my life. As an example, let's say I decide I'm going to quit my job, move across the country, and train to be a mixed martial artist with the goal of becoming an Ultimate Fighting Championship contender. None of this seems to have anything to do with the set of relations we call kinship, but of course it does. These decisions would impact my children and partner to say nothing of other friends and family who might be concerned about my new trajectory. How would I contribute to the household while pursuing my UFC dream? Where would we all live? How would this impact the social relations important to my family? What about my partner's job and her aspirations? What if I'm injured and have to be cared for over an extended period of time? Is this decision and the sphere of social activity it occupies about kinship, economics, individual choice, or something else entirely?

While many of us assume that kinship is all about shared bio-genetic substance (blood relations) and a corresponding code of conduct (responsibilities and obligations toward our relations), this cannot be assumed as corresponding to any given context without investigating it ethnographically in terms of how it is lived by people. As Schneider points out, if we examine how this works on the ground, we find that in many societies the borders between what we might call kinship and other social systems, like religion, nationalism, economics, and more, are blurry at best. That doesn't mean we cannot or should not investigate the way people relate to one another, live together, and organize and distribute the work of care, quite the contrary. What it does mean is that we cannot assume that these activities, roles, and responsibilities belong to some hived-off sphere of human activity that is universally understood as "kinship."

Anthropologist Marshall Sahlins refers to kinship as "mutuality of being," that is, "people who are intrinsic to one another's existence" (2011a, 2). This may seem like an awfully broad notion of kinship, but it's supported by a wealth of cross-cultural research on how people figure out their relations. Simply put, we know that any social status or relationship that is a product of "procreation, filiation, or descent" can also be made through "culturally appropriate action" (Sahlins 2011a, 3). In other words, kinship is fundamentally a socially constructed relationship, not a biologically essential one. In contradiction to the current fascination with DNA testing and the notion that genetic science can tell us who we are and where we come from, human kinship pays homage to the primacy of nurture over nature in terms of how we figure out to whom we are beholden and who is beholden to us in the context of collective social life. While genetic testing has popularized the idea of discovering family histories through genetic science, the basic concept of kinship and the way it's managed socially really hasn't changed. While genetic science appears to give us the facts of our ancestry and even our future if we're talking about genetic markers for disease, scientific theories of knowledge and methods are themselves cultural products that reflect basic understandings of what the world is and how we can know and explore it. More than this, what we do with whatever information we glean from genetic testing only has significance when we make sense out of it. As we saw in the previous chapter, white people claiming Métis identity by "proving" indigeneity through genetic testing that identifies a long-lost Indigenous ancestor is a social and political act of exercising power in the world, not an objective truth. If no Indigenous community recognizes me as a member in the context of lived relations of responsibility and belonging and I have no connections to these lived realities, does it matter that genetic science tells me that I, like every other human alive today, can trace their life to a diverse web of ancestors?

Turning to another example, the popularity and relatively new accessibility of genetic ancestry tests has attracted the attention of white supremacists, who see in it a way to scientifically prove their racial purity (Panofsky and Donovan 2019; Reeve 2016; Zhang 2016). This is a community that not only believes that race is a real, biological category but that racial differences are absolute, genetically hardwired, and arrange human groups hierarchically, with whites at the very top. That these beliefs have been consistently disproven by genetic and social science hasn't stopped fascists, racists, and other far-right groups from advancing them (ASHG 2018). What happens when white supremacists receive test results reporting they have some non-white or non-European ancestry? Wouldn't such results necessarily exclude them from the white nationalist/white supremacist community, given its belief in "race realism" and hard genetic lines between distinct human populations?

In a study focusing on discussion forums on Stormfront, one of the most popular and long-standing white nationalist websites, researchers discovered that people posting "bad news" of mixed ancestry genetic testing results were often met, not with rejection by other white nationalists, but with attempts to "repair" their threatened identities and reaffirm their belonging (Panofsky and Donovan 2019). In other words, white nationalists posting genetic testing results that proved they were something other than "purely white" are often met with replies that sooth their fears of not being white enough and that affirm their membership in the white nation. This repairing of threatened identities also serves to maintain the racist community itself, sustaining what we might think of as a form of kinship predicated on racialized supremacy and exclusion, ironically in the face of evidence that some members are less than purely white. This is accomplished through a variety of strategies, including challenging the validity of genetic testing; asserting the truth of racist ideology and its related forms of folk knowledge; and "creatively and critically engag[ing] genetic, statistical, historical and anthropological knowledge about human diversity, picking and choosing elements to generate their arguments about racial boundaries and hierarchies" (Panofsky and Donovan 2019, 22–23).

Faithfulness to the ideology of white supremacy trumps evidence that would seem to invalidate membership in the white nation in ultimate service to maintaining racist kinship. Given the "race realism" of white nationalists who espouse a belief in the existence of distinct, hierarchically ordered human groups and in the genetic basis for such ordering, one would anticipate more rigid and harsh responses when it comes to policing of group belonging and its boundaries. Instead, white nationalists end up creatively re-working white nationalism and redefining what constitutes "white identity" in order to keep their racist chosen family together, more or less. What's interesting about this case for our discussion of kinship is that it clearly shows how, even in the face of extremist and absolutist rhetoric to the contrary, collective identity, belonging, and affinity are figured in highly flexible, creative, and complex ways that are about social context, not biological essentialism.

As we can see from the examples of genetic ancestry tests and claims of indigeneity or "whiteness," our techniques and technologies affect our lives but they do not determine them. Various innovations are often fitted in to the dominant structures and relations shaping our lives. It's not surprising that genetic science has resonated so strongly in places like North America, where dominant notions of kinship are already strongly linked to blood and shared bio-genetic substance. However, living under the same roof, preparing and sharing food, spending time together, caring physically and emotionally for each other, and sharing experiences are ultimately much more powerful forms of social bond-making. Kaja Finkler (2001) offers a definition of kinship as the work people do in identifying a "significant same group" of others who are understood as family and kin and "who perceive themselves as similar and who consider themselves related on grounds of shared material, be it land, blood, food, saliva, semen, or ideological or affective content," with membership in such a group carrying "moral obligations and responsibilities" (2001, 236). The concept of shared substance, understood as both material and symbolic, is the crux of kinship.

This notion of belonging to one another is a critical element to kinship that goes beyond the kind of solidarities sketched by Durkheim and explored at the start of this chapter. We can feel affinity and solidarity for those with whom we live, but the sense of being run through by each other's lives is something that goes beyond this and is characteristic of kinship. It's common for those of us who live in highly individualized, modern, capitalistic societies to think of our kin relationships and statuses in terms of our own personal identities, as things we are and relations we possess. These relations also fundamentally mirror modern, North American notions of kinship as determined by shared bio-genetic substance, which are actually the exception rather than the rule if we look across the diversity of human societies (Finkler 2001, 237). I am a father. I have sons. I am a member of a defined set of individuals related by blood and marriage who constitute a family. This form of identification is not only ego-centred but reproduces capitalist property relations. But I am not essentially or intrinsically any of these things; they are all products of interpersonal relations that bring them into being. I biologically helped to produce my children with my partner, but it is our day-in, day-out collective coexistence and the relations of love, care, and responsibility that make us kin. Sahlins writes the following about the intersubjective nature of kinship: "To the extent they lead common lives, they partake of each other's sufferings and joys, sharing one another's experiences even as they take responsibility for and feel the effects of each other's acts" (2011a, 14). Our lives are run through by those of others, just as we run through theirs. This mutuality highlights the essential anthropological insight that kinship can be constituted in incredibly diverse ways, "from pure 'biology' to pure performance, and any combination thereof" (Sahlins 2011a, 14).

This is not the same as saying other ways of figuring out kin relations are close to "real" kin relations determined by blood. All kinship is about social relationships, and birth is no more a definitive marker of kinship than social coexistence. As Sahlins eloquently explains,

> If love and nurture, giving food or partaking in it together, working together, living from the same land, mutual aid, sharing the fortunes of migration and residence, as well as adoption and marriage, are so many grounds of kinship, they all know with procreation the meaning of participating in one another's life ... all means of constituting kinship are in essence the same. (2011a, 14)

The ethnographic record that supports this conclusion is incredibly broad and deep (Sahlins 2011a, 2011b).

For our purposes, two simple examples are illustrative. First, think about the way people who are identified as kin are often implicated in the deeds of their family members, fairly and not. Notions of family honour are symbolic manifestations of this "mutuality of being," as are collective feelings of guilt and shame for the misdeeds of our kin, either in the moment or historically. If a relative of mine is implicated in abuses against other people, I may well feel it's my responsibility to make amends for this legacy even though I didn't enact it. Similarly, I may tell the stories and celebrate the memory of a relative who carried out an act of bravery or sacrifice on behalf of others despite the fact that I had no role in it.

The second example is death. The passing of a relative, particularly a close one, often has profound and lasting effects. People often withdraw from the flow of daily life for a while in the wake of a close relative's death. They may avoid certain activities, adorn themselves in specific ways that publicly demonstrate that they are in mourning, and carry out ritualized activities like attending to the deceased's last wishes and memorializing them with other loved ones. The death of a loved one is mirrored in a kind of temporary social death of those left behind. Not everyone experiences mourning this way, but rituals around the death of a loved one symbolically testify to the impact of death on the social relations of the living. Again, we are run through by each other's lives in a way that extends beyond physical proximity and lived experience.

FAMILY MATTERS

To look at North America today one could be forgiven for assuming that small, disconnected family units are and have been the norm rather than the exception. After all, we often take for granted the contexts within which we are socialized; they become the largely unquestioned backdrop against which the rest of our lives play out. And yet the nuclear family, two parents living with their children, is not only historically very recent but linked to specific social, political, and economic processes. In other words, the family configuration that so many of us in this part of the world and at this point in time consider normal and natural is neither.

For those of us living in countries that have emerged out of historical processes of Western European colonization, our dominant form of family relation can be traced back to medieval Western Europe (Finkler 2001, 237). A hallmark of this way of figuring kinship and family is a belief in *bilateral descent* (tracing relations through both the mother's and father's descent lines), which is a feature of only a minority of human societies. More commonly, people have identified their relations through *unilineal descent*, either matrilineal (mother's descent line) or patrilineal (father's descent line). As we explored earlier in this chapter, societies organized around kinship are commonly considered simple, primitive, or non-modern, while the loosening of kinship ties, and their centrality to social organization and daily life, is seen as a quintessential feature of modern life. This is the classic Durkheimian distinction between mechanical and organic solidarity. While there are significant problems with this simplistic formula, it does point toward something worth considering in regard to how we relate to one another and what that means for daily life.

In societies that are more kinship-centred and utilize it as a central point of organization, "descent defines how property, status, and social obligations are transmitted and how marriage is contracted" (Finkler 2001, 236). In these societies, kinship is a central principle organizing critical elements of social life. It often matters little how individuals feel about one another personally or if they would choose to voluntarily recognize each other as kin. Property, status, responsibilities, and marriage are predicated on kin relations as the bedrock of sociality (Eriksen 2010).

In terms of North America, while kinship seems to be fundamentally bio-genetic (children are made up of their mother's and father's genetic material, the primordial kin relation), this seemingly straightforward map of kin relations is complicated by the fact that who gets identified as kin is greatly impacted by individual choice and emotional affect. The complexity and flexibility this brings to kin relations also carries important implications for if, how, why, and when kinship matters. Because for most people, kinship is not central to the way they live their daily lives outside of nuclear family life, it isn't charged with the same kind of significance as when it plays a critical role in organizing our proximity to wealth, power, privilege, and authority. In non-kinship-centred societies, shared bio-genetic identity becomes a symbol of deep, enduring connection and solidarity that, as we saw at the beginning of this chapter, serves as a metaphor for other kinds of intense solidaristic relationships. My best friend and I are "like brothers." My fellow union members are my "brothers and sisters." My teammates are "like a family."

It might seem that societies that base their understandings of kinship on a bio-genetic basis should be more objective or empirical in determining who is kin and who is not, but this is not the case. While shared bio-genetic identity is the basis for kinship in so-called modern societies, feeling and choice have a huge impact on the way kinship is lived and experienced. We all know people who are technically related (on a bio-genetic basis) to certain others but who do not recognize them as kin. Think of the "switched at birth" jokes you hear from people who talk about siblings who don't feel much affinity for one another. This flexibility and even degradation of kinship ties has been characterized as a feature of so-called complex and modern societies, with the modern individual understood as autonomous, independent, and detached from kinship ties (Finkler 2001, 237). As Finkler nicely summarizes, "The postmodern family is characterized by uncertainty, insecurity, and doubt; its arrangements are diverse, fluid, and unresolved, opening the way for an array of kinship relations" (236–37).

Divorce and gay marriage, to name only two significant phenomena, have also impacted the notion of "traditional families." In many complex and modern societies today, kinship is much more about families of choice than it is about a standardized model that reliably guides our kin relations and the status and responsibilities flowing from them. But as KelleyAnne Malinen explores in her intervention, the extension of dominant forms of social relationships and institutions like marriage and the family to those previously excluded from them is not always a simple story of progress and social justice. While "diversity" and "inclusion" have become watchwords for a host of institutions and organizations intent on affirming their liberal, progressive nature, social justice is not reducible to simply adding previously excluded ingredients to the mix and just stirring. What does kinship look like when the issue is not simply expanding the franchise but challenging and changing its very nature?

QUEERING THE FAMILY – *KELLEYANNE MALINEN*

SAME-SEX MARRIAGE IS one of the first themes often brought to mind by the phrase "queering the family." Indeed, the question of same-sex marriage "monopolized lesbian and gay activism" (Tremblay 2016, 28) in Canada from the late 1990s until this country became the fourth to legally extend marriage to same-sex couples in 2005.

This intervention first explains why vast political energy and capital has been expended to secure state recognition of same sex marriage in Canada and beyond. It then explains why many queer scholars and activists believe same-sex marriage is neither a desirable outcome nor a desirable objective for queer politics.

Why Same-Sex Marriage?

Marriage legislation includes practical benefits such as decision-making in medical or legal emergencies, spousal support, child support, and division of property upon dissolution of marriage. The importance of legal and medical decision-making became abundantly clear to LGBTQ+ communities during the HIV/AIDS crisis of the 1980s and 1990s. During this period, homophobic biological relatives of queer men dying from HIV exercised legal authority to prevent these men's friends and lovers from visiting, from claiming bodies of the deceased, and from attending funerals or memorial services. Today, many same-sex couples cite as a deciding factor in their decisions to marry the right to "care for a partner in the case of illness or injury" (MacIntosh, Reissing, and Andruff 2010, 80).

Others value marriage as the foundation of family. In the 1970s and 1980s, biological parents who came out or were outed as lesbigay in Canada were likely to be framed in court custody battles as immoral people and unfit parents and ultimately to lose access to their children (Epstein 2012, 368). Given this painful and recent history, many Canadian LGBTQ+ people are reassured to see same-sex marriage gain a place in the Civil Marriage Act of 2005, which states that "marriage represents the foundation of family life for many Canadians."

Finally, for many people in our culture, marriage is desired because it is seen to represent the penultimate stage in an intimate relationship – a stage of full, public, and exclusive commitment, recognized by society and the law. These characteristics are evidenced by the fact that it is illegal in Canada to be married to two people simultaneously and by the fact that a second legal procedure (divorce) is required to exit a marriage.

Butler summarizes the appeal of same-sex marriage as follows: "Everyone must let you into the door of the hospital; everyone must honor your claim to grief; everyone will assume your natural rights to a child; everyone will regard your relationship as elevated into eternity" (2004, 111).

Queering Marriage, or Co-opting Queerness?

If you detect a sarcastic note in Butler's notion of the marital "relationship as elevated into eternity," you are right. Like many queer theorists, Butler has reservations about the social and political potentials of same-sex marriage. Of course, the Civil Marriage Act of 2005 destabilizes to some degree the traditionally gendered roles of married coupledom. However, Butler is concerned that extending legal marriage to same-sex unions continues to leave forms of intimacy such as non-monogamy outside of legitimacy, while also continuing to ignore the life and death needs of single people. Using Gayle Rubin's (1984) terminology, we might say that same-sex marriage redraws the "charmed circle" rather than erasing it. Against the common assumption that same-sex marriage was first imagined in the 1990s, Warner shows that "queer thought before and after Stonewall" opposed same-sex marriage as a heterosexual norm belonging to "a state mandated hierarchy of intimacy" (2000, 120–21). Political preoccupation with same-sex marriage threatens a long-held queer tradition of constructing chosen families outside state recognition and regulation "from a mélange of biological family members, lifelong friends, and/or current and former lovers" (Sheff 2011, 495)

Anti-capitalist and feminist critiques of the nuclear family have also been articulated in response to same-sex marriage. We have seen that same-sex marriage advocates draw on the traditional view of the family as "the natural site for social reproduction" (Young and Boyd 2006, 219). Queer and feminist critical theorists problematize this framing of the family for allowing the state to download costs of health care and education onto the nuclear family structure. This downloading occurs in an economic system where only economically privileged families can afford quality health care and education and where women continue to provide the bulk of unpaid caring labour, often in single-parent households.

Lastly, queer activists and theorists problematize same-sex marriage as the focus of LGBTQ+ activist energies by arguing that our time and money would be better spent elsewhere and that the Civil Marriage Act of 2005 was too widely perceived as a final victory. On the contrary, in Canada, queer youth are overrepresented among homeless youth (Abramovich 2016) and hate crimes motivated by sexual orientation are disproportionately violent (Gaudet 2018). Furthermore, Canadian LGBTQ+ preoccupation with same-sex marriage allows us on the one hand to overlook criminalization of same-sex sexual acts in seventy-one countries around the world (Carroll, Mendos, and International Lesbian, Gay, Bisexual, Trans and Intersex Association 2017) while on the other hand engaging in "homonationalism" – celebration of the Canadian colonial state on the grounds that it treats its queers so well.

While patriarchal and heteronormative social relations reinforce the notion that having a family of one's own is a "traditional" value and an important threshold to adulthood, the result is not the elevation of the family-unit-as-collective but a co-optation of family life and relations by the dominant social logics of private property and hierarchy. Right-wing pundits often talk about the need to defend "traditional family values," but they are rarely questioned about what or whose tradition they are referring to or how in such an incredibly diverse world there could be a single set of family values that could somehow be universal. Of course, there is no such set of universal family values; the reference to traditional family values is really a dogwhistle for patriarchy, hierarchy, monogamy, and heteronormativity, wrapped in invocations of the Judeo-Christian religious tradition. The problem is not that such a value set exists per se, although anyone with an interest in collective liberation would probably raise good questions about it, but that it is projected as a universal package that all good people ought to adhere to.

As Élise Thorburn explores in her intervention, the capturing of family life by these logics of power and domination is not simply a matter of whose values get to set the baseline for acceptable social behaviour; it's very much about the material costs and consequences of who does what work and how the fruits of that labour are distributed. Many people still see the home and family life as a private space set off from the capitalist relations that structure our daily life in public. But just as kin-centred societies can draw no easy distinctions between what social scientists might call kinship systems and economics, politics, law, and other social spheres, neither can avowedly modern societies hive off private family life from the relations and forces that shape the rest of our existence. In fact, capitalism requires the unpaid labour involved in sustaining ourselves and our kin in order to generate the wealth it craves.

SOCIAL REPRODUCTION – *ÉLISE THORBURN*

SOCIAL REPRODUCTION IS A concept that clarifies the economic and social realms within capitalism and allows us to see how the two merge, operate together, and come into conflict with each other. It helps us to understand how capital reproduces both human labour and the social relations of capitalism while also creating the conditions of resistance and possibilities for post-capitalist ways of living. Social reproduction allows us to take seriously human and nonhuman actors in our movements and commits us to invoking feminist, anti-colonial, environmental, and anti-racist politics as key components of class struggle.

The concept of social reproduction traces its lineage through Marx and Marxism, appearing in cell form in Volume II of Marx's *Capital*. It was not until feminist militants and thinkers in the 20th century developed a detailed analysis of how capital reproduces itself and the conditions of capitalist social relations that the concept became a useful rubric to understanding the world beyond the workplace. Feminist thinkers such as Silvia Federici, Mariarosa Dalla Costa, and Selma James pointed to the home and the labour associated with it as a site of productivity and resistance within capitalism, removing the industrial workplace as the centrepiece of capitalist productivity and resistance and writing whole other activities into the sphere of class struggle.

Dominated by the labours of women, socially reproductive work in the home includes all the activities that allow labour power to be produced and reproduced each day. Because without reproductive labours there would be no labour power, these feminists argued that social reproduction forms the basis of all industrial work. Social reproduction had, heretofore, been largely invisible within Marxist thought, seen as part of the "wage bundle" of historically male workers or considered one of the "indirect costs" of production. In fact, Marxist feminist militants demanded, these hidden variables are essential to understanding capitalism as a process and seeing through it to sites of resistance.

In particular, Marxist feminist scholars have pointed to social reproduction as the necessary quotidian and intergenerational maintenance and reproduction of life. As well as attending to the actual biological facts of life – such as childbearing and rearing, caring for the elderly and sick – social reproduction is also the work of maintaining ourselves – through cleaning, preparing food, providing shelter – and can also be seen in the support we give to others – the regenerative activities of care we participate in and the work of satisfying emotional needs. It is both how we come to be human and how we come to be labour power and so is also resonant in the systems of producing human life that we collectively create, such as the school system, the health-care system, the welfare system, and even the prison system and borders. As a form of labour, it is physical, mental, and emotional; it is the web of social relations that maintains our relationships to each other but also to capital. For this reason, it has what Silvia Federici calls a "dual character," reproducing workers but also resistance, producing labour power alongside the social world of human beings. Social reproduction, she argues, has been as important to capitalist development as the factory system and commodity production and as important to resistance as factory organizing and wage struggles.

This feminist focus not only corrects a gender blindness at the core of most theories of the economy and class struggle, but it also suggests alternative modes of understanding capitalist and anti-capitalist relations that place caregiving at the centre. While not named as "social reproduction" precisely, such resistances have been part of materialist feminist analyses since at least the nineteenth century, when women's organizations challenged the separation of domestic and public spaces and the domestic from the political economy. Nineteenth-century materialist feminists formed new neighbourhood associations and housewife cooperatives, promoted new housing projects complete with daycare centres and public kitchens, and even demanded payment for unpaid household labour (Epstein 2012, 368). In the 1970s, the Wages for Housework campaign was begun in Italy by Marxist feminists Mariarosa Dalla Costa, Silvia Federici, Selma James, and Brigitte Galtier. The campaign soon spread to New York City, other parts of the northeastern US, and into Canada and demanded that reproductive work be considered work and defended state-funded welfare. The International Wages for Housework Campaign organized for compensation for unpaid work by women in the home, on the land, and in the community, and the Black Women for Wages for Housework (co-founded by Margaret Prescod) demanded remuneration not only for unpaid reproductive work, but also for the labours of slavery, imperialism, and colonialism.

These varied arguments did not necessarily envision incorporating these labours into the waged economy but rather demanded that reproductive work be recognized as work primarily so that it could also be recognized as a site of resistance, a site of refusal, and a "point zero" which grounds the conditions of existence for all other struggles and movements. The same can be said for many socially reproductive movements today – and the value of the concept of social reproduction is precisely that it expands our vision of what struggle looks like, where it resides, and what resistance must include. Movements often dismissed as "identity politics," land defence struggles, Indigenous resurgences, and anti-extractivist movements all become central components of a broader anti-capitalist struggle through the lens of social reproduction. Sites of resistance to capital begin to emerge outside of the traditional workplace setting, and "workers" emerge in the unlikeliest of places – as land defenders, as childbearers, as water carriers, as those who hold space and maintain culture. This is work and these people are workers. Only through the framing of social reproduction can we come to understand this and move our struggles to the next stage.

As Thorburn unpacks for us in her intervention, *social reproduction* is all about the collective work of care that goes into making social life – and hence economic activity – possible. But while we all do some care work for ourselves and others, some of us are much more burdened with this work than others. This, too, is an area where conservative and right-wing rhetoric about "traditional family values" serves to conceal relations of exploitation and oppression at the level of our most intimate relations. When this expansive, utterly necessary care work is figured as "natural women's work," a private "labour of love," or the sphere of poorly paid, unskilled, migrant labour, this isn't a rational, empirical judgement of the labour itself but a rationale aimed at justifying its super-exploitation. What could be more important from a human perspective than sustaining ourselves and our loved ones? As we saw in Chapter 1, the bedrock of our species' success on this planet is our sociality and capacity for cooperation. We are simply not built from an evolutionary perspective for individual survival, cultural myths about "man the hunter" or similar neoconservative stories notwithstanding. Furthermore, despite our cultural fixation with notions of blood ties and bio-genetic belonging as the root of family, it's clear that many people understand at an everyday level that family and kin ties are much more about affinity, the shared work of social reproduction, and collective care work.

THE UNEVEN TERRAIN OF SOCIAL REPRODUCTION

Outside of ideological and loaded claims to "traditional family values," the only true constant in family life is that it is constantly changing. As with other major social relations and institutions, family life and kin ties have been worked over by powerful social forces and processes. According to the 2016 Canadian census, 28 percent of

Canadian households are now made up of only one person, 26 percent are made up of a couple with their children, and another 26 percent are constituted by a couple without children (Statistics Canada 2017d). Single parent families make up 9 percent of all Canadian households, while 3 percent are extended or multi-generational, and 4 percent are households comprised of families of choice who are related by neither blood nor marriage (Statistics Canada 2017d).

Common-law unions as opposed to marriages are becoming increasingly usual across the country, with 21.3 percent of all couples in 2016 reporting common-law status, compared to only 6.3 percent in 1981 (Statistics Canada 2017e). This is a dramatic increase in recent decades. Canada's proportion of common-law unions is similar to that of the UK and France, below Sweden and Norway, and far above the US (5.9 percent in 2010) (Statistics Canada 2017e). In the vein of changes to marital status, same-sex couples represented just shy of 1 percent of all couples in Canada in 2016 (0.9 percent), but those reporting being in such a relationship increased dramatically after the passage of Civil Marriage Act in 2005 legalizing same-sex marriage (Statistics Canada 2017b). A third (33.4 percent) of all same-sex couples in Canada in 2016 were married (Statistics Canada 2017b).

Another significant change in domestic life in recent years has been the increasing proportion of young adults living with their parents, a dynamic that's repeated across other countries as well. In 2016, 34.7 percent of people aged 20 to 34 were living with their parents in Canada, up from 30.6 percent in 2001 (Statistics Canada 2017c). Fewer young adults are starting their own families, and, along with living with their parents, more are seeking alternative arrangements, like living with roommates or with other relatives (Statistics Canada 2017c). There's obviously a lot going on behind these figures, but one thing we can discern immediately is a trend away from so-called traditional family arrangements and toward other forms of living in common. Undoubtedly, the delayed departure of many young adults from their family homes also reflects a new period of austerity and precarity in global capitalism. But what about the increase in people living alone? What about the decline in marriage rates? What about smaller family sizes and more flexible arrangements in cohabitation?

One of the most striking statistics is that the biggest category of household type in Canada is now people who live alone. As we've discussed, this kind of solitary existence would have been unthinkable and almost impossible at other times and in other places. Is this shift over the last century unique to the Canadian context? What might account for it? The simple answer to the first question is that, no, it is not unique to Canada; it's a trend that is pronounced across overdeveloped, industrialized, capitalist nation-states. According to Statistics Canada, Canada's percentage of one-person households (28.2 percent) is in line with the United States (27.5 percent in 2012) and the United Kingdom (28.5 percent in 2014) (Statistics Canada 2017e).

These percentages are actually lower than those in France (33.8 percent in 2011), Japan (34.5 percent in 2015), Sweden (36.2 percent in 2011), Norway (40.0 percent in 2012), and Germany (41.4 percent in 2015) (Statistics Canada 2017e). Solitary living, what we might also think of as a characteristic of social atomization as collective life is eroded by capitalist alienation, is a clear trend across the most advanced capitalist countries in the world. But what are the factors that drive it?

Over the course of the twentieth century the size of Canadian households declined dramatically, from an average of 5.6 people per household in 1871 to 2.4 in 2016 (Statistics Canada 2017e). The kinds of living arrangements characterizing these households also changed over the same period. Like households elsewhere, Canadian households in the late nineteenth and early twentieth centuries tended to be larger and more flexible in their membership. They were more likely to be extended and multi-generational and were also likely to include non-family members like boarders, lodgers, and servants (Statistics Canada 2019).

A variety of forces came to bear on the Canadian household over the course of the twentieth century and particularly after World War II that shifted this configuration dramatically. The legislation of no-fault divorce in the 1960s, the development of a new life stage in-between leaving one's childhood home and starting a family, urbanization, social welfare policies, and household technological innovations all combined to make solo living possible in a way it simply hadn't been before (Tang, Galbraith, and Truong 2019). Along with increases in life expectancy, increasing rates of divorce and separation have played important roles in these changing household configurations. Among seniors (people 65 years of age and older), 33 percent of women were living alone as of 2016 compared to 17.5 percent of men (Statistics Canada 2017e). The rate of senior women living alone has fallen in recent years while that of senior men has risen. At the same time, more couples are living without children now than at any time on record, with 51.1 percent of couples living with at least one child in 2016 (Statistics Canada 2017e). Some of this gets chalked up to the effects of an aging population, particularly the aging of the baby boomers (born between 1946 and 1965), but this demographic bubble doesn't tell the whole story.

Women's access to birth control, abortion, and divorce have obviously had significant impacts on gender relations and family life, in general giving women more control over their lives and bodies and making them less dependent on husbands and fathers. Women's struggles for social, economic, and political rights and freedoms, best exemplified by the feminist movement, certainly afforded women more capacity to forge their own lives independent of men and the social conventions of patriarchy. It's important to position these struggles, their successes and failures, in light of the fact that they occurred unevenly on terrain profoundly shaped by the dynamics of race, class, sexuality, and citizenship status.

While it's part of Canadian nationalist mythos that women in Canada won the right to vote federally in the 1921 election, this victory explicitly excluded Indigenous and racialized women (particularly those of Chinese, East Indian, and Japanese descent) (Section15.Ca 1997). It was not until 1960 that all these women were formally able to vote in federal elections. This example highlights the fact that social change and what we often refer to as "social progress" never occurs evenly across the social landscape. Abortion was decriminalized in Canada in 1988, but, again, this did not mean that all women in Canada then or now have unobstructed access to abortion services (Ghabrial 2008). Women living outside large urban centres or coming from racialized, marginalized, or Indigenous communities often face significant barriers to accessing abortion services, which they are supposedly guaranteed under Canadian law.

While most people consider birth control and access to abortion services as central to reproductive justice, struggles by racialized, poor, and Indigenous women highlight that reproductive justice also has to extend to freedom from coerced sterilization and access to high quality, public health-care services before and after giving birth (Maynard 2017; Stote 2015). None of this is to downplay these advances but it is important not to tell a story about changing household, family, and kin configurations in the context of the Canadian state that simply takes the white, heterosexual, middle-class experience as a baseline for all others. Indeed, as more and more middle-class women entered the waged workforce during and after World War II, this did not occur as a result of men taking on a significantly greater share of domestic work and social reproduction but was facilitated by the explosion of migrant care workers, mainly racialized women from the so-called developing world, who were imported on work contracts, poorly paid, and subjected to appalling abuse with little or no legal recourse (Ehrenreich and Hochschild 2004). Progress for some is not necessarily progress for all, particularly when other relations of exploitation and oppression remain firmly in place.

As Élise Thorburn shows us, the household is a critical site of social reproduction where people, often women, do the necessary but intentionally devalued work of reproducing labour power. Much has been made in recent years of men taking on a greater share of domestic work, particularly child care, something that's been enthusiastically picked up in pop culture representations of the "new man" busting out of the confines of the old patriarchal mould. But does reality live up to representation? Since the mid-1970s, the proportion of dual-income households has risen from 39.2 to 58.8 percent (Moyser and Burlock 2018). This change has challenged traditional gender roles that assigned women the primary responsibility for the work of social reproduction and men that of waged worker in the public sphere. In the context of the nuclear family, this dynamic of overwhelmed parents desperately seeking worklife balance has become a running trope in much popular media, particularly that which focuses on middle-class lifestyles. While these shifts have happened, much else remains unchanged.

Women's participation in waged work outside the home is now encouraged and often necessary for financial survival. Nevertheless, mothers in particular are "expected to invest heavily in childrearing, spending plenty of 'quality time' with their children, fostering their children's development through exposure to a variety of extracurricular activities, and making constant efforts to enrich their children's environment." In 2015, women in Canada spent at average of 5.4 hours per day on all unpaid work activities, compared to 2.9 hours for men (Moyser and Burlock 2018). Women are still less likely to participate in waged work than men (82 percent of women participated in the labour market in 2015, compared to 90.9 percent of men) and, when they do, are more likely to do so on a part-time basis (Statistics Canada 2018). Despite egalitarian rhetoric to the contrary, when the total work burden for men and women in Canada was calculated in 2015, women were still doing 1.2 hours more work per day than men (9.1 versus 7.9 hours) (Moyser and Burlock 2018).

Across every meaningful metric measuring different aspects of social reproduction, women continue to do significantly more housework, care work, and child care than men. Women in Canadian households spend an average of 2.8 hours on housework each day compared to 1.9 hours for men (Moyser and Burlock 2018). Gender also has implications for the housework tasks taken on. Women's household tasks tend to be "routine and repetitive, such as cooking, cleaning, laundry, and shopping," while men's tasks "are more episodic or discretionary, such as taking out the garbage, house and car repairs, mowing the lawn, and gardening" (Moyser and Burlock 2018). Men are doing more housework than they have historically, but they are still doing less than women and have more freedom in determining what tasks they do.

Child care is another area where much has been made of men's increasing involvement compared to previous decades. Research confirms that men are spending more time with their children and, in fact, having more fun doing it (Stechyson 2019). While such accounts rightly celebrate the growing commitment from many men to caring for their children, this commitment doesn't extend to other aspects of care work or housework traditionally considered "women's work." In recent years, men have significantly increased the time they spend playing with their children, but they have not similarly increased the time spent on a host of other activities related to child care (laundry, cooking, scheduling, homework, etc.). The real story here is that more men play with their children more often and that's a benefit to both parents and children, but these fathers are not taking on more of the unpaid work of social reproduction overall.

These dynamics are replicated when we consider the work of caring for an adult family member or friend. Women are three times more likely than men to provide care for elderly, ill, or disabled adult family members or friends and, when they do, spend significantly more time doing so (Moyser and Burlock 2018). The gendered distribution of tasks that marks housework and child care is also reflected in adult care work, with women taking on all tasks (personal care, housework, scheduling care-related tasks, medical treatments, and transportation) more frequently than men, with the exception of household maintenance tasks. That's the patriarchal dividend continuing to pay benefits to men on the backs of women. It's a dividend that isn't just gendered; it's also positioned at the intersection of race, class, ability, and more.

CONCLUSION

Who are your kin, and why does kinship matter in society? In this chapter we explore these questions by unsettling some of the most taken-for-granted assumptions about family and kinship. For those of us born and raised in the overdeveloped North and West of this world, family and kinship are often considered synonymous with people who are related by blood and marriage. The primordial kernel of this relationship is often thought of as the nuclear family — parents living with their offspring. This bio-genetic essentialism is rarely questioned since it seems obvious to people. Of course, there are other kinds of relatives (adopted kin, for example) but the common-sense conviction for many people living in this part of the world and at this moment in history is that "blood relation" is the bedrock of kinship and family.

All it takes is a little poking and prodding around the edges of this "common sense" to reveal its problems. Even for those of us who take shared bio-genetic substance ("blood relatives") as the bedrock of kin relations, we all know that in practice things are more complex. I have people who are related to me by blood or marriage who I don't particularly like, rarely see, and largely want nothing to do with. They are family "on paper" but not in actuality. Other people in my life I have known for years; they are not technically related to me by either blood or marriage, and with them I share a relationship of mutual trust, love, and support. They are not recognized as family from the perspective of the state or dominant tradition, but they are my family of choice. Choice, affinity, proximity, and a commitment to mutual aid are all elements that stand outside of the formal kinship map we learn, but in many ways they are more important than the supposed bedrock of shared bio-genetic substance.

Part of the problem with kinship is that we think about it as if it's a specific, discrete part of a larger social machine. In this way we are encouraged to take the machine apart and see how it works. But is this a good metaphor for social life? My father's brother is my uncle. My mother's brother is also my uncle. They have the same title so this should mean they have the same relationship to me and I to them, but that's obviously rarely the case. Life interferes with our desire to make neat conceptual maps of our social worlds. This tendency to abstraction and system-making is convenient from an analytical perspective but doesn't actually map onto lived reality very well.

When we fall into seeing the world as a collection of systems and institutions, we make several critical mistakes. First, we swap simplified and idealized types for dynamic and messy lived reality. This may make our analysis look elegant, but it misrepresents the thing we are trying to understand. Second, we make social interaction between people look like machines running on tracks, but agency disappears from people individually and collectively as we become the products of monolithic forces, systems, ideologies, and institutions. Third, we deaden the social world by objectifying it. "Objectifying" something means you are turning the social world into a set of lifeless objects for your own use. Representing society as if it's nothing more than repertoires of thought and action, systems, and institutions that people act out like drones is analytically wrong and doesn't help us understand society. Fourth and finally, by retreating to the convenience and simplicity of abstraction and idealized types, we develop concepts and analytical categories that work in our models but aren't actually used by people in making their way through the world.

We might think of kinship as a system of relations based on shared bio-genetic substance tied to a corresponding code of conduct. That's tidy and conceptually coherent, but it gives us a false impression of what's going on. As David Schneider argues, "kinship" is only really a category that exists in the minds of social scientists looking to analyze societies; it isn't a category that people think and act with. This doesn't mean kinship and family are not real things in society or important to people. What Schneider means is that we can't understand kin relations without placing them in their proper, messy, crowded social contexts and understanding how those who inhabit those contexts think about and make use of these relations. Society is not like an engine made up of discrete parts working together to achieve a specific outcome. It's a dynamic field of action made up of relations, subjects, and institutions all acting on one another. It makes for easier analysis if we divide the world up into "private" and "public" spheres with different roles and types of activity attached to each, but this doesn't make the analysis true. With regard to kinship, as Marshall Sahlins argues, we know from a mountain of cross-cultural research that any kin relation that can be made through "procreation, filiation, or descent" can also be made through "culturally appropriate action" (2011a, 3). This is why Sahlins makes the case for understanding kinship as "mutuality of being," a relationship that is a product of people living common lives and being run through by each other. Shared genetic substance doesn't make for "real" kin versus symbolic or affective ways of working out kinship. Let's recall Kaja Finkler's definition of kin as a group of people "who perceive themselves as similar and who consider themselves related on grounds of shared material, be it land, blood, food, saliva, semen, or ideological or affective content," with membership in such a group carrying "moral obligations and responsibilities" (2001, 236). Shared, common substance, whether genetic, symbolic, ideological, or something else entirely, is the basis of kin relations.

Living in a capitalist, hetero-patriarchal, white supremacist, and settler-colonial society also skews our understanding of the nature and purpose of kinship. Like so many other social relations, kinship and family life are refracted through the lens of capitalist relations because capitalism colonizes our lifeworlds, and the logic of profit, private property, and the wage relation comes to infect our social lives, not just our waged working lives. Capitalism, as we will see in chapters to come, also encourages me to understand the social world narcissistically, with me the warm centre of it. Kinship in this formulation becomes all about having and being individually rather than doing collectively. I am a son, a father, a partner, a brother, a nephew. I have children, a partner, a sister, a mother, an uncle. But, I am not intrinsically any of these things; I take on the roles these words stand in for and live them into being through my actions, but I don't essentially embody them. The only reason we can believe such possessive, commodified fictions is that our social lives don't depend on them. Capitalism rips us up by our roots and alienates us from what we need to survive and from each other in order to sell survival and belonging back to us, at a profit of course.

While Durkheim's formula of organic versus mechanical solidarity is simplistic and problematic, it does point to the differences in ways of living in large-scale, industrialized, and capitalist societies versus smaller scale, non-capitalist ones. As someone embedded in a modern, capitalist, industrialized society, I still feel kinship's importance. I understand its significance because of the importance of my children and my partner to me and because of the work we do together in taking care of each other. I think about kin relations when I remember friends and family whom I love but who I also miss because they are physically distant from me. I consume media that constantly plays on the trope of family relations as one of its central recurring themes. But my life in this society is structured by logics of commodification, profit-taking, and private property, and this, too, has implications for kinship. Perhaps the most important one is that the family is the site of social reproduction, the social location in which we sustain ourselves and so our ability to labour. As Élise Thorburn shows us in her intervention in this chapter, the work of social reproduction – emotional and physical care work, housework, making food, socialization – is not tangential to capitalism, it's the real source of profit. Without this work, how could anyone labour? Without labour, where do commodities and the profit they are sold for come from? This work, feminized, degraded, unpaid, is some of the most important work we do with and for each other, and it's part of the reason kinship and the family are so very important to human experience.

Like the other social phenomena we consider in this book, what matters most about kinship is not what it is but what it does and what is done to it. Looking at families allows us to see the other forces and relations being brought to bear on us. Our survey of the changing nature of family living in Canada shows us many things: more people are living alone than ever before and that's especially true for older women; more young adults are still living with their parents, often well into their thirties; fewer people are choosing to marry and common-law unions are increasingly popular; more men are spending more time with their children; and more households are made up of a couple without children than at any time in the record. But these are only the most superficial markers of change. To understand what is driving them and what they mean, we need to look at the wider context.

If we do so, we see that the alienation, atomization, and precariousness that is a hallmark of capitalism has clearly impacted family life. Elders live by themselves in solitary dwellings and without support. Younger people delay starting their own families because they are constantly re-training for good work that never seems to materialize and can't afford both rent and debt payments. Women do more waged work but no less housework, while men play with their kids more but avoid taking up other aspects of the necessary work of social reproduction.

Other factors are also relevant. Equal marriage, no-fault divorce, birth control, and the rise of the dual-income household are often cited as evidence of liberation from the shackles of hetero-patriarchal tradition. But while white women won the vote in Canada by 1920, Indigenous and racialized women didn't secure this until the 1960s. While middle-class women entered the waged workforce during and after World War II, destabilizing the "man-the-breadwinner" axis of patriarchy, their places in the home were not occupied by woke husbands and partners but by poor women and women migrating as temporary care workers. While abortion was decriminalized in the 1980s, many women in Canada continue to be functionally denied access to such services because of unwilling or nonexistent service providers. Reproductive justice has typically been taken to mean the right to birth control and abortion services. For Indigenous, racialized, and criminalized women in Canada, their struggles for reproductive justice have also been about access to quality health care, child care, their own children, and freedom from forced sterilization. While many queer couples celebrated marriage equality allowing them to join the hetero-patriarchal and capitalist franchise, many others have been clear that the struggle for queer liberation was about the right to make the families we want, not the right to join an institution that belongs to the mainstream and seems fairly broken at that. Like a canary in a coal mine, family and kinship are sensitive detectors of profound changes in our lifeworlds. Far from homogenous, despite what conservative commentators would have us believe, our kin relations are as diverse as the experiments in human sociality. If we focus on their role as sites of social reproduction, perhaps we can even find ways of liberating ourselves from the toxic social relations wrought by heterosexist patriarchy, settler-colonialism, and capitalism and carve out other ways of caring and living in common.

KEY CONCEPTS

affinity: social relations figured through marriage or choice.

bilateral descent: tracing kin relations through both the mother's and father's descent lines.

consanguinity: social relations figured through "blood" or bio-genetic descent.

kinship: the term anthropologists have used since the late nineteenth century to refer to those social systems that tell us about who our relations are and what our obligations to each other are in the context of those relationships.

social reproduction: the collective work of care that goes into making social life – and hence economic activity – possible. Marxist feminists developed this concept to focus on the work that goes into reproducing labour power. Such work is often carried out by women, sequestered in the private sphere, and intentionally degraded and invisibilized, not because it is useless or marginal but because it is central to wealth-production.

unilineal descent: tracing kin relations either through the mother's descent line (matrilineal) or the father's descent line (patrilineal).

6

MAKING MEANING, MAKING SENSE

Communication and Belief

There are many ways that humans represent and convey their experiences in and of the world. We've seen some of them already in our explorations in this book. Whether we're talking about cave paintings created by our early human ancestors, mass produced books, or modern science, these are all ways of representing and making sense of the world. On a day-to-day basis, we take most of these for granted. That's a critical element of communication – once we're good at it we rarely think much about the way we do it. But if we consider it for a moment, the human capacity to communicate about the world is a truly remarkable thing.

Take spoken language, for example. Using complex combinations of sounds we convey worlds of possibilities. I can tell you what I did yesterday, what I'm doing now, what I plan to do tomorrow. I can talk about events I witnessed as easily as I can tell you about things I hope for, fear, or imagine. How do I do this? Most basically, I utter a series of sounds that the listener hears and then decodes. These sounds have no necessary connection to the thing they represent, and they can be cobbled together in essentially unlimited formations, yet we hear and decode them and thus derive meaning from them. The same is true for other forms of language, including sign language, written language, and even body language.

As we learned in Chapter 1, one of the most significant outcomes of our human evolutionary journey is the development of our large and complex brain. The complexity and relatively large size of this vital organ provides the biological basis for our species' sprawling ability to represent our experiences of the world in ways that extend far beyond simply conveying practical information. While all living things possess some capacity for communication, no other species, so far as we know, possesses the kind of facility for this that humans do. This chapter explores some of the critical elements in our collective capacity to make sense out of the world. Once we start to dig, it's amazing and a bit overwhelming to grapple with all the ways humans have elaborated to make meaning in the world. There's no way to discuss each of these forms in a chapter like this; instead, the aim is to examine some of the common threads binding these practices together.

A WORLD OF SIGNS

The capacity for symbolic thought is one of the hallmarks of human cognition. This means more than humans being able to think abstractly. It means that our interactions with each other and the world around us are mediated by an infinite and flexible symbolic economy. Simply put, we communicate through signs. By "signs" I don't just mean traffic signs, advertisements, or brand logos, although these are all kinds of signs. A *sign* is simply something that stands for or represents something else. For example, a dollar sign ($) represents Canadian currency, but it also represents wealth, power, success, and more. A brand logo obviously stands in for the company itself and the commodities it produces, but it can also represent a host of other ideas that have little to do with the stuff the company makes and everything to do with the values and sentiments advertisers work hard to associate with brands. Nike's swoosh can signify athleticism, glory, victory, and prowess. Of course, brand logos can also have other meanings depending on the perspective of the viewer. It might convey exploitation, conspicuous consumption, sweatshop labour, and capitalist excess. To some, a dollar sign might represent capitalist commodification of the lifeworld and the alienation of people from each other and what they need to survive. How could a sign do all this? The simple answer is that a sign has no single, immutable meaning; its meaning depends on the intentions of the one making the sign and on those who receive it, as well as the wider social context in which all these things are placed. How does this work? Let's break it down.

A sign is simply something that represents something else, and every sign is made up of two distinct parts: a signifier and a signified. The signifier is the form the sign takes in the world, the thing we observe. To return to the examples above, the signifiers are the dollar sign and the swoosh. In language, the signifier is the word itself or the gesture (in the case of non-verbal forms of language, like American Sign Language). The signified is the abstract concept to which the signifier points (Edgar and Sedgwick 2005, 357–58). Signs are crucial units of meaning-making in any act of communication, but it's vital to understand that the relationship between signifiers and signifieds is arbitrary, contextual, and mutable. By this I mean that there is no necessary connection between the thing we use to represent something and the thing being represented. That doesn't mean there aren't connections or conventions that govern these kinds of relationships but rather that none of these conventions are true, necessary, or unchanging.

Take the swastika. Today, it is impossible to separate this symbol from its association with Nazis and their genocidal legacy. The swastika was used in Hinduism, Buddhism, and other religious and cultural traditions long before the Nazis appropriated it for their Third Reich. It has had other meanings that have nothing to do with Nazism, fascism, white supremacy, or genocidal violence. Nevertheless, the incredible weight of Nazi horrors and the prevalence of the swastika in Nazi iconography means that it is freighted with meaning from which it simply cannot be divorced. The swastika was not somehow destined to be a key Nazi symbol, but since it was appropriated in this way it cannot now be used unproblematically to refer to something else. But why dwell on this example in the abstract when we can turn to the real world?

In 2019 a news story made the rounds about Steve Johnson, a resident of El Sobrante, California, who had a twenty-foot square black concrete swastika built in his front yard (Gander 2019). Neighbours were understandably shocked and outraged, but when Johnson was confronted by them and questioned by reporters, he claimed not to know much about the swastika's association with Nazism. He said he'd built it because he liked the symbol and was referencing Tibetan Buddhism, despite the fact he had no Tibetan ancestry or Buddhist affiliation. Pressed further, Johnson told reporters, "That Nazi [stuff] happened like 80 years ago" and people should "get over it," while also citing his rights as a property owner to do whatever he liked with his yard (Gander 2019). He doubled down on this line of argumentation, saying the swastika "doesn't represent anything" other than "me not having to pull weeds over in that part of my yard; that's what it represents to me. What does it represent to you?" (Gilmour 2019).

Keep in mind that the Nazi regime and its collaborators murdered 17 million people in the Holocaust, 6 million Jews and 11 million others drawn from a host of "undesirable" groups, a total that excludes soldiers and civilians killed in the massive industrialized warfare of World War II. The Anti-Defamation League (n.d.) calls the swastika "perhaps the most notorious hate symbol in Western culture." Johnson's implausible justifications aside, the issue is clearly not just what he associates with his giant swastika but the social, political, and historical context in which this and every other sign exists. The fundamentally dialogic nature of signs is in fact one of the key concepts introduced by theorists interested in their study (see Bakhtin 1981). Simply put, all communication is dialogic in the sense that it requires both a sender who puts something out into the world, and a receiver who can decode and make sense of it. This is why context matters and why the arbitrary nature of the signifier-signified relationship doesn't simply mean that anything goes in this symbolic economy. Regardless of what I think a given sign means or how badly I want to repurpose it, I can't make those decisions unilaterally because every act of communication involves not just the one sending out the sign but those receiving it. Johnson's rhetorical question about what the swastika represents to others is unintentionally perceptive. In his verbal fencing with reporters, Johnson gives away the fundamental problem with his personal denials of the history and significance of this symbol. Even if Johnson were entirely unaware of the swastika's significance, it would still be a symbol of genocide and hate because that's the context it's embedded in.

Eminent cultural studies scholar Stuart Hall (2007) captures the core of this communicative economy of signs when he considers the way messages are produced and disseminated through mass media like television. In his influential essay "Encoding, Decoding," Hall points out that no event simply speaks for itself; it has to be made into a story that not only can circulate and convey meaning but also conforms to storytelling conventions. As we've seen repeatedly in this book, every attempt to make sense of the world is basically a kind of storytelling. The tools, social relations, and conventions of different modes of storytelling are, of course, different but that doesn't mean they don't share common traits. Whether we're talking about academic research, conspiracy theories, national history, or current event news, all can be considered narrative genres with their own stylistic and substantive conventions.

Behind the scenes, these modes of storytelling also have their own means and relations of production, the tools and ways of organizing people and their labour to make these messages before they can be put into motion, consumed, and reproduced (Hall 2007). Production timelines, technical demands and expertise, the way the work of message-making is organized and distributed, and the profit motivation of the media conglomerates that own media outlets all bear directly on the messages being circulated. Mass-mediated messages also habituate those consuming them to particular narrative styles, tropes, and plot devices. Complexity and nuance often disappear from mass-mediated messages, giving way to simpler stories that, not coincidentally, frequently accord with the vested interests and power relations animating the status quo. This is as true in news media as it is in Hollywood films.

At issue is not merely whether any given account is accurate or factual but the way in which stories and our ways of telling them make sense within dominant power relations, institutions, and ideologies. Cultural studies scholar Henry Giroux describes movies as "powerful teaching machines" that "both entertain and educate" and are always "deeply imbricated within material and symbolic relations of power" (2002, 3). Whether we're talking about myths and legends that are hundreds of years old or the latest Hollywood superhero blockbusters, it's not hard to see these stories as forms of entertainment as well as moral and political parables about the world as it is or might be. These fictional stories are meant to convey lessons about the nature of the world and our place in it. Other forms of storytelling, such as journalism about current events, are supposed to occupy a different place, particularly in liberal democracies, where much lip service is paid to the virtues of an informed and engaged citizenry and the role played by journalists in holding the powerful up to scrutiny. In recent years, however, the phenomenon of "fake news" has taken on pressing significance, particularly in the age of social media. As Ian Reilly explores in the following intervention, the fake news phenomenon poses new and vexing challenges to media consumption and democratic participation that take us beyond the slippery nature of signs and the power relations embedded in every act of representation.

FAKE NEWS — *IAN REILLY*

FAKE NEWS HAS BECOME so ubiquitous a term since Donald Trump's presidential election win in 2016 that it has enjoyed an almost protean malleability. As a highly divisive and polarizing phenomenon (with a recent study suggesting that Americans cannot even agree on how to define the term) (Knight Foundation 2018), fake news has been used to describe false, misleading, or intentionally fabricated stories (Hunt and Gentzkow 2017); state-sponsored or corporate-funded propaganda (Khaldarova and Pantti 2016; Stauber and Rampton 1995); satire or news parody (J. P. Jones 2010); partisan or ideological commentary (Taub 2017); activist interventions (Reilly 2013); artificial intelligence-doctored text, image, audio, or video content (Reynolds 2018); and commercial or advertorial content masquerading as news (Hirst 2017). This is but the tip of the proverbial iceberg.

For each iteration of the term, there is a different set of applications and outcomes. Intentionally false stories and propaganda have attracted the lion's share of commentary because news items of this ilk have the capacity to misinform and deceive news-reading publics. The increasing proliferation of these stories simultaneously weakens citizens' purchase on truthful or reliable accounts of current affairs and contributes to a deepening erosion of trust in both journalists and news organizations (McNair 2018).

Responding to what they deem an impoverished news and information climate, satirical publications like *The Onion* and satirists such as Stephen Colbert, John Oliver, and Samantha Bee have actively criticized and ridiculed mainstream news media outlets for consistently failing to fulfill their fourth estate (i.e., watchdog) role. In drawing attention to news media's failure to serve as a critical check on corporate, state, and/or institutional power, satire channels the "fake news" format to playfully critique and reform its targets.

Partisan forms of fake news are leveraged to discredit and delegitimize stories, perspectives, and opinions that do not coincide with their own. For practitioners of (hyper-) partisan commentary (e.g., Donald Trump), the term fake news has been co-opted to mean anything they don't agree with — a feature (not a bug) of media discourse that risks normalizing lying and dishonesty in the political sphere (Crines 2017).

Activist groups such as the Yes Men and the Palestine Media Collective (PMC) created fake newspapers (*New York Times* and *Vancouver Sun*, respectively) to openly criticize news media performance and to register their dissent with broader publics. For the Yes Men, their fake *NYT* (2008) published stories they wanted to see in print and to advance utopian ideas (i.e., stories on universal health care, free access to higher education, climate change policy).

The expansion of artificial intelligence (AI) across all realms of cultural production has introduced even greater risks into the fabric of everyday news consumption. With AI-driven news bots producing and disseminating a wide range of news content — from seamlessly manipulated photos to algorithm-generated fake audio and video (Niemi 2018) — new challenges to correctly identify and interpret news content have arisen. Without proper vetting, labelling, or skepticism, AI tools may sow unwanted and unnecessary confusion.

Finally, advertorial content that masquerades as news may seem like the most benign form of fake news currently making the rounds, but its broader circulation is contingent upon news media's wholesale integration of press releases and video news releases. These covertly pitched products and services often appear without disclosure of the funding or production sources, giving unsuspecting audiences the impression that they are consuming legitimate news (Farsetta and Price 2006; Goodman and Goodman 2007).

The motives for creating, publishing, and recirculating fake news are by now well documented. The economic incentives are such that the creators of fake news content (and the platforms that give this content its visibility) stand to earn considerable sums of ad revenue and capital. During the 2016 US election cycle, Buzzfeed News uncovered a network of over forty websites responsible for more than 750 fake news stories (Silverman and Singer-Vine 2016). So pervasive was the network's influence that Buzzfeed labelled it a "fake news empire." During this period, a group of now infamous teens in Macedonia generated considerable profit from their pro-Donald Trump fake news narratives (Subramanian 2017). Capitalists aside, fake news is being leveraged by a broad range of practitioners: propagandists, hoaxers, hackers, partisans, satirists, and activists (Reilly 2018). While fake news is not inherently destructive in all of the above iterations, it has become increasingly important to properly decipher these activities. Citizens' abilities to do so will shape how well or how poorly we understand the world.

As Reilly shows in his intervention, the "fake news" phenomenon cannot be reduced to a single thing. Spanning a range from propaganda and partisan commentary to intentionally misleading news and activist satire, in the age of social media the fake news phenomenon has taken on even greater significance than it might otherwise have. There is legitimate reason to be concerned about the effects of fake news at a moment in time when other social, political, economic, and ecological crises are challenging the status quo and generating increasing levels of distrust, pessimism, and insularity (Marantz 2019). But we also shouldn't naïvely overstate the newness of this phenomenon. While modern technologies and media platforms have increased the possibilities for and circulation of fake news stories, there never was a golden age where journalists held the powerful to account and society was broadly informed about what was really going on in the world. In many ways, all that fake news embodies is an acceleration of already existing logics at work in relations of ruling. Making meaning is never free from larger relations of oppression and exploitation. As we will see in the next section, struggles over meaning are also struggles over power.

BATTLING OVER THE MEANING OF THE BATTLE OF SEATTLE

As David Solnit (D. Solnit and Solnit 2009) details, the way social change struggles are remembered rarely goes uncontested. Solnit was a key activist and organizer involved in the 1999 "Battle of Seattle," where a broad coalition of social justice movements came together to protest capitalist globalization and the World Trade Organization (WTO), the international organization vested with setting the rules for capitalist accumulation on a global scale. The Battle of Seattle was a high point in the cycle of struggles now known as the alter-globalization movement, a period that spanned the late 1990s until the early 2000s. In many ways, this period was a high-water mark for anti-capitalist, radically democratic movements for social justice on a global scale (Conway 2004; Kingsnorth 2004; Klein 2000; 2002; Notes from Nowhere 2003). While this upsurge of social movement activity built on previous currents of struggle, it was the Zapatista Uprising, which began on January 1, 1994, that was the real spark for this fuse of resistance to neoliberal capitalist globalization (Midnight Notes Collective 2001; Khasnabish 2008, 2010).

The Zapatistas began their armed uprising against the Mexican Army and the federal executive as the North American Free Trade Agreement (NAFTA) came into effect, binding Canada, the United States, and Mexico together in what was, at the time, the largest capitalist free trade area in the world. The Zapatistas, named in honour of Emiliano Zapata, the greatest hero of the Mexican Revolution (1910–17), declared NAFTA a "death sentence" for the Indigenous people of Mexico because it put an end to land reform and collective land ownership, so vital to Indigenous and peasant communities (Marcos 2002). The real grievances animating the Zapatista Uprising stretch back to the colonization of Mexico by the Spanish in the sixteenth century and include entrenched racism, grinding and enforced poverty, dispossession of land and autonomy, and brutal violence and state-backed terror in defence of ruling-class interests and property rights (Muñoz Ramírez 2008; Harvey 1998; Collier 1999;

Womack 1999). By the early 1980s, after decades of trying to organize peacefully for social change, Indigenous communities in the far southeast of Mexico were tired of having their efforts viciously crushed by private landowners' hired guns and the repressive arm of the state. Into this tinder box stepped urban revolutionaries from Mexico City, who had come to try to organize the peasantry as the southern flank of a larger revolutionary struggle. Instead of conscripting Indigenous communities into their national revolutionary struggle, these urban revolutionaries would end up being folded into the Indigenous realities and struggle in Mexico's southeast, and the Zapatista Army of National Liberation (*Ejército Zapatista de Liberación Nacional*, EZLN) was born (Harvey 1998; Muñoz Ramírez 2008; Khasnabish 2010; Gilly 1998). It would take a decade of clandestine organizing, training, and preparation before the thousands of insurgents of the EZLN would initiate their uprising to coincide not only with NAFTA but five centuries of colonialism, genocide, and capitalist violence.

The shooting war between the EZLN and the Mexican Army lasted only two weeks, with a unilateral ceasefire and calls for a negotiated peace issued by the government in the face of massive national demonstrations in support of the Zapatistas (see Muñoz Ramírez 2008; Ross 2000). The long tale of the Zapatistas' struggle for democracy, liberty, and justice is far beyond our scope here, but their experiment in building autonomy in Chiapas, Mexico, continues to set an inspiring example for radicals the world over. While the Zapatistas have remained an armed rebel movement, one of their most important accomplishments was initiating an enduring, expansive dialogue between the Zapatistas and those they described as rebels against neoliberalism in Mexico and all over the world (Conant 2010; Khasnabish 2008). Refusing to see their struggle as an isolated one, they called for the creation of an intercontinental network of resistance and rebellion "for humanity and against neoliberalism" and capable of building "a world where many worlds fit" (Marcos 2004). They held a series of encounters in rebel territory in the far southeast of Mexico to kickstart this network of struggles with thousands of others in attendance from across Mexico and around the world. Out of this initiative would grow the People's Global Action (PGA), one of the central anti-capitalist, direct-action networks responsible for organizing many of the major protest events that would become the hallmark of the alter-globalization movement. The Battle of Seattle is among the most prominent of these.

On November 30, 1999, 50,000 activists representing a diversity of social justice struggles from trade unions to direct action anarchists to environmentalists shut down the meetings of the WTO. That year, the WTO's member states were meeting in Seattle to hold key discussions aimed at setting the framework for a new round of multilateral trade agreements like NAFTA. Multilateral trade agreements had become central pillars of capitalist globalization with implications far beyond basic business interests, like the elimination of land reform and collective land ownership in Mexico. So-called "free trade" deals had direct and often sweeping implications on areas of social life extending well beyond the economy, including environmental regulations, labour rights, public services, democratic practice, and state sovereignty (McNally 2002; Ellwood 2010). This multi-pronged capitalist colonization of people's lifeworlds also served to catalyze a diverse array of organizations and groups to co-operate in an effort to oppose capitalist globalization and advance alternative visions of globalization centred on social justice, people's needs, and the planet's survival (D. Solnit 2004). Faced with this threat, feminists, anarchists, Indigenous people, racial justice and anti-poverty activists, trade unionists, environmentalists, and many, many more came together to work across lines of difference that had previously kept their movements segregated (Ayres 1998).

Months in advance of the WTO's millennial round meetings in Seattle, activists began planning their opposition to it. They did so to draw attention to the incredible and growing inequalities and injustices created by neoliberal capitalist globalization and to demonstrate the capacity for grassroots, democratic alternatives to the status quo advanced by people's social justice movements. Prioritizing direct democracy in organizing and direct action in practice, activists from a multitude of movements gathered in Seattle at the end of November 1999 to show they could block the capitalist pillaging of their lifeworlds and advance alternatives to it. Not content to limit themselves to familiar and performative rituals of protest like permitted marches, many activists and organizers came committed to the plan of shutting the WTO meetings down. If ordinary people had no say in the way their world was being organized by and for the interests of capital, the mouthpieces of those interests would not be allowed to go about their business in peace.

From November 30 until December 3, Seattle became a battleground between activists, police, and the US National Guard. Despite mass arrests, brutality, and the abundant use of tear gas and other chemical weapons, police repression was unable to defeat this burgeoning movement of movements that successfully disrupted the WTO meetings while insisting that resistance and alternatives were still possible. On December 3, without reaching agreement on the next stage of capitalist globalization in large part because of the vigorous and committed resistance being mounted outside the halls of power, the WTO meeting was concluded. The protests in Seattle in 1999 did more than express people's anger and outrage at the shape of the globalized capitalist order; they also struck a critical blow against institutions meant to legitimate and advance this order, such as the WTO. The Battle of Seattle was no mere spectacle of resistance; it was a manifestation of people's grassroots power against globe-spanning ruling-class interests that struck a critical and lasting blow against what had previously seemed to be untouchable and unassailable institutions and the interests they represented. In many ways, this is precisely why the battle over the meaning of the protests remains so significant.

A great deal has been said about the WTO shutdown coordinated by the Direct Action Network in the years since the Battle of Seattle, and I won't rehash that here. Instead, I focus on the way that the story of the Battle of Seattle has been told, retold, circulated, and contested in the years since it took place. As David Solnit (2009, 5) notes,

> The 1999 Seattle WTO shut down and resistance has become an icon – a story that gives other things meaning. What people think happened in Seattle shapes what they believe about protest, direct action, social change movements; about corporate globalization and capitalism; and about police, the state, and repression. Stories shape consciousness. Consciousness shapes the future.
>
> The story of Seattle WTO resistance has itself become a battleground. In the conflict, activists and movements fight the corporate media, police, and government disinformation myths used to stoke public fears and justify repression against grassroots movements across the US. It also remains a source of inspiration for people hungry for positive change across the planet.

As Solnit points out in his essay, the real drama of the Battle of Seattle was the clash between a corporate, capitalist vision of globalization and a people's globalization predicated on social justice. For many, particularly those not part of a cosmopolitan corporate and political elite, the vision of capitalist globalization forcefully advanced by the WTO meant a globalized freedom of movement for capital, commodities, and the rich, and greater immiseration for most everyone else. There are, of course, nuances to all of this, but there can be no real doubt about the fundamentally elitist, market-obsessed, profit-driven nature of the neoliberal globalizing project.

The organizing, training, and other preparation that went into mobilizing 50,000 activists from diverse locations and movements and made the WTO shutdown possible is another vitally important story. Predictably, corporate media focused almost exclusively on "violent riots" supposedly initiated by activists, including baseless allegations of activists throwing urine and feces at police. Activists were quickly characterized as know-nothing flat-earthers opposed to trade, and the careful, deliberate, year-long work of organizing the protest convergence was dismissed as a spontaneous, incoherent rebellion (D. Solnit 2009). These elements resonate with other cultural frames we are socialized into. In other words, they make sense to many of us because they fit with other dominant tropes and themes.

It's important to recognize that just because something fits into the way we've been taught to see the world and others in it doesn't make it true. Popular media is saturated with stories about heroic police officers, noble and inspired leaders, dangerous and shadowy threats, and the necessity for obedience and hierarchy to stave off chaos and civilizational collapse. Whether we're watching the news, the latest superhero movie, or our favourite post-apocalyptic zombie survival show, these tropes recur time and again and reinforce dominant narratives about society. We don't need to buy into conspiracy theories to understand why this is so. Powerful ruling-class interests animate powerful social institutions, and so it should be no surprise that the prevailing narratives about any significant social issue tend to reproduce those dominant, vested interests.

It's worth noting that stories of protestors throwing bottles of urine or feces at police officers is a recurring trope without any substantiated claims of it having happened at Seattle in 1999 or at other protest events (Wood 2014). Despite its falsity, the circulation of these stories has continued, often by police spokespeople themselves, and has important and intentional effects. As sociologist Lesley Wood notes in her path-breaking study of the militarization of protest policing,

> Whether or not the spokesperson believes the story, the telling dehumanizes protesters, and the idea that the protesters are somehow less than human can spread through the media to law enforcement, civilian authorities and the public, triggering a whole cascade of reactions before the protest event, including restrictions on protest, and increased police spending, and afterwards, justifying charges against and the use of militarized tactics against protesters. (2014, 151)

The point to the story of protestors throwing urine or feces at police is that it "dehumanizes and depoliticizes" the protestors, associating them with disgusting, degrading activities that even children know better than to engage in (Wood 2014, 160). Given the taboo nature of any form of "play" with human waste, the notion that protestors were planning to throw it at rank-and-file police officers sets the protestors up as people willing to violate basic standards of sociability, respectability, and hygiene. More importantly, imagine the powerful effect such stories have on the mindset of police officers deployed in such contexts. It appears to matter not at all that no police department in North America or any media outlet that has participated in circulating these stories can turn up a single verifiable piece of evidence supporting these allegations. The story exercises a powerful emotional pull on those receiving it. The symbolic charge associated with human waste transfers to the protestors, who are, in this telling, willing to weaponize it. It tells us these are people who have crossed the line of basic civility and, in so doing, place themselves outside the bounds of dignified treatment. In a context where activists are often regarded distrustfully by mainstream society, stories of them intending to fling human waste at police officers can "transform distrust into disgust and horror" (Wood 2014, 160). This not only makes it easier to employ more brutal tactics to control them, it also facilitates the under-cutting of a host of grassroots struggles for social justice as activists in general come to be associated with degrading and disgusting behaviour. This, too, is ultimately a story about signs in a larger economy of social meaning-making.

The story of the Battle of Seattle provides another interesting example through which to explore the power-laden work of meaning-making in society. As another demonstration of the protest's iconic status, it was even made into a feature-length film, *Battle in Seattle* (2008), directed by Stuart Townsend and starring, amongst others, Charlize Theron and Woody Harrelson. Once activists involved in the actual WTO shutdown became aware of the film's production, they sought to contribute to it in an effort to preserve their side of the story and prevent it from becoming yet another formulaic Hollywood tale (D. Solnit 2009). Direct Action Network organiz-er David Solnit even travelled to the filming location in Vancouver, BC, to read the script and offer comments and suggestions to the filmmakers.

Solnit highlights five key areas that were far off the mark in the script: the portray-al of activists; the erasure of movements from the *Global South*; protestor violence (including the ubiquitous urine-throwing myth); the conflation of anarchism with black bloc tactics; and a fundamental misrepresentation of why the shutdown was successful (2009, 36–39). Without getting into the specifics of his assessment, these five areas all suffered from a replication of Hollywood convention and wider social myths. For example, the film offers a narrative about the protest's success as due to city officials being caught by surprise by the numbers of protestors and their tac-tics, the leniency of key city officials like the mayor in authorizing more aggressive policing tactics, and insufficient numbers of police (2009, 38). In effect, the deeper meaning is that the rabble won against the powerful because the powerful were too soft, too indecisive at critical moments, and chose not to deploy the force they had at their disposal. In response, Solnit writes:

> In actuality, our plans and indications of our numbers were very public, even if authorities did not utilize the information well. We won because we were strategic, well organized over six months, were part of strong local, region-al, national, and international networks and alliances. We also won because leaderless networks are stronger and more flexible than the top-down hier-archies of the police, city, state, and federal authorities. (2009, 38)

Without suggesting that Solnit's counter-narrative ought to be accepted without question, the distance between the two accounts serves as an important reminder that one can tell very different stories conveying very different messages while utilizing the same basic series of events. This matters because it is through the telling and retelling of stories that we learn about the world as it is, our place in it, and how it might be otherwise. Control the narrative and control the meaning that people take from it, including the sense, or lack thereof, of their own collective power. In his intervention about independent media, Scott Neigh delves into the way the organization and underlying principles of media-making, particularly news-making, shape the form and content of the stories it tells.

INDEPENDENT MEDIA — *SCOTT NEIGH*

WE LIVE IN A profoundly unjust world, in which violence and harm are organized into many lives and unearned benefit into others. We live in a world, moreover, where the most readily available resources that we have for learning about what lies beyond our own immediate experience often do little to expose this injustice or equip us to fight for a better tomorrow.

There are individual people and outlets within the dominant media that sometimes do important work, of course, but most of the time the overall landscape supports the unjust status quo. The norms and practices of the profession of journalism deserve careful critique, and hierarchical organizational forms, a capitalist business model that is interlinked with other powerful capitalist enterprises, and broader oppressive social relations all shape how media institutions do their work. But on a certain level, all we need to know is the outcome: The voices and stories of people who are oppressed and exploited tend to be erased, downplayed, or distorted, and the importance of collective efforts to struggle for justice is rarely reflected.

The term "independent media" captures projects that attempt to produce and circulate knowledge about the world using approaches that are in one way or another different from the norms dictated by this dominant media landscape. Independent media projects that are grounded in a commitment to justice and liberation take a wide range of forms. On the most obvious level, the content of what is made and circulated is different. The voices, stories, and struggles of oppressed and exploited people are centred, and their standpoints are the basis for the visions of the world that are advanced. Injustice is acknowledged, justice is valued, and collective struggle is often an important part of the narrative.

Many projects emphasize a difference in practices from the dominant media, though exactly what this looks like varies tremendously. It might include a prioritization of different forms of written, audio, and video texts than is commonly seen in the mainstream. If a journalistic form is still used, it might include different expectations for how a story gets put together, how to select which voices are centred, and how to evaluate significance and meaning. It might include more justice-focused standards for relating to sources and to entire groups and com-munities. Or it might reject journalistic forms altogether, perhaps in favour of first-person accounts or collaborative creation in which people who would nor-mally be reduced to quotable sources or topics are involved in co-creating what-ever media is being made.

In some projects, those actually doing the work and making the decisions are significantly different than in the mainstream. People who are usually marginalized, both in society as a whole and in dominant media institutions, may be the ones doing the writing, editing, and producing. And independent media projects can take on different organizational forms – a non-profit, a cooperative, a loose collective, or something else – which can create conditions for enacting different kinds of social logics than those reproduced by hierarchical and capitalist media enterprises.

At their best, independent media projects exist in dynamic relation with so-cial movements and communities-in-struggle and actively seek to answer what it might look like to make and circulate knowledge in ways grounded in a commit-ment to decolonization, gender justice, racial justice, anti-capitalism, and all of the other axes of struggle alive in our world.

Independent media is inevitably a work in progress. Precisely because of the frequent need to invest significant amounts of unpaid time into the work, inde-pendent media-making is often disproportionately done by people who are mid-dle-class and white. Too often, our projects do not embody in their own function-ing the kinds of values and social logics that we centre in our content. Too often, the demands of deadlines and lack of resources mean that we remain safely in established practices and forms rather than pushing boundaries. And too often, we depend on corporate social media platforms to circulate our work, and even then, our reach is orders of magnitude less than it needs to be.

This may seem discouraging, but I don't think it is. Social movements and com-munities-in-struggle themselves do not exist apart from the oppressive social re-lations we struggle to transform – we exist within them, while also struggling against them, and pointing to a world beyond them. Independent media ground-ed in a commitment to justice and liberation similarly exists within, against, and beyond our oppressive present. Through commitments to experimentation, dia-logue, critical questioning, staying in relation with movements, and radical listen-ing to the voices of ordinary people, we play a part in the transformations that the world so desperately needs.

COMMUNICATION AND POWER

As Neigh shows in his intervention, the way we go about organizing our meaning-making in the world is deeply connected to prevailing relations of power. Anthropologist Sherry Ortner offers a powerful example of this principle in her research on the social enterprise production company Participant Media, whose mission is to produce films that "change the world." Ortner's research explores a new kind of "woke" business model that is nevertheless situated squarely within a neoliberal landscape "that systematically, and almost inevitably, constrain[s] its intention to do good" (2017, 529). Despite the noble mission and even the sincere good intentions of Participant Media's employees and owners, the kind of "good" they can contribute is dramatically impacted by the environment they operate in and the power relations they abide by. As Ortner describes,

> Films that could have been political were softened up, and films that were more overtly political were undercut by the marketing and even sometimes by the redirection of the social-action campaigns. Social-action campaigns in turn were almost entirely technologically driven, seeking low-level, quantifiable fixes that never challenged the larger status quo. (2017, 536–37)

Who gets heard, what stories are told, and what significance is derived from them are not merely outcomes of better ideas winning out in the marketplace of ideas, as many liberal pundits are so fond of repeating. Anyone with a social media account can probably see the fallacy in assertions like this.

Since the mid-2000s, social media has rapidly displaced legacy news media. Facebook, Twitter, Reddit, YouTube, and many more social media platforms are not simply convenient and fun digital tools allowing us to connect with family and friends. They are vast meaning-making ecologies that have thoroughly disrupted the reigning mass communication paradigm without touching power relations at all. Many have celebrated social media's disruption of the informational gatekeeping characteristic of traditional news media, casting it as a tool for media and communicative democratization. From this perspective, users are liberated from the filters, hierarchies, and vested interests of legacy media, and information becomes freer. But just because social media has challenged one type of hierarchical power relation (for example, editors making decisions about which stories make the news and which do not) does not mean it's not prey to others. Facebook, Twitter, YouTube, and the vast ocean of other social media platforms are not public goods; they are for-profit corporate entities whose purpose is not democratization, enlightenment, community-building, or personal empowerment — it is to keep users on their platform as long as possible (Marantz 2019).

While social media may have disrupted legacy media gatekeepers, it didn't simply create a realm of perfect digital freedom in their place. In a digital environment where different platforms are competing for users' time and attention, clickability and virality, not factualness or public relevance, are key metrics of a given post's worth (Marantz 2019). As more and more people are connected to and through social media, it has become a key way that people learn about the world and, often, a key gateway to the Internet itself. People use social media to join groups focusing on their favourite hobby, keep up with friends and family, and stay abreast of celebrity gossip. They also rely on this media for their understanding of current events and pressing social issues and struggles.

Social media also has the ability to connect an individual user not only with information but with a virtual community of others who are also accessing, sharing, and commenting on it. Whether we're talking about fans cosplaying as their favourite comic book hero, people obsessed with exploring abandoned buildings, or neo-Nazi insurrectionists preparing for their longed-for racial holy war, these digital communities and the sentiments they breed can be the basis for action in the world (Evans 2019). The algorithms that sort the posts each of us sees on our social media feeds are not innocent tools neutrally assessing information; they are designed to promote emotionally activating posts over low-arousal posts since this is key to keeping users on site (Marantz 2019). This means the gatekeeping disruption of social media has put in place its own profit-driven hierarchy of value, with dramatic consequences for us individually and socially. Rarely is communication about a dispassionate exchange of positions. Communication, particularly mass communication, is a function of power.

Another way to examine this relationship between communication and power is to examine language loss. *Language* is the system of arbitrary symbols that people use to encode their experiences of the world. Note that this definition doesn't only apply to spoken languages but to any symbolic system used to encode experiences of and in the world, such as American Sign Language or written language. Current research suggests that by the year 2100, half of the approximately 7000 languages currently spoken on this planet will have died out, while the global spread of English, Mandarin, and Spanish will have increased (Rymer 2012). If we look at communities of speakers the picture is even more stark. Of the approximately seven billion people on Earth, 78 percent speak one of the 85 most popular languages, while the 3500 smallest languages are spoken by a mere 8.25 million people (Rymer 2012). More than a thousand of these languages are identified as "critically" or "severely" endangered, set to slide into oblivion as their current communities of speakers die away (Rymer 2012).

What are some of the consequences of language loss? When a language dies, humanity loses a unique repository of knowledge, experience, and perspective on what it means to be human in the world. From vocabulary to grammatical structure, languages are not simply an interchangeable set of codes we can swap out to express the same thing; they are stores of cultural and contextual knowledge and insight (Eschner 2017). While translation applications give us the illusion that words or phrases in any given language can simply be ported into any other, anyone who has ever done any translating or has learned a language other than their mother tongue knows that this is not at all the case.

When I was learning Spanish in preparation for my first fieldwork trip to Mexico in 2001, I remember my surprise at discovering there was no way to say "I like" in Spanish. If I wanted to say "I like coffee" I would say "*Me gusta café*," which translates literally to "Coffee pleases me." The difference at first may seem insignificant, but let's consider its implications. In the English construction I am the subject of the sentence. I do the liking, I am the agent, the actor, the entity imbued with intention, consciousness, and significance. Coffee is a thing, an object to be liked or not by me, something in the world but inanimate, without agency or significance of its own.

Now let's consider the Spanish phrase. In that case, "*Me gusta café*" ("Coffee pleases me"), it's coffee that does the acting, that is the subject of that sentence, while I am acted upon. This distinction may seem subtle and may not have profound implications for the day-to-day existence of Spanish and English speakers, but it does signal a fundamentally different conception of the world. In the English phrase we have a world made up of objects which I consume and which I either like or don't. In the Spanish phrase those objects have the capacity to engender feeling in me, to act on me, to generate consequences in the world. In this mundane example, we have two very different worldviews crystallized. Imagine this instance repeated across all those 7000 languages and across an infinite number of examples. Languages are not simply collections of words that refer to things and that speakers use instrumentally to navigate day-to-day interactions. They are also storehouses of culturally specific knowledge, concepts, and worldviews, and when they disappear the collective ways of being in the world that they embody are fundamentally threatened too.

Of course, it's long been understood that language is a vital storehouse of culturally specific knowledge about the world. This is precisely why colonizers always target the native languages of the populations they seek to dominate and exploit. In the Canadian context, the state's longstanding policy of assimilation directed toward Indigenous Peoples was explicitly aimed at cultural dispossession as a route to turning them into Canadian citizens to "solve" the "Indian problem." One of the key mechanisms through which this was attempted was the Indian residential school system. These schools, run by the Canadian state and various churches, operated for 150 years and involved ripping over 150,000 Indigenous children away from their communities and families and placing them in institutions where they faced overcrowding, abuse, and deprivation (NCTR n.d.). Indigenous children were not allowed to speak their language or practise cultural activities since these schools' explicit mandate was to compel assimilation to settler-colonial culture and society. While genocide is often thought of as mass violence directed at an identifiable group of people to destroy their physical existence as a group, tactics like language deprivation are fundamental and powerful aspects of it as well.

Polish lawyer Raphäel Lemkin coined the word "genocide" in 1944 as a response both to the Nazis' system of mass murder aimed at the extermination of specific groups of people and to other instances of mass violence aimed at the killing of whole groups of people. The term is made up of the Greek prefix *genos*, meaning race or tribe, and the Latin suffix *cide*, meaning killing. In 1948, the United Nations General Assembly issued the Convention on the Prevention and Punishment of the Crime of Genocide. Critically, the definition of genocide involves not only the killing of members of an identifiable group but also activities such as "deliberately inflicting on the group conditions of life calculated to bring about its physical destruction in whole or in part," "imposing measures intended to prevent births within the group," and "forcibly transferring children of the group to another group" ("United Nations Office on Genocide Prevention and the Responsibility to Protect" n.d.).

The Canadian state is guilty of all of these acts in relation to Indigenous Peoples, and the Indian residential school system is but one instance of the genocidal settler-colonial logic (Daschuk 2013). It's in this light that we need to understand language loss and the power dynamics it signals. Maliseet scholar Andrea Bear Nicholas (2011) shows that the policy and practice of linguicide, the destruction of languages, continues unabated in Canada today with respect to Indigenous Peoples. While most Canadians assume forced assimilation of Indigenous people ended with the closing of the last residential school, Bear Nicholas shows us how "submersion education" of Indigenous students in the settler-colonial public school system perpetuates it. Bear Nicholas describes this approach as submerging "Indigenous children in both an alien language and an alien culture" and then leaving "them to sink or swim." With dropout rates over 50 percent, Indigenous students are either pushed out of public education by a hostile, though not openly violent, settler-colonial pedagogy or forced to assimilate in order to find success on the system's terms (Bear Nicholas 2011). By compelling instruction in dominant, settler-colonial languages, Canada's public education system is essentially participating in the destruction of Indigenous Nations through linguicide and assimilation, to say nothing of the deleterious effects of these toxic relations on Indigenous youth.

State officials have clearly long understood the link between "solving" the "Indian problem" and eradicating Indigenous Peoples as distinct, identifiable groups. Whether Indian residential schools, the adopting-out of Indigenous children to non-Indigenous families as part of the infamous Sixties Scoop, extinguishing Indigenous identity through the gendered and bureaucratic violence of the Indian Act, the denial of basic infrastructure to Indigenous reserves, or the fact that Indigenous people are massively overrepresented in the Canadian prison population, the cumulative effect of Canada's orientation to Indigenous Peoples has been genocidal in nature. In this sense, the eradication of language is a key index of the existence of oppressive power relations. It's also why language reclamation is such an important aspect of an Indigenous politics of resurgence today (Alfred 2005; Coulthard 2014; Bear Nicholas 2011). It's vital to understand the dramatic reduction in the number of languages spoken by humanity not as a referendum on which languages are best since the only real metric for measuring languages is the extent to which they facilitate information exchange between those using them. Instead, the dominance and spread of some languages are linked indelibly to routes traced by imperialist and colonialist adventures as well as to the force of contemporary culture industries.

Communication dynamics bear the marks of power relations in a multitude of ways. Communication is, for example, powerfully gendered. "Mansplaining" refers to "the act of explaining something, usually by a man to a woman, in a manner that is patronizing or sexist under the presumption that the female audience is uninformed on the subject matter or topic at hand" (Know Your Meme n.d.). While this term is new, the phenomenon is not, something that author and activist Rebecca Solnit (2012) famously pointed out in her essay "Men Explain Things to Me." This of course is not to say that men somehow inherently or innately seek to diminish women in conversational interactions; rather, "the intersection between overconfidence and cluelessness" so generously afforded to men under patriarchy furnishes abundant conditions for this to happen.

Studies in professional settings in North America consistently confirm the presence of dynamics of power and privilege that shape communication in fairly predictable ways. Men talk more, take up more time and space, and interrupt each other and, especially, women with considerable frequency (Goodwin 2018; K. Snyder 2014). Women interrupt each other but rarely male co-workers, and when they do their behaviour is far more likely to be framed as abrasive, rude, or unintelligent than when similar behaviour is engaged in by a man (Goodwin 2018; K. Snyder 2014). In a study focusing on democratic deliberation, communication, and gender, the researchers observed: "Even if men and women enter deliberation with the same preferences and equal formal rights, the disproportionate exercise of these rights by men erodes the political and civic standing of women, a group not yet equal in society" (Karpowitz, Mendelberg, and Shaker 2012, 13).

Public speech is profoundly shaped by prevailing relations of power. Whether we are talking about language survival, public speech acts, mass media, or symbols, making meaning in society is always about power dynamics and the relations of ruling to which they are attached. Take the "free speech wars" on university campuses across North America. Conservatives and other right-wing commentators have frequently expressed vexation about the supposed war on free speech on university and college campuses. The basic narrative is that mobs of left-wing students all across North America have become so blinded by "political correctness" and "woke" culture that they are incapable of reasoned, civil engagement and debate with others whose ideas they may find challenging or even offensive (Uyehara 2018; Yglesias 2018; Sachs 2018). Amidst a rising tide of far-right political movements, right-wing pundits have made complaining about the alleged war on free speech a lucrative endeavour. They have assailed "social justice warriors," "triggered snowflakes," and "libs" for their supposed inability to grapple with difficult ideas and issues and deal respectfully with those who express a position different from their own.

What does the evidence tell us about the nature of this conflict? According to political scientist Jeffrey Sachs (2018), "Young people and university students are generally supportive of free speech … university enrollment is associated with an increase in tolerance for offensive speech, and … a small number of anecdotes have been permitted to set the terms of public debate." Drawing on a variety of national-level surveys about attitudes toward free speech in the United States, Sachs and other analysts have found what can only be described as a strikingly consistent and even growing support for free speech and free expression over time (Sachs 2018; Yglesias 2018). While youth are regularly singled out by right-wing commentators as radically intolerant of ideas and speech they find offensive, this characterization isn't supported by the data. In fact, survey data consistently shows that people with left-wing political commitments are more tolerant than those on the right and that educational attainment is associated with greater, not less, tolerance for challenging ideas and free speech (Yglesias 2018). Over all, analysts who examine data have found that the so-called "free speech wars" are largely a fiction of the right-wing pundit class, who have successfully weaponized and monetized this non-issue (Uyehara 2018). This phenomenon of right-wing pundits advancing the spurious notion that free speech is somehow under attack has led to them being labelled "free speech grifters" as the moral panics they fuel allow them to rack up massive social media followings, opportunities for publication and platforming, and monetary benefits (Uyehara 2018).

One area where there are clear and divergent consequences for exercising free speech on campus pertains to faculty. In his research, Jeffrey Sachs (2018) looked at "45 cases from 2015 to 2017 where a faculty member was fired, resigned, or demoted/denied promotion due to speech deemed by critics as political." Twenty-six of these cases occurred in 2017 and, as Sachs discovered, the clear majority (nineteen) of these cases involved a faculty member being censured over liberal, not conservative, speech characterized as being "anti-white" or "anti-Christian." Sachs emphasizes that these numbers probably significantly underestimate the scope of the problem. Nevertheless, the clear picture we get from this is that, as has been true historically, faculty espousing left-wing politics are far more likely to face censure, including loss of employment and being blocked from future hiring elsewhere, than their conservative and right-wing counterparts. The data gives a very different picture of the issues bearing on freedom of expression than the free speech grifters would have us believe.

BELIEVE!

We've spent a lot of time in this chapter looking at the way social meaning is made through a vast landscape of signs. This work of collective, social signification is the bedrock of our human capacity for communication. *Human communication* refers to the transfer of information from one person to another, with or without the use of language, spoken, signed, or written. As we've also explored, these signs and the work of meaning-making they facilitate are also looped into prevailing power relations. It's no exaggeration to say that acts of communication and representation are also acts of power. The examples we've used to explore these dynamics also demonstrate the way meaning-making is deeply embedded in historical context. While the relationship between signifiers and signifieds in any system of meaning-making is arbitrary, the social meaning signs become freighted with is not. Nor is this symbolic economy innocent of prevailing relations of ruling. There are a host of large-scale, widespread, powerful institutions and systems of belief that are also deeply implicated in systems of meaning-making that we need to include in any survey of how humans make sense of their social worlds. Language is one of these foundational forms of human communication that we've already briefly explored. Language is not simply a way of encoding and decoding our experiences in the world; it's also an index of power and a powerful tool in its own right for shaping social life.

Religion is another of these powerful systems of belief and it's certainly not limited to the "world religions" made up of billions of believers around the world. If we understand religion expansively as "a set of beliefs concerning the cause, nature, and purpose of the universe, especially when considered as the creation of a superhuman agency or agencies, usually involving devotional and ritual observances, and often containing a moral code governing the conduct of human affairs," it should be obvious how many different iterations of it could exist on a global scale (BBC n.d.). The majority (84 percent) of the world's population identifies with a religion, a group that tends to be younger and produces more children and so is actually growing, not shrinking (Sherwood 2018). This is interesting because it flies in the face of common-sense understandings of the modern world as becoming more secular, rational, individualistic, and technological.

It should also remind us that there is no necessary contradiction between religious belief and scientific thinking. What it really highlights is that both as individuals and societies we are capable of sustaining multiple, overlapping, and often contradictory beliefs. Indeed, looking at the structure of belief systems by themselves and in the abstract is a problem to begin with. As scholars of fascism have pointed out, examining beliefs that people espouse in the abstract is far less useful than examining how they manifest those beliefs through action (Paxton 2004). In this sense, it's much more important to look at the interaction between any given belief system and the material realities it validates than examining it in terms of doctrine or abstract principles.

What does the landscape of religious belief look like on a global scale? According to research by the Pew Research Center, while Christians remain the world's largest religious group, at 31.2 percent (2.3 billion people), that's followed closely by Muslims, at 24.1 percent (1.8 billion people), and Hindus at 15.1 percent (1.1 billion people) (Hackett and McClendon 2017). Only 16 percent of people on a global scale identify as "religiously unaffiliated," including atheists and agnostics (Pew Research Center 2017). In Canada, Christians are the single largest religious group, representing 67 percent of the population, followed by those with no religious affiliation, at 24 percent, and Muslims, at 3 percent (Statistics Canada 2013). These statistical snapshots give a sense of the outlines of religious affiliation, but they tell us very little about how these avowed affiliations affect people's lives at the level of daily reality. Certainly, they show us that religion continues to be a common and significant form of belief, but they don't say much about why and with what consequences.

Much like kinship, the more social researchers have explored the dynamics of religious belief and affiliation, the more it becomes clear that such systems of belief are only part of a much bigger, more complex, and highly interactive process of making meaning in the world. Religion can have a number of different social effects. Most basically, it offers an explanation for the way the world is and authorizes a particular vision of how it ought to be. It is a force for social control and cohesion, providing its adherents with a set of moral and cultural coordinates for navigating social life. It can provide comfort, solace, and emotional release, particularly in the face of difficult, challenging, or tragic circumstances. It can even be a tool for cultural revitalization and adaptation, particularly in the case of marginalized or oppressed groups.

Just like every other system of belief, religion can be both empowering and oppressive. The moral compass and sense of unity that religious affiliation can impart to a community of believers can also dehumanize and degrade non-believers or others who do not conform to its standards of belief and behaviour. Such systems of belief can even degrade, dehumanize, and oppress believers themselves if some members of the community are understood to be fundamentally subordinate to others. Religious belief systems can advance conceptions of the world that reject rational thought, critical inquiry, and empiricism, promoting authoritarianism and dogmatism. But none of this belongs exclusively to religious belief; the same could be said of any number of fundamentalist forms of belief in the realms of politics, economics, philosophy, and more.

The case of Bill 21 in the province of Quebec serves as an interesting example through which to explore the tensions and contradictions between different systems of belief. In June 2019, the ruling *Coalition Avenir Québec* (CAQ) passed Bill 21, known in English as "An Act Respecting the Laicity of the State." "Lacity" is an archaic English word so for clarity it's worth turning to the French title of the Bill. As Supriya Dwivedi (2019) explains, *laïcité* "is a specifically French tradition of secularism based on a strict separation of government and religion" that "implies and demands commitment to an inherited understanding of French identity above all things." Essentially, the law prohibits those in "positions of authority," such as public school teachers, police officers, government lawyers, and judges from wearing religious symbols at work. Because freedom of religion is a protected right under the Canadian Charter of Rights and Freedoms, Quebec's CAQ government invoked the "notwithstanding" clause, which provides legal grounds for governments to declare an exception to the Charter and restrict Canadians' fundamental rights. Framed publicly by its defenders as a law promoting the liberal democratic tradition of separation between religion and state as well as Quebec's traditional values, this bill was only the most recent effort in a series to pass such a "values" law in Quebec (Dwivedi 2019).

Critics were quick to point out that it wasn't just any and all religious traditions that were being singled out by the ban; it was specifically those belonging to immigrants, who had long been accused of diluting the "authentic" cultural values of Quebec as a distinct society. Speaking the familiar language of the defence of social values that has become so common on the political right, Bill 21 is conspicuous in banning certain kinds of religious symbols in certain contexts while studiously avoiding others. As one writer summarized, "Community organizations, civil rights groups and opposition politicians have pointed out that while the bill theoretically treats all religious symbols as equal, by far the largest pool of people affected are non-Christian women who wear scarves or veils, giving it a distinctly xenophobic and sexist edge" (Uprichard 2019). This has led some observers to label Bill 21 "selective secularism," since it explicitly excludes "the emblematic or toponymic elements of Québec's cultural heritage that testify to its history" (Dwivedi 2019). Symbols of Catholic faith, such as the 30 metre cross atop Mount Royal in Montreal, are interpreted under this rubric as cultural and historic rather than religious. As Dwivedi (2019) notes, "The practice of Christianity is in no way impeded by this bill, while that of other religions is: Bill 21 has the practical effect of targeting only minority faiths, such as Judaism, Sikhism, and Islam, in which adherents are required to wear certain garb or symbols. This isn't a question of simply removing religious symbols — it interferes in the actual practice of religion."

The passage of Bill 21 provoked protests and legal challenges from a variety of groups, including the Canadian Civil Liberties Association and the National Council of Canadian Muslims even as it remains very popular among residents of Quebec in general, according to a range of opinion polls (Shingler 2019). The most important thing about this conflict for our purposes is the way it casts into sharp relief the clash between different systems of belief. Superficially, one might say that this is a conflict between secularism and religious identity, but the selectiveness of the ban's application tells us much about it. While Catholic symbols of identity and worship are interpreted under the ban as "cultural," "traditional," and part of Quebec's "heritage," symbols like the hijab or turban are associated with conspicuous religiosity, foreignness, backwardness, and culture loss.

The recourse to traditional liberal values about the separation of religion and state, which many of us might agree with, doesn't let us escape charges of ethnocentrism and cultural chauvinism. Liberal democratic values are not somehow neutral or universal but clearly culturally rooted in their own way. To make matters worse, the effect of the ban has obviously been to force those people who wear what are identified through the law as "religious symbols" to choose between their employment and their beliefs (Shingler 2019). While a Catholic person in Quebec could easily work in a public position of authority while wearing a cross around their neck that could be concealed when necessary, a Muslim woman wearing a hijab as a cultural or religious expression could not successfully pass in this way. Furthermore, one set of values is presented as authentic tradition while others are depicted as invading forces that threaten the very fabric of Québécois culture and heritage. None of this is to suggest communities should not have open conversations about religion and public life or about the values we want to see at the heart of our societies. But we cannot use one set of cultural and religious values to trump another or assert that a dominant group gets to cast its own values and institutions as an unproblematic civilizational baseline while all others are aberrations. That's not merely contradiction; that's xenophobia masquerading under the banner of secularism and progress.

The example of Bill 21 aside, given the global reach of capitalism, we do not need to look very far to see formally secular beliefs that perpetuate dehumanizing, degrading, authoritarian, and dogmatic orientations to the world and those with whom we share it. As Naomi Klein explored in *No Logo* (2000), the most successful corporations no longer sell commodities, they sell lifestyles and identities packaged as brands. Brand loyalty and a prevailing obsession with brand identities no less constitute a structured system of belief than political or religious affiliation. In fact, branding may even be a more powerful and pervasive form of belief in many parts of the world today than religious or political affiliation given the way capitalism has enclosed and commodified people's lifeworlds. The alienation, atomization, and authoritarianism cultivated by capitalist relations is something that critical theorists have long recognized (Marcuse 1964).

As we've seen in preceding chapters, nationalism, too, is a system of belief that has proven itself more than capable of generating all manner of xenophobic, violent, colonialist, and imperialist forms of thought and action. Today we can even see forms of secular thought grouped under the label the "new atheism," which advance intolerant, authoritarian, and dogmatic beliefs in the name of science and rationality. These examples should remind us that there is no realm of human belief that is free from the potential for authoritarianism, oppression, and domination. While this may seem discouraging, I don't think it is. As we've explored through this chapter, it's not the signs or systems we use to make meaning in the world that are at issue; it's the context in which they are embedded and the power relations that animate them that make them tools of liberation or oppression. Whether we're discussing language, stories, symbols, or systems of belief, every act of representation is also an act of power.

CONCLUSION

The capacity for abstract, symbolic thought is one of the hallmarks of human cognition. It's central to our ability to make meaning in the world. Whether we're talking about political symbols, language, news, popular media, or foundational forms of belief and meaning-making, such as science, religion, and myth, humanity is truly a meaning-making species. One of the most interesting aspects of this work of meaning-making is that it relies on a vast symbolic economy to convey significance. We live in a sprawling world of signs – things that are used to represent something else. Every sign is made up of two parts, a signifier (the specific representational form) and a signified (the thing being represented), and not only do we successfully use them to encode and decode our experiences, we use them to share these experiences collectively. This amazing process allows us to represent and transmit things we're living through, things we can only imagine, our hopes and fears for what is to come, the meaning of what has come before, and so much more.

One of the things that is so interesting about the act of communication is that the signs we use to encode and transmit meaning are themselves embedded in a social and historical context. That means that they acquire baggage over time. While the relationship between signifier and signified is always arbitrary, signs of all kinds become freighted with meaning, and we can't just wish that meaning away. As we saw with the swastika, some symbols become associated with such heinousness that they simply can't be reclaimed. History and context matter. More than this, signs and the systems of belief and communication they make possible are always embedded and never free from the power relations that make up society. Communication is fundamentally an act of power.

If signs are sites of power and struggle, the same is true for the larger stories they are used to create. As we saw in in both Reilly's fake news intervention and the story of the Battle of Seattle, narratives of all kinds are aimed not merely at convincing people of something but at shaping social reality. In fighting over how an event like the Battle of Seattle is understood, we are fighting not only about how history is remembered but about how we understand our present and imagine the future. Activists, elites, police, and media-makers were not just battling over how an event was going to be remembered but how power is understood. If we understand that activists shut down the WTO meetings in Seattle in 1999 because the ruling class and its agents were too soft, failed to act appropriately, or were hamstrung by a liberal, overly permissive political sensibility, we come to very different conclusions about social change and social justice than if we understand the WTO shutdown as a product of a carefully organized manifestation of people's grassroots intelligence and power. What we must remember is that it's not just the story that gets told about any given event that's at issue; it's also the way those stories are told. As Neigh points out in his intervention about independent media, the meaning of stories is shaped by the dominant social institutions, relations, and conventions through which they are told. Who are our storytellers, what are their conventions, and what are the relations and conditions of work? We cannot understand the work of meaning-making, particularly in mass-mediated societies like ours, without answering these questions.

From signs like the swastika to language to systems of belief like religion and science, the terrain we've surveyed in this chapter is fundamentally one shaped by power. Whether we consider language survival, mansplaining, or the free speech wars on campuses across North America, acts of communication and the systems of belief to which they are attached are run through by prevailing power relations. This doesn't mean we have to be cynical or pessimistic about our collective capacity to make meaning in the world. It means that this work of meaning making is another route to building a more just, equitable, democratic, and peaceful society. It can, of course, also be a route leading in precisely the opposite way to more oppressive and exploitative social relations. No act of meaning-making is inherently oppressive or liberating; its significance can only be found in its social, political, and historical context. Absolutist arguments about the purity of one belief system over another fall apart when exposed to this kind of critical, contextual scrutiny. Rather than feeling nihilistic about all this, the contingency at work here should remind us of our responsibilities to each other and the society we want to inhabit.

KEY CONCEPTS

Global South: like Global North, less a geographical concept than one denoting countries that share a set of socio-political and economic characteristics. The Global South is made up of so-called "developing" or "emerging market" countries, many of which were formally colonized by Global North countries and especially Western European powers. This group includes countries such as Afghanistan, Argentina, Bangladesh, Brazil, Cameroon, Cuba, Egypt, Haiti, India, Iraq, Palestine, and South Africa.

human communication: the transfer of information from one person to another, with or without the use of language, spoken, signed, or written.

language: the system of arbitrary symbols that people use to encode their experiences of the world.

sign: something that represents something else and made up of two distinct parts: a signifier and a signified. The signifier is the form the sign takes in the world; the signified is the abstract concept to which the signifier points.

7

MAKING A LIVING
Economies and Ecologies

Think about the last meal you ate. Who prepared it? Where did the ingredients come from? Look at the tag on an item of your clothing. Where was it made? Who made it? What is it made of? Think about your home. Who built it? Who maintains it? What is it made of? How is it heated? Consider your form of local transportation. Who built it? Who maintains it? What fuel does it run on? Some of these questions may be easy to answer, but in all likelihood many of them aren't. This isn't because they are fundamentally unanswerable or that the answers aren't important. It's also not because we are bad or ignorant people that these answers seem mysterious. It's because in large-scale, complex, capitalist societies, the web of relations that bring social life into being is both vast and intentionally obscured in the service of those who have the most power and derive the most benefit from the current order.

In this chapter, we explore that diverse bundle of human activity that we often refer to as "economic activity" but which I prefer to simply call "making a living." More than this, we explore how that activity is wrapped up in the larger natural world. Rather than thinking about these things as separate, we need to understand them together. Like all other life on this planet, nothing about our existence as a species can be understood in isolation from other forms of life which live here. Even thinking about all the life around us as "nature" or the "environment" is a problem because it makes it seem as if these things are discrete entities or backdrops, something external to our experience and activity. As we will see, that's completely incorrect. When we talk about society and nature, what we're really talking about is that sprawling web of relations among different forms of life in specific contexts, or what we call ecologies. What we think of as our productive or economic activity is in no way separate from these ecologies, so we consider them together in this chapter.

The ways societies divide and assign work, allocate resources, and produce, distribute, and consume the goods and services created from them, all of which happens embedded in a much larger web of life, is what we might call "making a living." If we think of the incredibly diverse work of sustaining ourselves and each other as making a living, we end up with a very different perspective on this work than if we reduce it to economics as it's conventionally understood. Take, for example, the well-worn conservative mantra, "It's the economy, stupid." For years elites have repeated this phrase ad nauseum to any and every challenge raised to the status quo, reducing complex and pressing social justice issues to the incredibly narrow and shortsighted metric of economic growth. From this perspective, there is no issue that cannot be solved by increased economic prosperity. But prosperity for whom? Defined and measured in what ways? Generated with what consequences and at what costs? What, for example, is a livable planet worth? What's a good price for decolonization and learning to live with justice and dignity alongside Indigenous Peoples? At what price point is an anti-racist, non-misogynist society a good deal? How much is universal health care, public schooling, robust public infrastructure, and high quality, accessible child care worth? If we fall into the trap of reducing everything to the incredibly narrow metric of economic growth, nothing that isn't profit-making is worth anything. Our notions of value become dangerously skewed as we learn to valorize industries and activities that are antithetical not just to justice, democracy, and basic notions of dignity but to our very survival on this planet.

MAKING A LIVING

One of the biggest problems with reducing the sweeping, diverse work people do to "the economy" is that it takes this vast array of collective labour that is responsible for creating the social reality we inhabit and reduces it to an imaginary thing that seems to stand apart from us. The economy appears as something with its own momentum, needs, and intentions, and people must find ways to serve it. Not only is this a factual mistake, it is also in the interests of the ruling class to mystify the real interests being served by arrangements of work and the goods and services produced from them. A third significant problem posed by this way of thinking is that work comes to be figured as only those activities that are profit-generating for the owning class. Thus, forms of labour that are absolutely critical to social life, like the work of social reproduction (see Chapter 5), are devalued, disparaged, and degraded, while some activities that are frivolous or destructive are celebrated as the highest forms of economic activity. In our capitalist society, the work of taking care of the old, sick, and young is rarely even considered "real work" despite its exhausting, difficult, and essential nature, while financial speculation, weapons manufacturing, and corporate law are seen as high status, aspirational, and important forms of economic activity. This maladaptive fiction is impossible to sustain if we consider the totality of human labour involved in the daily work of creating and re-creating our societies.

Take the questions with which we started the chapter. Basic elements of social existence like food, clothing, transportation, and shelter are not just things out there in the world that magically manifest when we want or need them. They are the products of our collective ability to create things together. They are also the outcomes of a vast web of interdependence. Finally, they are tied into relations of extraction and exploitation that are historically deep and often rooted in legacies of colonialism that are foundational to modern, globalized capitalism (Wolf 2010).

The coffee and tea I prepare in the morning for me and my family are commodities that were produced by people I will never personally know but whose labour nonetheless directly shapes my life. The water and electricity I use to make these beverages come from publicly built (though increasingly privatized) infrastructure that is maintained by a small army of workers. The food that my kids pack into their lunchbags comes from farms, fields, and factories near and far, where people and animals work to produce them. Other workers deliver that food in complex distribution networks that span the world. The clothes that we pick out, the cars we drive, and the fuel we rely on to make our vehicles go and to heat our homes also emerge out of human labour, the life and activity of nonhuman species, and the processes of the natural world. My activity is not only implicated in the activity of other humans; it's also implicated in the activity of the nonhuman world too. Thinking of humans as somehow outside of nature is a modernist conceit, but as both climate change and the COVID-19 pandemic have shown, it is a dangerous fiction. Human activity produces even as it is produced by nature, and this fact makes the abstraction of "the market" or "the economy" as something that exists outside of or above human relations doubly absurd (Moore 2015). As environmental historian and political economist Jason Moore argues, "The economy' and 'the environment' are not independent of one another. Capitalism is not an economic system; it is not a social system; it is *a way of organizing nature*" (2015, 2).

Focusing on how people through time and across geographical distance have sought to make a living — to sustain themselves and others — encourages us to look past narrow capitalistic notions of wealth accumulation and to consider the labour we do with and for each other. It also reminds us that the terms, conditions, and outcomes of these diverse ways of making a living are never simply matters of free will or choice. We are not free agents able to pick and choose what we want to do to continue to live in systems not of our own making. We are not all equally to blame for the consequences of such systems, just as we do not all benefit equally from them. Once again, we come around to the fact that we are not dealing with discrete spheres of human activity but with relationships (between people, between people and nonhuman life, between society and nature) that are always relations of power. As Jason Moore tells us, "The stories of human organization are co-produced by *bundles* of human and extra-human nature. Humans build empires on their own as much as beavers build dams on their own. Both are 'ecosystem engineers.' Neither exists in a vacuum" (2015, 7). The focus on power raises questions about who works, who creates value, and who appropriates it. It's useful to think of an *economic system* as the basic processes of allocating resources, and producing, distributing, and consuming the goods and services that are created from them. Nothing about economic systems is "natural"; any given system is produced out of a matrix involving settlement patterns, ecosystems and their carrying capacities, work and the division of labour, social relations and structures of power, privilege, and inequality, and the construction of "needs" and "wants."

CAPITALISM AND THE PREDATORY LOGIC OF ACCUMULATION

All economic systems are really relations of power. As we've already explored in this book, power isn't a thing, it's a relationship (see Chapter 3). Creating items of value in the world is an exercise in power, as is living off someone else's labour. To use the vocabulary we learned in Chapter 3, bringing something of value into the world, whether individually or collectively, is an exercise in "power-to." *Exploitation*, the act of living off someone else's power-to, is an exercise in "power-over." While slavery, sex trafficking, and child labour stand out as particularly odious and extreme forms of exploitation, there is no economic act or system that isn't also an ethical and political one. That doesn't mean that some systems of relationships aren't better than others; all these ways of making a living are always about our common understanding of what is right, how the world works, and how we are supposed to relate to it. As feminist economic geographers writing under the pen name J.K. Gibson-Graham astutely observe,

> Decisions about how much time to put into food gathering or into cultural and community practice, how much of a wage increase to bargain for, how much is a "living wage," how much of one's harvest can be set aside for household needs, are all decisions about what should be seen as "necessary" to subsistence. (2006, 89)

These decisions are made in social and cultural contexts in which notions of what is right, necessary, and ethical are already in play.

Since these decisions about making a living are always already contextual and ethical, we may as well start there. There is no objective or neutral position from which we could claim to be making such decisions; to say otherwise is simply mystifying the status quo and the power relations that make it up. The dangerous abstraction that the economy is something out there, independent of us, an entity that needs to be served in particular ways, seems even more absurd in this light. What kind of system of making a living accords with the kind of society we want to live in? What are the values that underwrite its practices? To what ends should this activity be directed? What are its limits? These questions are far from the kinds of discussions about the economy and how people can make a living that dominate the media today. At a moment when we have created more wealth, possess greater technical ability, and have access to more knowledge and resources than at any other time in human history, genuine sustainability and security have rarely seemed further away. In order to understand why this is so, we need to take a look at capitalism.

Capitalism is an economic system and ideology based on the production of *commodities* for sale on the *market* in pursuit of *profit*. Critical to this system is the *alienation* of workers from the *means of production*, forcing them to sell their *labour* in exchange for a *wage* in order to survive. Today, capitalism is a globe-spanning system, but it germinated in Western Europe and superseded feudalism as the dominant economic system beginning in the fifteenth century (Federici 2003; Linebaugh and Rediker 2000; McNally 2002). Unlike feudalism, which was predicated on the ownership of land in exchange for service, capitalism rests on the exploitation of labour to generate profit.

You'll notice that in the definition of capitalism above some words are italicized. Capitalism is complicated, and it's important to take it apart systematically if we want to understand it and the effects it has in our world. Karl Marx (1818–1883), theorist, social critic, and revolutionary, made this a central part of his life's work. While Marx's work has been built on over the last century and a half, it remains unsurpassed in terms of understanding capitalism not simply as an ideology or an economic order but as a system of relations predicated on re-working and re-imagining the world in the endless pursuit of profit. In the first volume of his masterwork, *Capital*, Marx details the way capitalism as a system of relations remakes the world through the process of making it exploitable. From the structure of the standard work day to family relations to the mental acrobatics required to standardize work time and the wage, Marx shows how the world under capitalism is literally re-constructed to make profit-taking and systematic, large-scale exploitation possible.

People didn't just wake up one day with one group owning the tools necessary to produce all the things we need and another group able to use those tools to make things and willing to hand those things over to the owning class to sell them for their own benefit, while the working class takes a fraction of that value in the form of a wage. The process of making the working class and the owning classes took a long time and was often bitter and violent. It certainly had nothing to do with natural orders, progress, or inevitable outcomes. All societies have a *mode of production,* a combination of productive forces and social and technical relations of production that are put to work to create what is considered necessary and desirable. *Productive forces* refers to the raw materials, human labour, tools, and equipment, while *relations of production* are the ways people are organized and taught to relate to each other in any given mode of production. Capitalism is a specific mode of production, one that rests on the vast majority of people compelled to sell their labour power to a much smaller group of people who own the means of production.

To create a group of people who must work but do not own the means of production (tools, raw materials, and infrastructure), masses of people were forcibly dispossessed of land and autonomy so that they could be compelled to sell their labour for a wage. This process of divorcing people from the tools and resources they need to survive is known as *alienation*. We're used to talking about alienation most often as a psychological state, a feeling of being disconnected from others, disaffected by the status quo, and generally feeling like society has no place for us. Another way to understand alienation is as the experience of being torn away from the things that sustain us. This can be applied materially in terms of our day-to-day activity of making a living. Only once people could no longer survive independently of having to sell their ability to work to someone else was capitalism able to truly take root. This was a violent and protracted process everywhere it was carried out; elites tore up whole communities and their social lives to create the dependency and desperation necessary for capitalist exploitation. It also involved the historically unprecedented shift in understanding that assigned a standardized value to people's generic ability to work. That's what an hourly wage is: a monetary value assigned to a standardized unit of time. We all have our distinct talents, abilities, and limitations, but the wage relation doesn't care about any of this because it is essentially the act of one class of people renting the lives of another. It isn't our talents, our passions, common survival, tradition, or socially necessary work that drives capitalism. It is the unending, insatiable quest for the frenzied hoarding of wealth that lies at the root of this economic system.

THE MARKET AND VALUE

There have been many, many forms of economic exchange across the breadth of human experience on this planet. Despite the mantras regularly repeated by capitalism's high priests, there are many alternatives to the status quo. While some of those alternatives were crushed to facilitate capitalism's rise and dominance, others have persisted and are even a regular part of our lives. We will come to some of these soon. One of the reasons regularly offered in defence of capitalism is that markets are an efficient way to adjudicate between competing interests. Despite the increasingly glaring contradictions and destructive tendencies of capitalism, we are told that open exchange between producers and consumers through a free market is an elegant, efficient, and innovative path to a free and prosperous society and that history bears this out. But is this true?

To answer this question, it's useful to specify the lynchpin of this vision: the market. A *market* is simply a place where actors engage in impersonal exchanges mediated by money. As we will see, unlike other forms of exchange, no social ties or obligations are created. Note that there is nothing in this definition of markets that identifies their intelligence, efficiency, or magical ability to adjudicate the best outcome out of competing options. They are simply places where people come together to procure things they want or need from others who have them using some form of all-purpose money. Only under capitalism has the market been elevated to the status of mystical arbiter of all that is good and true.

Under capitalism, anything that can be bought and sold on the open market is a *commodity*. When something becomes a commodity, it no longer has worth because of its use value, the practical purpose it serves, but rather because of its exchange value, what it can be sold for. Under capitalism, most of us come to conflate the worth or value of something with the price we pay to own or access it. We are told that the price given to things is the outcome of free markets, where what something is worth is set by what people are willing to pay for it. This seems simple enough, and were it true it might even be elegant, but, as with most social phenomena we've examined in this book, the truth is more complicated and much more power-laden than this. As academic and activist Raj Patel writes,

> There is a discrepancy between the price of something and its value, one that economists cannot fix, because it's a problem inherent to the very idea of profit-driven prices. This gap is something about which we've got an uneasy and uncomfortable intuition. The uncertainty about prices is what makes the MasterCard ads amusing. You know how it goes – greens fees: $240; lessons: $50; golf club: $110; having fun: priceless. The deeper joke, though, is this: The price of something doesn't measure its value at all. This prickly intuition has become entertainment. An alien from another planet would find it strange that one of the most popular TV shows in dozens of countries is one that trades on the confusion around what something's worth: *The Price Is Right*. In the show, the audience is presented with various consumer durables, and asked to guess the retail price of each. Crucially, you don't win by correctly guessing how useful something is or how much it costs to make – prices are poor guides to use and true costs of production. You win by developing an intuitive sense of what corporations believe you are willing to pay. (2009, 10–11)

Patel's game-show example is a perfect illustration of the myths we internalize as we are socialized into the capitalist lifeworld. The point is not to develop a sense of value in the world that actually corresponds to the things necessary to a decent, sustainable, dignified, just, inclusive, and supportive common social life. The point is to develop an intuition that corresponds to the profit-motivated desires of capitalists to sell us things.

The flipside of prices in a capitalist economy is the *wage*, the money workers are paid for a specific amount of time spent expending their labour power for someone else. Think about it as your boss renting those hours of your life and the productive capacities involved therein. If prices are supposedly a measure of the preciousness, scarcity, and desirability of a given commodity, the wage can be thought of as a quantitative measure of the value assigned to different kinds of work. Just like prices, while wages may seem at first glance to reflect some kind of rational accounting of the value of certain types of work over others, a closer inspection of this dynamic reveals a very different truth. Why, for example, do finance bankers and corporate lawyers make more than paramedics, early childhood educators, and firefighters? Why do professional athletes and pop culture celebrities make orders of magnitude more in compensation for their work than plumbers, teachers, nurses, and garbage collectors? Obviously, the wage paid to these different workers cannot simply be equated with an objective measure of the value brought into the world by these different activities. Is teaching children less valuable than being able to shoot a puck or sink a jump shot? Is being a first responder to emergencies less valuable than buying and selling stocks to make your clients richer? Is collecting garbage, recycling, and compost produced by a dense, urban population and attending to a city's sanitation needs less valuable than negotiating corporate mergers? Clearly, wages are not simply a measure of important or socially useful labour.

We can learn much about markets and the capitalist faith in them as the highest form of human interaction through concrete examples. In January 2020, a novel coronavirus emerged and spread rapidly around the world with deadly consequences. The COVID-19 pandemic did what up to that point had seemed nearly unthinkable: it effectively reversed capitalist globalization as governments, with notable exceptions, scrambled to respond to this public health threat by imposing lockdowns, closing borders and businesses, and generally bringing life as usual to a halt. As reports of the pandemic and measures to combat it spread, one particular commodity suddenly became very scarce: toilet paper. Logistical and labour challenges did indeed threaten the availability of some products, but this was not the case with toilet paper. Neither was there any suggestion that those suffering from COVID-19 required access to greater amounts of toilet paper than normal. Nevertheless, in the first months of the pandemic, across the overdeveloped Global North, news reports circulated not only of chronic toilet paper shortages but of fist fights in grocery store aisles, anti-social hoarding, and predatory price-gouging by both corporations and individuals looking to turn a quick profit.

What was going on? If markets are so good at providing access to products, adjudicating between interests, and leading us to the best outcomes, why were people in the midst of a pandemic suddenly confronted with a lack of toilet paper? Conditioned to act as atomized individuals rather than members of a larger social collective, many people responded to the fear of what the pandemic might bring by hoarding a commodity that many associate with the bare minimum of a civilized existence. Ironically, this made the fear of it being scarce a reality. As Simon Springer (2020) explains, "We might be inclined to laugh at the implausibility of the whole scenario, but whether the situation is real or imagined is beside the point. The truth, which in this case may appear stranger than fiction, is that markets operate in the sweet spot between scarcity and fear." In the face of a global pandemic, many who could afford it took the route of hoarding supplies (toilet paper only being the most prominent) in pursuit of their own comfort and security and at the expense of others'. Of course, this behaviour was not only irrational and unnecessary but provoked other anti-social behaviour, like predatory price gouging on basic commodities and fist fights in grocery stores. So much for the myth of efficient markets and a path to a freer and more prosperous society.

The lessons we can learn from the interruption of capitalist business as usual by the COVID-19 pandemic are legion. For example, as emergency rooms and intensive care units filled up it quickly became clear that a decades-long policy of treating health care as a commodity (even in countries like Canada, where access is supposed to be universal) was that these systems were woefully unprepared for a large-scale public-health emergency. As Springer illustrates in his essay, the same logic that drove the run on toilet paper also animates many other aspects of our daily lives. Springer encourages us to look at housing, "where those who did not get in early must pay inflated prices, subject themselves to an ongoing extraction of their means in the form of rent, or find themselves homeless." This is the logic of predatory accumulation under capitalism. Individual wealth exists at the cost of mass deprivation. Whether or not you need or can use something has no bearing on whether you invest in it. We are bombarded with messaging encouraging us to see everything, including ourselves, as an opportunity for profiteering. The misery and deprivation of others in this context aren't conditions to rectify but opportunities for wealth accumulation. As Max Haiven explores in the next intervention, the extension of this profiteering logic into every nook and cranny of society is accelerating, with dramatic consequences for our lives, individually and collectively.

FINANCIALIZATION – *MAX HAIVEN*

FINANCIALIZATION IS THE PROCESS that transforms everything in society into an investment. Think of your own education. Likely you've been told that it is an "investment in your future," and it is likely that, as a student at a Canadian university, you've taken out a loan or borrowed money from your family in order to make this "investment." There are debates in major newspapers about whether this investment is worth it and what sort of degree program is the best investment to get a job after graduation (to repay those loans). But let's set aside these questions for a moment and think about "investing in education" in three related frames: discursively, in terms of political economy, and sociologically.

Examining something discursively means asking: why do we talk about things in a certain way? When did we begin to do so? And what can the way we talk about things tell us about our society? The idea that we are "investing" in important things, or of thinking about choices in terms of a "cost/benefit analysis," or of "leveraging" our skills and abilities to get some sort of payback is very new. It's a set of terms that have been imported from the world of business (and specifically the world of banking and high finance). This form of discourse is a symptom of neoliberalism: as corporations dominate our society, their ideas, language, and ways of understanding society also come to dominate our imaginations. In part, this occurs through how we use language to communicate. The popularity of the idea of investment is part of this process.

Why do we frame education as a private investment that is oriented towards the graduate having a better chance at competing (with other graduates) for a job? Even as recently as twenty years ago, it was much more common to talk about education as a public good, as the responsibility of a society towards its young people. It was also common, among the working classes, who had been denied access to universities, to talk about education as a means of personal and collective liberation.

If, today, education is spoke of as an individualized investment, what does that mean for how we, as a society, organize and provide education? For one, universities become less and less like public institutions and more and more like corporations offering a service for hire. Students and professors are encouraged to imagine what they are doing as the transfer of knowledge and skills, rather than the cultivation of broad, worldly knowledge and critical ideas. University education becomes oriented towards getting the credential (the degree) rather than transformative education.

Political economy is the term we use when we want to think about the way the capitalist economy we live under is shaped by power, and in turn helps shape

183

power. In terms of political economy, financialization means the vastly increased power of one particular part (or sector) of the capitalist system, the so-called "FIRE" sector, which stands for high finance (like investment banks on Wall Street and Canada's Bay Street), insurance and real estate. Over the past forty years, this sector's power over the economy and society has grown tremendously on at least three levels. First, the FIRE sector has a profound power over the corporations that produce or distribute most of the world's goods and services: when CEOs talk about "shareholders" demanding ever more ruthless corporate behaviour (like laying off workers or dumping toxins in the rainforest), they are pointing the finger at finance.

Second, the FIRE sector has huge disciplinary power over governments, which they use to demand neoliberal policies, which entrench and expand the FIRE sector's power. For instance, all Canadian governments (federal and provincial) are deeply in debt to international financial markets and go deeper into debt (i.e., run budget deficits) every year. The FIRE sector uses this influence to demand corporate tax cuts, deregulation of corporations, and more freedom for money to move around the world.

Third, the FIRE sector is transforming everyday life through the expansion of consumer debt or through speculative gambling on urban real estate, which drives up housing prices and rent. Today, the prices of most of the world's most basic materials and foodstuffs, like aluminum and rice, are the objects of intense financial speculation on futures markets: indeed, the rights to these things are often traded hundreds of times while they sit in warehouses. As ever, it is ultimately the world's poor, who have no influence over the FIRE sector, who pay the price as the value of the things they need fluctuates wildly and without warning.

This political-economic transformation is both facilitated by and at the same time helps to drive onward a profound sociological transformation in the way individuals and social institutions (like universities) approach and interact with the world. The financialization of society means that each of us feels responsible to master the future, to act as if we are each financiers "investing" in education and other areas of life. Reality television is full of shows that celebrate the savvy house hunter or antique collector who buys low and sells high. Self-help books advise us to treat romantic relationships or parenting as an "investment" of care. Public-health propaganda suggests we see our body as an "investment": eat right and exercise today for future payback. Even arts and culture are reframed as an "investment" in creativity and the imagination in the hopes that they will inspire market-oriented "innovation."

The ultimate problem is that financialization represents a method for recrafting society in the shadow of extremely powerful, undemocratic forces. It's not just

> that the evil CEOs of the FIRE sector have too much influence or that they're ruining the economy because all they care about is short term gains, not long-term growth. That's true enough, but the problem is also that, to the extent the FIRE sector's power grows, its ideas and ideologies become the norm in almost every social institution and for many individuals. This ideology is hyper-individualistic, consumerist, competitive, and reduces the complexity of the world to a brutal economic calculus. This is why it's important to resist the idea that university education is an "investment" and that you are an "investor."

The way we see ourselves and our activity in the context of society is never neutral, natural, or free of powerful interests. As Haiven makes clear, the extension of the logic of financialization into every facet of social life is neither an objective description of human nature nor some inevitable stage of development. What's so interesting about capitalist logic is that it is imposed on top of a whole array of non-capitalist ways of working in common that are critical to it and collective social life. Despite what capitalism wants us to imagine, none of us are rugged individual free agents evolutionarily primed to maximize self-interest. As we've seen throughout this book, our evolutionary journey as a species is defined by cooperative, collective life. Human survival on any other terms is simply not possible. Capitalism replaces none of this. It exists parasitically on top of it, living off our collective, shared capacities like a vampire.

CAPITALIST EXPLOITATION AND APPROPRIATION

As we explored in Chapter 5, the work of social reproduction is at the centre of our social life together, including our economic activity. Social reproduction refers to all the work of care (physical, emotional, social) that goes into producing and reproducing *labour power*, our ability to exert power to create individually and collectively in the world. It's the work of birthing babies, raising children, caring for the sick and infirm, making food, cleaning, emotionally sustaining ourselves and each other, and so much more. This work is the bedrock of all social life and it's absolutely central to capitalism. As a consequence of its central importance, it is intentionally sequestered and super-exploited, to say nothing of the way it's also powerfully shaped by oppressive relations like sexism and racism. For us to be able to get out of bed each day and head back out into the waged work world requires an incredible and diverse array of work. If you've ever been primarily responsible for the care of the very young, old, or sick, you know this intimately. Without this sustaining work, it wouldn't be possible for us to enter the market to sell ourselves and our labour. This is precisely why this work is intentionally degraded and devalued in public discourse: so that it can remain a vital pillar of profit-taking under capitalism. Imagine, for a moment, if so-called housework was paid even minimal wages. If you find yourself balking at remunerating this work, ask yourself why. Why pay for children to go to daycare but not for the same work when it takes place in the home? The simple answer is, of course, that if we were to redistribute wealth in a way that acknowledged the essential work of social reproduction, it would dramatically cut into the profits reaped by the owning class.

If *profit* basically comes from the gap between what a commodity costs to produce and what the owner (note, not the maker) of the commodity can sell it for, where does this gap come from? While entrepreneurial creativity and technological innovation can account for some of this gap between cost and price, the reality is that this gap is the smoking-gun evidence of exploitation. Squeezing what owners pay workers is one obvious source of this gap, which becomes profit for those same owners. But beyond this, capitalists profit by conscripting unpaid labour in a whole variety of ways from social reproduction at home to slave labour in precious mineral mines. Whole populations are kept intentionally outside waged labour markets not because they simply haven't been included yet but because their position there advantages the owning class. Housework isn't paid not because it isn't really work but because it is essential to making all other work possible. Child labour, sweatshops, and slave labour all persist not because of a failure of development, the human capacity for greed and cruelty, or misfortune but because they are all critical sources of wealth appropriation for capital. As Michael Truscello explores in his intervention, capitalist relations extract wealth from what is common and shared, like our labour and the natural world, only to enclose and privatize it as profit, while returning all the negative consequences of this toxic relationship back to us.

EXTRACTIVISM – *MICHAEL TRUSCELLO*

FOR LEWIS MUMFORD (1964), the famous sociologist and philosopher of technology, mining

> originally set the pattern for later modes of mechanization by its callous disregard for human factors, by its indifference to the pollution and destruction of the neighboring environment, by its concentration upon the physico-chemical processes for obtaining the desired metal or fuel, and above all by its topographic and mental isolation from the organic world of the farmer and the craftsman, and the spiritual world of the Church, the University, and the City.

The destructive capacity of mining "closely resembles warfare," and its organization of labour and environmental devastation would migrate to the manufacturing industries of capitalism (Mumford 1964). Extractive industries that remove oil and gas, minerals, metals, and other materials from the earth presaged the ecocidal relationship with the land embedded in all capitalist enterprises and colonial conquests. When Christopher Columbus reached what is now the Dominican Republic and Haiti, he wrote, "There must be an infinite number of things that would be profitable" in such lands (Bury and Bebbington 2013, 28). In the centuries that followed the arrival of European settlers, "a global system of extraction, exchange, and production" was organized for the benefit of colonial powers (Bury and Bebbington 2013, 36).

The ecological devastation of the neoliberal era of capitalism — the post-1950 destruction so pervasive scientists have described it as The Great Acceleration, "the most rapid transformation of the human relationship with the natural world in the history of humankind" (Steffen et al. 2015, 82) — accompanied an extraction of resources for human use that tripled between 1970 and 2010 (Kirby 2016). Saskia Sassen (2014) describes the neoliberal mesh of extractive industries and high finance that produced the current global order of destruction as "a world where complexity too often tends to produce elementary brutalities." While scientists continue to debate the onset of the Anthropocene, some date its beginning to 1950 and the postwar Great Acceleration, which included the radioactive fallout from testing nuclear bombs, as well as the transformation of the planet from the distribution of "plastic pollution, aluminium and concrete particles, and high levels of nitrogen and phosphate in soils, derived from artificial fertilisers" (Carrington 2016). The rapidity with which these signals of a new geological era have embedded, sometimes irreversibly, in the earth is unprecedented. In the past twenty years alone, for example, global construction has consumed more than half of the concrete ever produced (Vaughan 2016). The more than 50 billion tonnes of concrete that has been produced is enough to pour a kilogram of concrete on every square metre of the planet (Wong 2016). So much concrete is being produced today that there is actually a global shortage of sand (*Economist* 2017; Beiser 2015; Owen 2017). Extractive industries now comprise a "vast assemblage of humans, animals, plants, highways, railroads, power lines, energy infrastructure, communications networks, exploration equipment, mineral processing facilities, refineries, pipelines, storage facilities, and ports" to "support activities that locate, extract, process, and transport extracted materials across the region and into the global system of production and consumption" (Bury and Bebbington 2013, 54).

To avoid catastrophic global climate change, we must leave 80 percent of the remaining oil, gas, and coal in the ground, according to climate scientists

(McGlade and Ekins 2015). This would require capitalists leaving trillions of dollars in future profits on the table, which they are very unlikely to do. Global capitalism already proposes a commitment to industrial infrastructure over the next twenty years that *The Economist* (2008) calls "the biggest investment boom in history," with much of it concentrated in the BRIC countries, and almost half of that spending occurring in China, whose Belt and Road Initiative is the largest infrastructure scheme in history. Only a radical commitment to preventing new extractive enterprises from emerging, and shutting down most of the existing projects, will afford humanity a chance of existing beyond the next century. This commitment to the "brisantic" politics of shattering extractive assemblages must be accompanied by alternative, anti-capitalist social formations (Truscello 2020). To that end, social movements such as Idle No More and Indigenous communities such as the Kichwa people in Ecuador, the Embera people of Colombia, the Lumad of the Southern Philippines, and other Indigenous forms of resistance across the planet represent the front lines in the struggles against a centuries-old monstrosity that will not willingly change its "callous disregard" for life on earth.

Capitalist profiteering also relies, ironically, on the socialization of its costs. The myth of the free market as the best arbiter of social as well as economic good promotes a vision of a society based around economic transactions and maximizing self-interest, all carried out by industrious individuals. As British Prime Minister and arch-neo-conservative Margaret Thatcher famously intoned in an interview in 1987, "There's no such thing as society. There are individual men and women and there are families. And no government can do anything except through people, and people must look after themselves first" (*Guardian* 2013). But this ideology doesn't measure up to reality. The bare facts of our existence as a species (see Chapter 1) disprove the idea that there is nothing to human existence beyond the individual and the nuclear family. In fact, nothing could be further from the truth.

While capitalism as an ideology and set of material relations makes it seem like we are all profit-maximizing free agents, like all economic systems, all ways of making a living, capitalism is a way of organizing society and nature. As environmental historian and political economist Jason Moore demonstrates in his powerful book *Capitalism in the Web of Life* (2015), capitalism isn't some system imposed on nature or society. It is a way of organizing nature, including our human nature. For profitability to be maintained for those with access to capital and power, this way of organizing depends on appropriating – taking, but not paying for – what Moore calls "Cheap Natures": food, energy, raw materials, and labour power.

Think, for example, of the way damming a river produces hydroelectric power, the way foisting child care and housework on women subsidizes the process of raising new workers, or the way colonies fed raw materials like lumber or precious metals directly to colonial centres of power. Intentionally lax or nonexistent environmental regulation allows corporations to use the atmosphere and oceans as dumping grounds for all manner of toxic products. Slave labour mines yield precious metals like coltan, without which smartphones, laptops, and an array of wireless devices could not exist. Vast animal populations are imprisoned and brutalized in order to feed the factory farming industry, which, in turn, produces the mountains of food necessary to sustaining the army of industrial, urbanized waged workers. A river flowing in course, animals living their lives, and minerals being created by geological forces and processes don't fit what most of us have been conditioned to see as "work," but it is vital to understand just how critical these sources of unpaid work and energy are to capitalist accumulation. Without them and capitalism's constant search for new frontiers of appropriation of unpaid work/energy, there is no profitability and this form of organization falls apart. This is, in part, why seeking capitalist solutions to the climate crisis is a fool's errand. There is no way for accumulation and profitability under capitalism to be sustained without relying on the appropriation of the "Four Cheaps," as Moore refers to them. To put these contributions in economic terms, unpaid human work, overwhelmingly delivered by women, has been calculated to equal 70–80 percent of world gross domestic product (GDP), while the work/energy provided by nature equals 70–250 percent of world GDP (Moore 2015, 64). By this measure, the value produced by unpaid work vastly outstrips that produced by conventional economic activity. This is staggering, but it is almost entirely invisible in most of our day-to-day conversations about economic, social, and environmental issues.

Many people can see the problematic effects of capitalism that manifest in workplaces and society more generally, even if they believe capitalism is the best economic system we've got. The problematic outcomes produced by capitalism that it disavows responsibility for are commonly known as "externalities." An example of such an externality is structural unemployment. Capitalism relies on a reserve army of the unemployed to keep workers in line and depress wages. Full employment is never achieved under any capitalist economic order. But under- and un-employment have all kinds of consequences. People cannot live without food, water, and shelter, whether or not they can find waged work that will allow them to access these things in a capitalist society. But without access to waged work in a capitalist society, you are immediately rendered vulnerable to all kinds of life-threatening hardships. Corporations and other capitalist agents wash their hands of this entirely; they externalize them, leaving them for others to deal with. But the homelessness, addictions, social violence, abuse, and ill health that flow from capitalist relations are real and must be dealt with somehow. Someone bears these costs; they do not simply disappear because capitalists don't take responsibility for them.

This is important, but what is much harder and more important to see is the way that capitalism relies on the taking of unpaid work/energy in ways that vastly outstrip these more obvious effects. If externalities like unemployment and environmental pollution have all kinds of negative effects, what about systemic misogyny facilitating the appropriation of women's unpaid socially reproductive labour, the racism that makes slave mining possible, and the degradation of whole other species so the horrors of factory farming can be rationalized? Under capitalism the exploitation of waged labour rests on the appropriation of unpaid work/energy. In order to appropriate this unpaid work/energy, whether carried out by humans or not, this work/energy has to be devalued (Moore 2015). As Moore notes, "The history of capitalism flows through islands of commodity production, developing within oceans of unpaid work/energy" (2015, 54). The world as we know it has been made through capitalism. Our understanding of ourselves, our world, and those with whom we share it is all wrapped up in this specific way of organizing nature and society. We cannot address the spiraling crises of capitalism, whether economic, social, or ecological, within the parameters of this organizational logic. In addition to developing new ways of organizing ourselves and the natural world, we also have to learn new ways of valuing the world and those with whom we share it.

LEARNING ABOUT VALUE THROUGH THE LENS OF A PANDEMIC

The COVID-19 pandemic provides a useful lens through which to examine questions of value, socially necessary activity, and the way human societies are implicated in larger webs of life. According to a tracking project run out of Johns Hopkins University, by December 2021 the novel coronavirus had infected more than 272 million people globally and killed more than five million. Spreading easily, the virus led authorities around the world, though not everywhere, to implement lockdown measures that restricted people to their homes and shuttered businesses and public institutions in a desperate attempt to contain the spread of the disease. The globalized lockdown conditions were without precedent as many countries, confronted with the reality of mass infection and overwhelmed medical systems, effectively resorted to the last line of defence by telling people to stay home. In effect, the COVID-19 pandemic brought everyday life to a grinding halt and did so for weeks and even months before lockdown measures were lifted.

As scientists raced to understand the virus and worked to develop effective treatments and a vaccine, the pandemic also went to work on human societies, suddenly making uncertain almost everything people had come to take for granted as inalien-able features of everyday life. Work, commuting, travel, schools, shopping, nightlife, gyms, concerts, cultural events, and so much more were all suspended. Many of us believed that our wealth, technological prowess, and technical knowledge gave us great power and control over the world, and the pandemic offered a harsh reminder that we remain very much embedded in a larger web of life. The lockdowns and oth-er suspensions of what passed for normal activities were like pushing pause on the perpetual motion machine of the status quo, opening up a valuable opportunity for reflection on many aspects of what previously had seemed inevitable and unalterable.

Much of the public discussion around COVID-19 presented it, intentionally or not, as something that was impacting us from the outside, something that was being done to us. This is wrong, but it's also an important reflection of the way we have been taught to think and act in the world. Like humans or any living species, viruses are a part of our global ecology. While viruses can have devastating effects on the lifeforms they inhabit and use to propagate themselves, that, too, is not so different from the impact humanity is having on the world and the life with which we share it. This is not to advance an argument about how "humans are the virus." It is, however, worth recognizing that the conditions that made this pandemic possible, and which will undoubtedly give birth to future ones, are of our own making. Researchers have pointed to the fact that a decline in biodiversity due primarily to habitat loss provides fertile ground for the emergence of new diseases like COVID-19. What is the pri-mary source of declining biodiversity and habitat loss? Human activity, particularly extractive industries, capitalist industrialization and agriculture, and urbanization. As David Quammen argues in a *New York Times* opinion piece in a passage worth quoting at length, the circumstances that gave rise to the COVID-19 pandemic are all right in front of us:

> Current circumstances include a perilous trade in wildlife for food, with supply chains stretching through Asia, Africa and to a lesser extent, the United States and elsewhere. That trade has now been outlawed in China, on a temporary basis; but it was outlawed also during SARS, then allowed to resume — with bats, civets, porcupines, turtles, bamboo rats, many kinds of birds and other animals piled together in markets such as the one in Wuhan.
>
> Current circumstances also include 7.6 billion hungry humans: some of them impoverished and desperate for protein; some affluent and wasteful and empowered to travel every which way by airplane. These factors are unprecedented on planet Earth: We know from the fossil record, by absence of evidence, that no large-bodied animal has ever been nearly so abundant as humans are now, let alone so effective at arrogating resources. And one

consequence of that abundance, that power, and the consequent ecological disturbances is increasing viral exchanges — first from animal to human, then from human to human, sometimes on a pandemic scale.

We invade tropical forests and other wild landscapes, which harbor so many species of animals and plants — and within those creatures, so many unknown viruses. We cut the trees; we kill the animals or cage them and send them to markets. We disrupt ecosystems, and we shake viruses loose from their natural hosts. When that happens, they need a new host. Often, we are it.

The list of such viruses emerging into humans sounds like a grim drumbeat: Machupo, Bolivia, 1961; Marburg, Germany, 1967; Ebola, Zaire and Sudan, 1976; H.I.V., recognized in New York and California, 1981; a form of Hanta (now known as Sin Nombre), southwestern United States, 1993; Hendra, Australia, 1994; bird flu, Hong Kong, 1997; Nipah, Malaysia, 1998; West Nile, New York, 1999; SARS, China, 2002–3; MERS, Saudi Arabia, 2012; Ebola again, West Africa, 2014. And that's just a selection. Now we have nCoV-2019, the latest thump on the drum.

Current circumstances also include bureaucrats who lie and conceal bad news, and elected officials who brag to the crowd about cutting forests to create jobs in the timber industry and agriculture or about cutting budgets for public health and research. The distance from Wuhan or the Amazon to Paris, Toronto or Washington is short for some viruses, measured in hours, given how well they can ride within airplane passengers. And if you think funding pandemic preparedness is expensive, wait until you see the final cost of nCoV-2019. (Quammen 2020)

This powerful passage hammers home the fundamental realization that as the pre-eminent "ecosystem engineers" on this planet, humans have created the conditions for our own imperilment. This is why we cannot separate what we call economic activity from environmental issues or questions about how we live. We are one living species among many more embedded in a massive web of life on this planet. But humanity's capacity to impact the global ecology positions us at a dramatically different level than other ecosystem engineers, like ants or beavers.

None of this should be taken to mean that disaster is inevitable. The conditions that give rise to pandemics and that are, crucially, also implicated in bringing on the climate emergency are tied to the same institutions and relations that rob people of dignity and autonomy and make life precarious. In his powerful article about the devastating impact of COVID-19 in the United States, Ed Yong (2020) traces the pathways carved by prevailing relations of oppression and exploitation that facilitated the novel coronavirus's transmission and amplified its deadly impacts. Summarizing only some of his important insights, Yong argues that the pandemic "defeated" America as a result of a confluence of structural factors, none of which are conspiratorial or biological in nature:

> A sluggish response by a government denuded of expertise allowed the coronavirus to gain a foothold. Chronic underfunding of public health neutered the nation's ability to prevent the pathogen's spread. A bloated, inefficient health-care system left hospitals ill-prepared for the ensuing wave of sickness. Racist policies that have endured since the days of colonization and slavery left Indigenous and Black Americans especially vulnerable to COV-ID-19. The decades-long process of shredding the nation's social safety net forced millions of essential workers in low-paying jobs to risk their life for their livelihood. The same social-media platforms that sowed partisanship and misinformation during the 2014 Ebola outbreak in Africa and the 2016 U.S. election became vectors for conspiracy theories during the 2020 pandemic.

These are not mysterious, external forces that shape our lives and societies. Prevailing relations of ruling, the interests of the ruling class, and capitalism's insatiable appetite for profit are all critical aspects of this predicament.

These same power relations extend well beyond the pandemic. For example, between 1970 and 2000, the number of privately owned jets multiplied by a factor of ten, with each of these private jets emitting six times more carbon per passenger than normal commercial airliners (Pizzigati 2018). In Canada, the top-earning 1 percent of households generate three times more greenhouse gas emissions than average households, while on a global scale the richest 1 percent have a carbon footprint 175 times deeper than the poorest 10 percent (Pizzigati 2018). The richest 1 percent of Americans, Singaporeans, and Saudis on average emit over 200 tons of carbon dioxide per person per year, "2,000 times more than the poorest in Honduras, Rwanda, or Malawi" (Pizzigati 2018). These figures provide a snapshot of the kind of incredible injustice levied by those with the most hoarded wealth against the rest of us. It also paints a stark picture of the relationship between unrestrained, ever-expanding consumption and the costs to the rest of the lifeworld.

The capitalist response to this kind of challenge often rehashes some version of the achingly familiar cliché of the "free" (that is, capitalist, privately owned, for-profit) market as a "tide that lifts all boats." But does it? COVID-19 provides a rich context in which to test this assertion. Many people experienced the initial wave of the epidemic and the lockdowns it necessitated as a profound economic shock. Many lost their jobs or experienced deep cuts to hours, security, and earnings. But, just like the Great Recession of 2008, pandemic economic pain was not felt equally. In fact, COVID-19 was great for the super rich. In Canada, the top twenty billionaires managed to hoard an average of an extra $2 billion each in wealth even as the bottom fell out of the economy for many workers (Hemingway and Rozworski 2020). Even as front-line service workers were forced back to work without adequate protection and declared "essential services" in order to keep shelves stocked, the idle rich continued to rake in massive profits. Despite the stock marketing tanking in early 2020, comparing the wealth of these billionaires in 2019 and 2020 reveals that they collectively pocketed more than $28 billion in wealth gains in a year that saw many lose jobs, homes, and basic security (Hemingway and Rozworski 2020). This happened at a time when 1.1 million lost their jobs in Canada, while another 713,000 found their hours dramatically cut, with the worst impacts being felt by women, racialized people, and the working poor (Hemingway and Rozworski 2020). Today, the richest 1 percent of Canadians control 26 percent of all wealth in the country, while the richest families hold 4448 times the wealth of the average ones (Hemingway and Rozworski 2020). If a few boats are clearly being lifted by this tide, most are being swamped by it.

A study by the RAND Corporation, a think tank closely linked to US military and industrial interests, examined wealth distribution in the United States over the last half century, painting a picture massively tilted toward the very richest. A full-time worker in the US making the median taxable income, with half the population making less and half making more, currently earns approximately $50,000 per year (Wartzman 2020). Had the fruits of economic productivity continued to be distributed under the terms that held between the end of World War II and the 1970s, that same worker today would have been making somewhere between $92,000 and $102,000 USD. Analysts at RAND discovered that this maldistribution of wealth held for the bottom 90 percent of wage earners over the last half century, concluding that "the bottom 90% of American workers would be bringing home an additional $2.5 trillion in total annual income if economic gains were as equitably divided as they'd been in the past." If the same dynamics of wealth distribution held for the richest 1 percent, analysts concluded that their average yearly income would fall from $1.2 million to $549,000 USD. This situation translates to an annual theft of $2.5 trillion USD from 90 percent of workers to the very richest. This picture should surprise no one. Decades of successful class war waged by capitalists against all those who sell their labour to survive has yielded entirely predictable and appalling results.

AGAINST AND BEYOND THE CAPITALOCENE

The term *Anthropocene* has recently gained considerable traction among those studying the climate crisis and humanity's relationship with the world we share. Coined in 2000 by Paul Crutzen and Eugene Stoermer, the Anthropocene names an unprecedented geological epoch where humanity – the *anthropos* – has become the primary force shaping the Earth's geology and ecosystems (Moore 2016, 3). The term remains informal in scientific circles but has become common in popular usage as human-driven climate chaos accelerates. The power and popularity of the concept lies in its unabashed identification of human activity as a central, driving factor in shaping our global ecology and, perhaps, ultimately rendering it unlivable for the very species at the forefront of transforming it. As others have pointed out, however, the concept is limited and even dangerous, suggesting that humanity as some kind of undifferentiated whole has been responsible for the current predicament. As we've seen repeatedly, we are not equal beneficiaries of the prevailing order and its relations of ruling, nor are we equally responsible for it.

Other terms for our crisis-ridden age have been proposed, but perhaps none is more apt than the *Capitalocene* – "the Age of Capital." As Jason Moore explains, "The Capitalocene signifies capitalism as a way of organizing nature – as a multispecies, situated, capitalist world-ecology" (2016, 6). Mass industrialized civilization deserves to be indicted here since the climate crisis we currently face is most certainly a product of that paradigm too. Yet it is impossible to understand our collective predicament or the powerful interests committed to sustaining the world ecology responsible for producing and reproducing it without centring capitalism. As we've already seen from the examples explored in this chapter, capitalism is not just a profit-generating system; it's a way of relating to the world and each other that elevates profit above all else. In this pursuit, exploitation of all work (human and nonhuman) and the alienation of each of us from those relations and ways of living that sustain us are at the very heart of what passes for normal life. This means in order to effectively address the spiraling crises that plague us and pose alternatives to the increasingly broken status quo, we must first confront and then find ways of moving beyond the capitalist paradigm.

One of the most powerful tools the ruling class deploys against the ruled is to entrench the notion that there is no alternative to the way things are. After all, if you are convinced that nothing is possible other than what is in front of you, no matter how miserable that might be, why would you risk struggling for something else? If, as Margaret Thatcher once infamously intoned, "There is no alternative" to the status quo, it would be the height of irrationality to struggle against it and try to build alternatives. The enclosure, conscription, and colonization of our collective ability to imagine life as it might be otherwise is one of the most important functions of dominant institutions. After all, it is far more effective to convince those being oppressed and exploited that their condition is inevitable and their resistance futile than to confront and attempt to defeat organized struggles for alternatives to the status quo. Capitalism and capitalists in general have proved quite adept at this.

As we've explored in this chapter, one of the ways capitalist relations are maintained is through the elaboration of potent myths that invert reality, presenting us with a distorted view of what is valuable and how and by whom such value is created. Whether we are talking about who works and creates wealth, how that wealth ought to be distributed, what is valuable, and what ends our economic activity ought to serve, capitalist myth-making presents us with a funhouse mirror vision of the world, warped and distorted to conform to the interests of the ruling class. You don't have to look far for examples of this kind of fantastical storytelling. Popular media is awash in aspirational spectacle about the lives of the absurdly rich and famous. If we're not consuming the flood of media that elevates police, lawyers, doctors, and judges to the status of heroes, we are inundated with stories that tell us we live in a land of endless opportunity, accessible to all if only we work hard enough, have a novel enough take on something, and are willing to pull up those bootstraps. We're bludgeoned by superhero story remakes that endlessly recapitulate the same underlying narrative of an exceptional class of people who are invested with the power and therefore the right to save us from terrors the rest of us puny humans are incapable of comprehending let alone confronting. We're fed a diet of human-interest stories that tug on our heartstrings and tell us that the world is a tough and heartless place and we need to hunker down and not look much farther than our front doors and our immediate circle of kin. The basic message is: obey your rulers, demonstrate loyalty to the established order, keep your head down, don't make trouble.

Writing from his prison cell, where he had been put by Mussolini's Fascist regime in the 1920s, Italian Marxist organizer and theorist Antonio Gramsci coined the term hegemony to refer to the process of cultural and ideological domination of the ruling class over the masses. Gramsci realized that in liberal democratic and capitalist societies, relations of ruling were rarely organized primarily through open coercion and violence. Instead, in such societies, ruling is organized through a web of dominant institutions such as schools, organized religions, the media, and other civic organizations. Essentially, those ruled over in such societies come to identify with the interests and values of those doing the ruling as a result of being saturated by the ideological conditioning perpetuated by these dominant institutions. Force is reserved for the maintenance of the dominant order only in exceptional or emergency situations when cultural myth-making and ideological conformity have failed. We learn to crave our own subjugation.

But there's a deeper truth here. The fact that such elaborate ideological mystification is required to prop up and justify the ruling class is also the admission that there are in fact alternatives to the status quo. Indeed, the seeds of many of those other ways of making a living are already all around us. In many cases, they are the foundation upon which relations of exploitation have been imposed. For example, our capacity to work together, to exercise our collective power-to, exists prior to and lies at the heart of capitalism. Our collective capacity to work is what is conscripted under capitalist relations. Capitalism in this sense doesn't create anything; our collective labour creates all wealth and brings value into the world. Capitalism takes what we've made, gives us a fraction of that value back as wages, and then compels us to buy our survival through the market. But the fact remains that we – all of us who work – are the source of all this wealth.

While we are socialized from birth to accept a social order ruled by the profit motive and market relations, we all know at a lived, personal level that the most precious moments of our lives and our most meaningful relationships are not mediated by the market. If you were to conduct every social interaction as an opportunity for profit maximization, you would probably find yourself isolated and alienated from others pretty quickly. Exploitative and oppressive relations of ruling are imposed on our human capacities; they don't constitute them. The work of social reproduction that we've come back to time and again in this book is a striking example of this. As a species, we care for each other. Care is primary, essential labour. The very long period of infant dependency on caregivers alone highlights the fact that our very existence as a species hinges on the caring work we do for one another. And while conservative narratives spin this reality to reinforce a toxic patriarchy, we are misled if we imagine the heteronormative nuclear family as the primary unit of human sociality. Our survival as a species could not possibly have hinged on the autonomous success of isolated kin groups but rather our collective capacity to care, communicate, problem solve, innovate, and, perhaps most importantly, cooperate. This is what constitutes the bedrock of our humanity. Exploitative relations like capitalism are imposed parasitically on it.

Oppressive and exploitative relations do tremendous damage and certainly shape social realities, but they live off our collective power-to. It isn't necessary to create alternatives to our increasingly violent, insecure, unlivable, crisis-ridden status quo out of thin air. Instead, the real struggle is to liberate our individual and collective power-to from the parasites that are currently stifling and feeding off it. In other words, our alternatives are, to some extent, already here with us.

Think about how we deal with others we care about. If we're a good friend or kin, we're there when our people need us. Whether it's helping out with moving house, giving someone a ride, making food for others, being emotionally supportive, showing up for others when it matters in good and bad times, or any one of an unending diversity of other possibilities, we participate in what we might call a social economy of care that isn't rigidly quantified or accounted for. When we show up for others out of care and concern, we know that they will also show up for us. This form of social interaction is called reciprocity. *Reciprocity* is an ancient and enduring form of human sociality that involves the exchange of goods and services (to use the dry and dusty language of commodities) between actors that aims to cultivate lasting social ties of responsibility and obligation. When we drive our friend to an appointment, we undoubtedly know that we can expect that friend to provide support when we need it too. Crucially, under terms of true reciprocity and the enduring social ties it helps cement, no one keeps score, much less a ledger of debts owed. If we do, we probably don't have many social ties to rely on because such narrow accounting is universally objectionable among people who see each other as kin or friends.

Think about last week. How many interactions can you remember, most of them entirely mundane and unremarkable, that you participated in that fall into this category? Probably quite a few. Any time we help each other out without expecting a reward or payment, we are engaging in solidaristic social activity that is already pushing beyond the narrow and dehumanizing bounds of capitalism and its profit motive. We are already demonstrating our capacity to ground our social and economic activity in something other than the narrow calculation of self-interest.

As social researchers have demonstrated, these non-capitalist interactions and exchanges constitute the vast majority of most people's day-to-day activity, even if we are intentionally encouraged by capitalist hegemony not to think of them this way (Gibson-Graham 2006). More formally, *redistributive networks* gather resources from the community, usually by specified agents, and redistribute them to community members. In large-scale societies like our own, one of the most familiar forms of such networks are taxes, but examples include food banks and other charities. Redistributive networks don't tend to have the same pro-social outcomes as reciprocity because of the role the intermediary agent plays in collecting and then redistributing resources, but they are nonetheless another example of a decidedly non-profit-motivated form of economic exchange that plays a crucial role in modern societies.

Unlike reciprocity, which tends to foreground the social relations that make life worth living, redistributive networks can also serve a variety of conflicting interests and, in highly unequal and stratified societies like our own, can serve as a central pillar for relations of ruling. Think, for example, of the use of money collected from individual taxpayers that subsidizes corporate profiteering or the allocation of public funding without meaningful public consultation to punitive and coercive institutions such as the police and the prison system, which are then deployed against the most oppressed and marginalized members of that very same public. Nevertheless, the very idea of obtaining resources from the collective to redistribute in service to some larger interest is a non-capitalist practice that takes place in even the most profit-obsessed and wealth unequal societies. In his intervention, Ajamu Nangwaya examines anti-capitalism as a political, social, and economic orientation by exploring its roots in the cooperative movement. Much like reciprocity and redistributive networks, cooperatives emerged as an attempt to meet collective human needs in a decidedly non-profit-obsessed way that also cultivated the terrain for non-coercive, non-exploitative forms of human life in common.

ANTI-CAPITALISM AS A LONGSTANDING TRADITION OF RESISTANCE — *AJAMU NANGWAYA*

ANTI-CAPITALISM DRAWS ON many ideological traditions that critique capitalism and offer prescriptive programs or solutions to this system of exploitation. Anarchism and state socialism (Marxism, Maoism, etc.) are principal ideological systems of thought that nourish the tree of anti-capitalism. The publication of *The Communist Manifesto* in 1848, on the eve of the revolutions that broke out across mainland Europe, exposed the oppressive nature of capitalism and offered socialism/communism as its antidote. Another source of anti-capitalist ideas and resistance was the International Workingmen's Association (or the First International), which was formed in 1864. It was a site for the articulation of the anarchists and state socialists' competing visions of the path to the stateless, classless, and self-organized (communist) society.

Anti-capitalism as a term in contemporary popular consciousness might have had its genesis with the Global Justice Movement of the late 1990s and early 2000s, as reflected in media coverage of the June 18, 1990, protest in London against the G8, the seven richest industrialized capitalist nation-states plus Russia, and the November 30, 1999, mass demonstrations in Seattle against the World Trade Organization, a regulating instrument of global capitalism (Harman 2000). However, anti-capitalism's true origin is, much like fine wines, of a much older vintage. The discourse and activism against the anti-humanistic, inequitable, and soul crushing character of capitalism can be traced to, at a minimum, the resistance of the cooperative movement, starting in the 1820s.

Economic cooperation was an expression of opposition by the working-class in Britain to the sharp business practices of capitalist shopkeepers and the dehumanization and callous treatment of workers in the workplace. According to Robin Thornes, economic cooperation among Frantz Fanon's "wretched of the earth" had an explicit anti-capitalist orientation:

> The origins of the co-operative movement are, indeed, traceable to the early writings of Robert Owen. In these Owen formulated a critique of competitive capitalism and advocated the creation of villages of unity and mutual co-operation – communities in which inhabitants would receive, by direct exchange the full value of their labour. First advocated as a means of dealing with unemployment and pauperism, he came to see in communities the key to the creation of a rational and equitable society. (Thornes 1988, 29)

These working-class cooperators developed retail stores and producer cooperative or worker self-managed firms to afford themselves a measure of autonomy and self-determination against capitalist economic assault.

One may deduce certain principal concerns or themes of anti-capitalism from an October 1827 educational handbill produced by the Brighton Co-operative Benevolent Fund Association in Britain. It critiqued the "difficulties and uncertainty of procuring a moderate supply of the necessaries of life" by the labouring classes in spite of the productive capacity of labour through human capital development as well as technological developments (Durr 1988, 12). Poverty, or the inability of people who sell their labour power to bosses in the capitalist and state sectors to afford the goods and services that provide a decent standard of living, has been a constant feature of capitalism.

The anti-capitalism of these cooperators put forth the idea of economic activities that are focused on meeting human needs and not the generation of profit as the reason for their existence. In the abovementioned handbill, these agents of cooperative as opposed to capitalist economics asserted that "it is in their [the working-class] interest, both as producers and consumers, that there should be the greatest possible quantity of useful articles made with the greatest possible saving of labour." When the purpose of the production of goods and services is done to meet human needs, the introduction of labour-saving technology allows for people to put less labour into work, while giving them to access the resources they need to live decent and satisfactory lives free from the dog-eat-dog competition of capitalism and liberalism.

Another anti-capitalist critique common to both the early cooperators and current critics of capitalism is of the underlying demand for competition that negates the sociality within people and the cooperation that is the basis of human development and social evolution. According to the Brighton cooperators, the labouring classes "see that those engaged in distributing commodities can become rich only by a profit on cost price," and this practice has "introduced competition into all the transactions of life." Liberalism, as the ideological enabler of capitalism, has sanctified the relentless, robust, and muscular competitive pursuit of individual interests with little or no regard for the social and economic impact on large sections of society.

An additional theme highlighted by the forces of anti-capitalism past and present is the degrading of labour in the capitalist workplace and society at large. The Brighton cooperators assert that the working-class "see that this general competition has the effect of putting human labourers on the same footing as the inanimate objects they work upon, and of subjecting human labour, the source of all wealth, to the rise and fall in price" (Durr 1988, 13). Workers are bossed, bullied, directed, and infantilized under capitalist work relations, which serve to destroy the idea of the dignity and humanness of labour.

As "the source of all wealth" and in recognition of the inalienable right of the people to exercise self-determination over their common affairs, the most radical forces of anti-capitalism call for self-management in the workplace and all other social spheres:

> Direct democracy, or horizontal organising is valued within the anti-capitalist movement and tools for direct democracy such as consensus decision-making are used to promote more egalitarian social relationships. Although little acknowledged, these values and tools have been passed down directly from the peace and feminist movements of the 1960s. A main impulse here is towards autonomy, literally self-legislation. Yet this is not individual self-management or autonomy in the liberal-individual sense embedded in enlightenment values where individuals are cut adrift from responsibility and acquire a legal right to maximise profits freely in the market. Rather, it is self-management that builds times and spaces to bring autonomous individuals together, undermining the logic of private ownership and which allows us to recognise our needs and differences. This kind of collective self-management and the common ownership and management of spaces and services are devices to erode the capitalist logic of accumulation for individual gain. (Chatterton 2010, 12–13)

All in all, anti-capitalism provides a big tent for different critiques of capitalism. However, it is important for the forces of anti-capitalism to explicitly name the ideological source of the solution they are offering. If one is advocating for anarchist communism, state socialism or Marxism, or social democracy (capitalism with a human face), one should overtly do so and explain to the people why the prescribed ideological path is the best way to rid society of racism, patriarchy, heteronormativity, capitalism, and other forms of oppression.

As Nangwaya shows, there are a multitude of experiments in other ways of organizing ourselves to meet our needs that orbit around a broad anti-capitalist ethic. Each of these alternatives has its own specific orientation and consequences that need to be thoroughly examined by those seeking to put them into action, but their very presence testifies to the enduring desire to find a way of living non-alienated, non-commodified lives. The long history of social movements the world over stands as an archive of attempts to build ways of living otherwise. Recalling that "radical" means to "get to the root" of whatever phenomenon is under consideration, radical social justice movements have often centred not only issues of economic justice under capitalism but forms of economic production, distribution, and consumption beyond capitalist relations (Khasnabish 2008; Foran 2003; Maeckelbergh 2009; Juris 2008; Klein 2002; Sitrin 2012; Graeber 2013; Haiven and Khasnabish 2014; Haiven 2014; Holloway 2002; 2010; Sen 2017; McNally 2002). This anti-capitalist orientation is often a defining feature of Indigenous Peoples' struggles for resurgence (Coulthard 2014). This is, in part, because despite the incredible brutality of white supremacist, heteronormative, settler-colonial capitalism, Indigenous Peoples continue to sustain social, political, and economic practices driven by an orientation to each other and the wider world that are not reducible to the profit motive. This is not to suggest that any human group is somehow essentially or intrinsically immune to capitalism or any form of exploitative or oppressive relation. This is about people who have sustained alternative ways of knowing and being in the world despite attempts to destroy their unique collective identities and associated lifeways and to dispossess them of their autonomy and territory (Alfred 2005; Coulthard 2014).

As we've explored already, there are a multitude of experiments in non-capitalist ways of making a living in the world. From many of our everyday, small-scale experiences in reciprocity and redistribution to bigger projects involving barter economies, time banks, community gardens, skill shares, local currencies, fair trade, and cooperatives, alternatives to profit-based accumulation abound (Gibson-Graham 2006). Social movements of many kinds have often also advanced alternative models for making a living in the world in non-exploitative, non-oppressive ways (Sitrin 2012). As Nangwaya mentions in his intervention, the turn of the millennium witnessed a global wave of creative, direct-action protest and prefigurative politics on a mass scale that sought to contest capitalist globalization in favour of socially just, radically democratic, anti-capitalist alternatives to it.

This "movement of movements," often referred to as the "global justice movement" or the "alternative" or "people's" globalization movement, was sparked by the Zapatista Uprising, an Indigenous insurgency and radical social movement based in Chiapas, Mexico, that exploded onto the world stage on January 1, 1994 (Khasnabish 2010; Notes from Nowhere 2003; Midnight Notes Collective 2001; D. Solnit 2004).

Opposing the notion that life is nothing more than the relentless pursuit of profit, activists the world over connected their struggles not to impose a single alternative to capitalist globalization but, to borrow a phrase coined by the Zapatistas, to build "a world in which many worlds fit." Over a decade, activists around the world built a struggle "as global as capital" to resist the neoliberal capitalist order being imposed by a globalized ruling class and to advance myriad alternatives to it (R. Solnit 2012; D. Solnit 2004; Kingsnorth 2004; Sen 2017).

This movement of movements successfully opposed the neoliberal capitalist globalization blueprint, directly challenging powerful institutions like the World Trade Organization and a transnationally networked ruling class. Like all waves of social movement activity, this one eventually crested through a combination of factors. These included movement victories, ruling-class repression and co-optation, burnout and fatigue, and the emergence of new challenges in a post-9/11 world. Nevertheless, the legacy of the global justice movement is a powerful one, indelibly marking waves of social movement activity that would follow, inspiring people's radical imagination of the politically possible, and demonstrating convincingly that there are always alternatives to the status quo.

In the late 2000s, the Occupy Movement, deeply inspired by grassroots democratic uprisings in the Middle East known as the Arab Spring, exploded around the world in response to the 2008 global capitalist crisis. While occupations of public space and democratic assembly models often took centre stage, one of Occupy's hallmarks was its call for a movement of the "99 percent" against the wealthiest "1 percent" (A. Taylor et al. 2011; Graeber 2013). Occupy centred a diverse set of concerns raised by those who took part in the occupations and the assemblies without trying to distil a single line of struggle. For some, this was a great democratic strength. For others, it was a fundamental weakness that diluted the movement. Without getting into this debate, it's sufficient to note that this high-profile social movement directly advanced a horizon of economic and political organization that served the needs of the majority of society rather than only its wealthiest members. It also put front and centre questions of how we might organize ourselves to make a living in ways that advance a vision of sustainable, grassroots, community-led development.

In the wake of Occupy, we have seen the rise of many new and powerful movements, most of which build on the work of generations of radicals and revolutionaries. Of particular note has been the increasing centrality and visibility of struggles for Indigenous resurgence and Black life. While we will explore social movements and the challenges and alternatives they pose to the current order in the next chapter, it is important to recognize that these movements have taken aim not only at the relations of oppression that have systematically attempted to dehumanize them but their deep enmeshment with capitalism as a system of exploitation.

While it's easy to get lost in the drama of our current moment, struggles against oppression and exploitation have roots that run decades, centuries, and even millennia deep. As author and activist Chris Dixon (2014) details, contemporary struggles that form what he describes as the "anti-authoritarian current" have their roots in women-of-colour feminism, prison abolition, and anarchism, political traditions that stretch back generations. It is no exaggeration to say that people invested in opposing exploitation and oppression and building a collectively liberated world are part of a long standing, diverse, and rich political tradition (Zinn 2005; McKay 2005). These mass-based struggles for radical social change offer us windows onto how life might be lived otherwise. They offer us glimpses of what life lived in common might look like if our principle for organizing society was collective liberation rather than profiteering and individual acquisitiveness. Rarely do these movements offer blueprints for a non-oppressive, non-exploitative society. Instead, they are laboratories for a multitude of ways of living otherwise, windows onto worlds that lie just beyond the thin and increasingly fractured veneer of the status quo.

CONCLUSION

We do ourselves a grave injustice when we talk about the economy and the environment as if they are external to us and not intimately bound up with each other and with our human existence and activity on this planet. This isn't just because we attribute agency, intention, and solidity to things that aren't autonomous entities but because this has real implications for how we understand social, political, and economic possibilities and what priorities ought to guide our collective action. When we make the mistake of locating the economy and the environment outside of ourselves, we mystify rather than clarify what's at stake. Too often we hear about what the economy needs, what it demands now, what we are required to do to protect, grow, and serve it. We hear endlessly about its health or lack thereof, measured by indicators of growth or contraction that are intoned by the high priests of capitalism – bankers, financial analysts, economists, and captains of industry. Our imaginations and memories are conscripted by powerful agents and institutions such that we come to understand ourselves as serving the economy rather than the point of economic activity being to serve and sustain our collective existence.

As for the environment, we come to see it as a backdrop against which our lives are set. We are taught to see the environment as like the set for a play, something that exists apart from and largely independently of us, the passive background to our activity. When we are encouraged to see value in this context, it is largely in the form of resource extraction and other human-centred recreational or utilitarian purposes. But as we have seen time and again through this book, there are no passive backdrops in the story of human existence on this planet. Rather than environments, it is much more accurate to understand our position here relationally, as one species in a web of life.

In this chapter we have explored the collective human activity of making a living in the context of this web of life. We also critically explored notions of value – what we value and how we know what is valuable – under capitalism and beyond it. Using the COVID-19 pandemic as a lens, we investigated how we understand human life in relation to the other life with which we share this planet, paying careful attention to the consequences of dominant ways of figuring this out. In all of this, a critical and rigorous examination of power relations and prevailing relations of oppression and exploitation were front and centre.

By now it should be abundantly clear that we cannot understand how society works without attending to the dynamics and operation of power. This chapter revolves around the recognition that capitalism is not merely an economic or social system but a way of organizing nature. This effort to organize nature extends to our own inner nature, as we saw through an exploration of the logic of financialization to the way we see ourselves, our purpose, and every facet of our social lives. These powerful and persuasive mythologies – about our role as the dominant species on this planet, about the primacy of wealth accumulation, about the naturalness of hierarchies, about the compulsion to prove one's worth by endlessly toiling for someone else – are crucial to maintaining relations of ruling and the ruling class that benefits from them.

The Capitalocence, the age of capital, has been marked not only by the production of fantastic wealth and material abundance but by shocking levels of inequality, ecological devastation, alienation, suffering, and violence. The pandemic that swept the world beginning in 2020 brought this picture into focus for those willing to look. Not only were the conditions for the pandemic fashioned by capitalist ways of making a living, a culture of hyper-individualism, alienation, and commodification greatly exacerbated its impacts and undermined common-sense efforts to socially and collectively mitigate it. In spite of what seem to be great advantages in technical and scientific knowledge and capability, many of the wealthiest, most overdeveloped countries dramatically failed to combat the spread of the virus. Hollowed-out health-care and social welfare systems, decrepit public infrastructure, social media platforms that specialize in conspiracy theorizing and misinformation, and an increasingly polarized and antagonistic populace proved fertile ground for the pandemic, with appalling consequences measured in deaths, long-term infirmities, and social suffering.

None of this is inevitable. As we explored in this chapter, there are abundant alternatives to a globe-spanning system of oppression and exploitation. Some of those alternatives exist right now; we practise them all the time, and capitalism even lives parasitically off them. Reciprocity is a powerful, everyday example of such a practice. So, too, are redistributive networks. They may be mundane and unexciting, but they demonstrate the existence of non-exploitative and non-oppressive alternative ways of making a living. More dramatic examples of alternative ways of making a living abound, as we briefly explored at the end of this chapter. There is a rich and thriving living tradition of bold experiments in making a living that promote solidarity rather than profiteering and collective liberation instead of individual enrichment. Contrary to the myths of ruling relations, there are a multiplicity of alternatives to the status quo. It is up to us to build them.

KEY CONCEPTS

alienation: the process of divorcing people from the tools and resources they need to survive. The experience of being torn away from the things that sustain us.

Anthropocene: a term coined in 2000 by Paul Crutzen and Eugene Stoermer, naming an unprecedented geological epoch where humanity – the "anthropos" – has become the primary force shaping the Earth's geology and ecosystems.

capitalism: an economic system and ideology based on the production of commodities for sale on the market in pursuit of profit. Critical to this system is the alienation of workers from the means of production, forcing them to sell their labour in exchange for a wage in order to survive.

Capitalocene: a term identifying capitalism, rather than an abstract "humanity," as a world-changing force, as a way of organizing nature on a global scale, often with disastrous effects.

commodity: anything that can be bought and sold on the open market under capitalism. When something becomes a commodity, it no longer has worth because of its use-value, the practical purposes it serves, but rather because of its exchange value, what it can be sold for.

exploitation: the act of living off someone else's labour.

labour power: our ability to exert "power-to" create individually and collectively in the world.

market: a place where actors engage in immediate and impersonal exchanges mediated by money. Unlike other forms of exchange, no social ties or obligations are created.

means of production: the tools, raw materials, and infrastructure necessary to any given production process.

mode of production: a combination of productive forces and social and technical relations of production that are put to work to create what are considered to be necessary and desirable.

productive forces: the raw materials, human labour, tools, and equipment involved in any given mode of production.

profit: the gap between what a commodity cost to produce and what the owner (note, not the maker) of the commodity can sell it for.

reciprocity: an ancient and enduring form of human sociality that involves the exchange of goods and services that cultivates lasting social ties of responsibility and obligation.

redistributive networks: gather resources from the community, usually by specified agents, and redistribute them to community members.

relations of production: the ways people are organized and taught to relate to each other in any given mode of production.

wage: the money workers are paid for a specific amount of time spent expending their labour power for someone else, a quantitative measure of the value assigned to different kinds of work.

8

POWER AND ORDER

Inequality, Injustice, and Paths Beyond

What is the social order and how do we know whether it's good or not? What are some of the characteristics that distinguish a good society from a bad one? How do we identify them and who is responsible for achieving them? How do we come to know about and accept the way our society is organized? Is it true that inequality is inevitable and even necessary? What about violence, whether interpersonal or structural? What about alternatives, large and small, to the way we live? Where do we get our sense of political possibility from and how do we come to know about what is realistic?

The social order, the structure of society, seems solid, natural, and inevitable, but the truth is very different. In the 12,000 years since the last ice age ended, there have been a great many experiments in human civilization, and the social order we currently inhabit is only one of those. In this book we've spent a lot of time examining how we come to know ourselves as social beings and some of the key institutions and relations that characterize our social lives. In this chapter we take a critical look at the way our social relations and institutions are structured and how that is deeply shaped by prevailing power dynamics.

If we want to understand how societies work, we first have to look at whose interests are being served by any given social order. If we are serious about addressing pressing social problems, from misogyny to racism, economic inequality to violence, we first have to examine how the social world that we reproduce on a daily basis is structured. It's vital to understand that the social reality we inhabit is only one possible iteration of reality and that there were, are, and could be other ways of organizing and arranging ourselves in this thing called society.

CONVENIENT FICTIONS

Some stories get told so often that we come to accept them as true even if we have no evidence to support them and have never stopped to seriously consider why we believe them. One of these stories is about our current political order and how we got here. In the broadest of brush strokes, it goes something like this. About 12,000 years ago, the last of the great ice sheets retreated and the last ice age ended. As the climate warmed, humans began to domesticate plants, animals, and ourselves. Permanent settlement, agriculture, and pastoralism all followed. The capacity to produce more than was necessary for immediate needs led to trade and wealth accumulation and, ultimately, capitalism. Permanent settlement, a division of labour, and hierarchy led to the earliest states, the form of political organization we know today.

This is a story not only about human civilization but human nature. It offers a vision of who we are that draws a straight line between domination of other species, the land, and each other and what we regard as the fruits of civilization today. The relatively short time period over which all this occurs appears to testify to the power of domination, accumulation, and hierarchy. Whether we like it or not, goes the unspoken moral of this tale, progress lies in achieving dominion. This story offers a narrative about where we have come from and also where we are going. If life is a war of all against all, survival is the prize for those who dominate and exploit best.

But what if this story isn't true? What if there is no straight line of domination charted by human experiments in civilization and life is more than a war of all against all? What if this story we have been told about how we got to where we are today is built on partial and selectively interpreted evidence? As James C. Scott (2017) discusses in his important book *Against the Grain: A Deep History of the Earliest States*, the archaeological evidence supporting this civilization-through-domination narrative has become more dubious over time.

For example, if domestication and agriculture led directly to sedentary settlement and states, why is there a 4,000-year gap between the first crop domestications and the earliest states? We need to always be critical about what we think we know about the history of human social, political, and economic organization, particularly the assumptions that underwrite these narratives. As Scott explains:

> That states would have come to dominate the archaeological and historical record is no mystery. For us – accustomed to thinking in units of one or a few lifetimes, the permanence of the state and its administered space seems an inescapable constant of our condition. Aside from the utter hegemony of the state form today, a great deal of archaeology and history throughout the world is state-sponsored and often amounts to a narcissistic exercise in self-portraiture. Compounding this institutional bias is the archaeological tradition, until quite recently, of excavation and analysis of major historical ruins. Thus if you built, monumentally, in stone and left your debris conveniently in a single place, you were likely to be "discovered" and to

dominate the pages of ancient history. If, on the other hand, you built with wood, bamboo, or reeds, you were much less likely to appear in the archaeological record. And if you were hunter-gatherers or nomads, however numerous, spreading your biodegradable trash thinly across the landscape, you were likely to vanish entirely from the archaeological record. (2017, 13)

Because our lives are structured by states as the principal form of political organization, it's all too easy to see human history through this lens. We are, effectively, constantly looking for evidence that looks like the world as we know it.

From massive stone structures to royal lineages to tax records, archaeological investigations have always privileged not only durable evidence that can survive in the ground over hundreds and thousands of years but that which, over the course of much more recent history, has come to be associated with civilization as opposed to barbarism. Because we assume we are civilized, the things that characterize our society are projected backward onto previous ones. Notably, when it comes to the markers of civilization, we are not talking about art, sewers, or clean food and water; rather, the assumption is that hierarchy, wealth accumulation (and so inequality), and sedentary settlement signify dawning civilization. One problem with this is that the vast majority of human experience gets ignored. For most of humanity's time on this planet we have not organized ourselves into states. The *state* as we know it today is a bureaucratic apparatus that exercises political sovereignty over its defined territory, collects taxes, and monopolizes the legitimate use of violence within its own borders. It truly only comes into being in the 1600s. Until that time, most of humanity lived according to other political formations, and the states that did exist were small, isolated, and ephemeral. This leaves us with a vast blind spot in terms of understanding our collective human history on this planet. Beyond ignorance, this state-centrism makes hierarchy, domination, domestication, exploitation, and enforced settlement appear as paragons of civilizational virtue.

It isn't that our understanding of our political pasts and possible futures is wrong, only that it is partial and deeply affected by where we currently stand. As Scott (2017) argues, the supremacy of the domestication story teaches us not to see the other possibilities of human social and political organization. This isn't to deny the significance of the state as a form of human political organization, but if we generously date the ascendance of the state to the last four hundred years, that leaves a whole lot of human activity unconsidered. Following Scott, perhaps the most interesting possibility is that it isn't a choice between romantic barbarian utopias versus powerful, freedom-crushing states but a hidden history of complex and often fruitful negotiation between divergent forms of social and political organization.

Measured "not in centuries but in millennia," Scott argues, there was a "golden age for barbarians," dating from the emergence of the earliest states to about 1600 CE, that would have been characterized by "physical movement, flux, an open frontier, and mixed subsistence strategies" (2017, 253). This tells us that there is considerably more room for alternatives to the status quo and many more interesting possibilities for human freedom than we have been led to understand. Again, this is not to argue for one form of human political and social organization over another on the basis of the values we might impute to it. It is only to remind us that every representation of our past, present, and future is an exercise in power. That stories shape our imagination of what is possible is something we have seen time and again in this book. The power to assert a given account as the authoritative one isn't distributed evenly across society, so the responsibility of good social science has to be to hold those accounts up to careful scrutiny. We are not simply quibbling over how the past is remembered; we are fighting over what our present and future hold.

WHOSE ORDER? WHOSE POWER?

When we talk about *social and political orders*, what exactly are we talking about? Most basically, we are referring to how people organize themselves collectively beyond the sphere of kin relations. Whether we accept radical critiques like Scott's of the supremacy of the trinity of domestication-hierarchy-state with respect to the history of human organization, it's clear that a great deal about the way humans have organized themselves has been systematically sidelined. What happens when we look at social order from the margins?

Roughly speaking, social orders can be divided according to whether they are egalitarian, ranked, or stratified. These types reflect how prestige, power, and wealth are distributed. *Egalitarian* societies are the most equal, with the fewest divisions in status, power, and wealth between individuals and groups. *Ranked* societies are those in which status and prestige are unevenly distributed, but wealth and power remain equal. *Stratified* societies are those marked by significant differences in status, wealth, and power between individuals and groups. These broad types are not perfect descriptions of any particular society, and they can, to some extent, overlap. While modern capitalist nation-states are most certainly stratified societies with incredible divisions between people and groups in terms of access to wealth, power, and social status, this dominant reality holds within it many examples of other ways of relating to each other.

Whether we're talking about volunteer organizations, urban gardening collectives, martial arts clubs, amateur sports teams, grassroots political groups, or a slew of hobby and special interest groups, much of our lives actually take place in spaces not defined by vast differences in wealth and power, even as we remain located in a wider context marked by pronounced and widening inequality. For example, I am a member of a martial arts club. The class is divided into youth and adult groups, and each group is subdivided according to the proficiency of each member, which is designated by different coloured belts, which begins with white and moves through yellow, orange, green, blue, brown, and black. Promotion to the next rank is earned when a member is formally tested according to our club's curriculum. Regardless of how much money, social standing, or access to the levers of power any member might have outside of the club, when we train together the only distinction recognized between members is martial arts proficiency, visually marked by the colour of belt worn with the uniform and the skill demonstrated in our various techniques. We all work together when we train, and it's expected you will partner with many different people at all levels of skill during your training. It is also expected that senior members will help instruct junior ones. This is a good example of a ranked social order, where there is indeed a distinction made between members of the group in terms of prestige or status but there is no difference in the access to power or wealth based on that distinction. In fact, the higher your belt rank, the more expectation there is that you will contribute to developing more junior members and take on more responsibility within the club. Such responsibilities are rarely paid; they're seen both as privileges and as obligations in the service of keeping the club and its techniques alive.

This is only one example of a ranked social order that exists as a microcosm in the context of a society that is profoundly unequal in terms of status, wealth, and power. There are many other examples of ranked or outright egalitarian islands existing in a larger sea of stratification, whether they be activist or community organizations, art collectives, book clubs, or a wide array of interest groups. The point is that despite our society's veneration of ostentatious displays of status, conspicuous consumption, and wealth hoarding, just below the surface there are all kinds of thriving instances of cooperative, non-hierarchical social activity.

What are we to take from this brief exploration of egalitarian, ranked, and stratified orders? First, it's clear that this is not a simple linear progression with more advanced forms of social and political order pushing out earlier ones. Much like capitalism is touted by those who benefit most from it as the highest form of economic development, even as it exists parasitically off a vast array of non-capitalist work, the most dominating, hierarchical, and rigid forms of rule are advanced as the only realistic type of order by those who see their interests best defended by them. When we ask whether a particular order is good or not, we have to consider the interests it advances.

There is no natural or inevitable form of political organization for humans, and what dominant historical narratives obscure is just how contingent any given form of social and political order is. While we are socialized in large-scale, industrialized, capitalist, and state-based societies to see politics as the province of professionals engaged in the work of governing the unruly masses who cannot be trusted to manage their own affairs, the domain of politics from a cross-cultural perspective means something very different. *Political organization* refers to the ways in which societies are organized to plan group activities, make decisions, select leadership, and settle disputes within and outside the group. There are many ways of doing these things and thus many ways of doing politics. There is no doubt that the modern state is a very powerful bureaucratic apparatus of mass rule, but just because these huge, centralized political units are capable of organizing the lives of millions and even billions of people does not mean they are the best forms of political organization. There is no single best political form of organization; such assessments depend on who is doing the evaluating and according to what measure. States may be the basic unit of the global order we know today, but that doesn't mean they are the only or best form of political organization for achieving democracy, social development, peaceful coexistence, ecological sustainability, or any other goal.

If we accept large-scale, industrialized society as the only viable version of collective life, then states make a lot of sense. But as we've examined in other chapters in this book, there are good reasons to explore other models of life lived in common. While much tends to be made of the role of states in maintaining a legal structure and system of rights, which is often posed as the line separating civilization from barbarism, the age of nation-states (roughly the last four centuries) and particularly the twentieth and twenty-first centuries have been the bloodiest in history. The mind-boggling carnage of the First and Second World Wars, with more than 100 million dead, is impossible to understand outside of the bureaucratic, industrialized capacity for war-making and devastation made possible only by the state form. If states and their systems of laws and citizenship have at times served as important protections against violence and suffering (see Snyder 2016), then it is equally true that only states are capable of mobilizing people and resources in such a way as to make such large-scale violence and devastation possible in the first place.

Aggression and violence are certainly aspects of the human condition and existed long before the era of nation-states, but they become managed and integrated into the operation of states in ways that make them infinitely more deadly and dangerous. This is because the scale that states are capable of acting at is so much greater than other forms of human community. Not only is scale an issue, so too is the way the interests of the ruling class come to be embedded and enacted through the legal, repressive, and bureaucratic architecture of states. For a common person living under the rule of their feudal lord, pharaoh, or priest-king, there was no question about the absolute and personified authority their lives were subordinated to. Rulers were seen, in one way or another, as the embodiment of divine power on earth. In the modern age of nation-states and the world system they make up, that's changed considerably without empowering the world's majorities in any significant way.

While states are supposedly a form of modern, rational governance where sovereignty, political power, and legitimacy arise from the people, the history of this age testifies to the fact that the state is an incredibly effective mechanism of class rule. Rather than the awe-inspiring power of divine rulers, modern states seem boringly bureaucratic. Even in authoritarian contexts, political elites are required to at least periodically solicit the consent of those ruled over, even if such efforts are merely performances (see Hett 2018). Constitutions, federal executives, parliaments, courts, and bureaucracies exist to regulate the operation of power within the state and give the appearance of impartiality, transparency, and predictability.

But as we've seen in many examples in this book, that's not actually the way the state works. We don't all have the ability to inform policy or to whisper in the ear of politicians. We don't even have an equal opportunity to represent our fellow citizens as any cursory survey of the composition of legislative bodies demonstrates. These institutions aren't populated by a diverse cross-section of the population they govern: they draw overwhelmingly from a narrow segment of the population both in terms of demographic makeup and, more importantly, the vested interests they embody. In any case, this is less an attempt to criticize the state as a form of political organization and more an effort to simply lay bare how skewed our imagination of what is possible tends to be. Indeed, even within this power-laden world system all kinds of interesting possibilities lie latent, awaiting the right combination of circumstances and collective actors to activate them.

ACCUMULATION BY DISPOSSESSION

For those who believe a society without coercive, hierarchical authority would leave us at the mercy of the most predatory, it is worth considering the political-economic order referred to as *globalization*. The word itself means simply to make something global, but it has come to refer to some of the most prominent features of the post-World War II world and the global dominance of capitalism. Tellingly, globalization does not refer to the right of free movement for all people but rather the ideology of allegedly free markets and the increasingly frictionless movement of capital, goods, and services across borders. This is why at the turn of the millennium social justice activists across the world declared themselves to be against corporate, capitalist globalization and in favour of an alternative globalization dedicated to advancing social, political, economic, and environmental justice (D. Solnit 2004; Notes from Nowhere 2003; Juris 2008; McNally 2002; Klein 2002).

Depending on where you were born and what passport you carry, the world can look like a playground or a prison. When I did my fieldwork in Mexico in the early 2000s, I regularly crossed the Mexican and US borders. As someone carrying a Canadian passport, I navigated these borders relatively effortlessly and never once was I stopped or detained. As I waited in customs lines, particularly on US soil, I would often look at the much longer lines of Mexicans waiting for much more muscular, intense vetting by border agents as they attempted to enter the US. I was not nor am I now a particularly wealthy or powerful person, but by virtue of being a citizen of one of the wealthiest, most powerful countries on the planet, my right to travel to places other people could never even dream of entering was rarely called into question. Even when I was on Mexican soil, I was the beneficiary of my high-status citizenship. Living and working in the southeasternmost state of Chiapas, next to Guatemala, I regularly witnessed Mexicans and other Latin Americans being stopped by immigration agents on public buses to have their ID and right to be in the country confirmed. While the official rationale for this often orbits around anti-drug-trafficking efforts, it is abundantly clear that what was really being regulated is the movement of desperate people looking for better lives in other places. As a citizen of a wealthy Global North country, I often passed through such checkpoints much more easily than Mexicans, Guatemalans, and other Latin Americans, despite my ambiguously racialized identity. Even outside of my own country, I enjoyed greater security of my person and freedom of movement than many Mexicans in their own country.

Activist and author Harsha Walia (2013) describes the hierarchy of the current world order as "border imperialism," pointing to the way that borders police the movement of bodies, particularly racialized and poor ones. More than this, borders are intrinsic to practices of colonialism and imperialism, containing "undesirable" populations while facilitating the extraction of wealth and resources from their territories. No border is a natural phenomenon; all are products of relations that structure the movement of people, goods, services, and capital in the interests of the powerful. As Walia notes, "Borders are not fixed or static lines; they are productive regimes concurrently generated by and producing social relations of dominance" (2021, 6). In the words of scholar and activist Robyn Maynard, "The imposition of different categories of citizenship, in effect, delineates who 'belongs' to the realm of humane treatment and state protections, and who is excluded – deemed 'temporary,' 'illegal' and disposable" (2017, 159). Maynard points out that "(dis)ability, sexuality, race and class have historically played an integral role in determining which migrants were desirable and which should be excluded" (2017, 159).

Criminalizing the movement of people does not actually address the reasons people feel compelled to move or stop them from moving; it only makes their movement more dangerous. This reality is particularly hypocritical and galling considering many of the richest, most powerful countries were founded on the displacement and dispossession of Indigenous Peoples by European settlers and then built by slave, indentured, and forced labour of racialized and poor people (Coulthard 2014; Linebaugh and Rediker 2000; Maynard 2017; Roediger 2007; Walia 2021). The very processes of violent dispossession and wealth accumulation, driven prominently by Western European powers in pursuit of colonies, that have so defined the last five hundred years not only grossly enriched some people in some parts of the world, they also immiserated and impoverished a great many others. In the 1890s the British politician, white supremacist mining magnate and ardent imperialist Cecil Rhodes opined, "We must find new lands from which we can easily obtain raw materials and at the same time exploit the cheap slave labor that is available from the natives of the colonies. The colonies also provide a dumping ground for the surplus goods produced in our factories" (Ellwood 2010, 16). This description could as easily apply to what is referred to as "globalization" today as it does to the historical dynamics of colonialism.

These processes of wealth extraction have always been coupled with relations of oppression that have entrenched white supremacy while degrading the humanity of racialized others. As revolutionary and psychiatrist Frantz Fanon (1982) writes about so powerfully in *Black Skin, White Masks*, colonization isn't just a political or economic process of draining the colonies to feed the imperial centre but also a psychic process of cultivating and then internalizing relations of superiority and inferiority. White supremacy/racialized inferiority is a structured social relation of oppression that exists to justify the theft of labour and resources that would otherwise be unconscionable. After all, if those we are busy exploiting and oppressing are not fully human, then they aren't capable of autonomy and self-determination anyway. They need a firm, guiding hand. This pernicious paternalism is the most kindly face of colonial and neocolonial relations, and it needs to be understood as no less odious than its more unapologetic varieties. The overdeveloped enclaves to which so many desperately seek entry today in search of a measure of security and opportunity only exist by virtue of this ill-gotten and jealously hoarded wealth. The age of colonialism has come to an end, but the globalized capitalist system that has succeeded it has only entrenched the relations of exploitation and oppression that ushered it in.

One form this structured injustice takes is in the hierarchy of citizenships. While the idea of a discrete hierarchy of races has been rightly and roundly rejected as the basis for decent and free societies, differential citizenship status and the inequality between citizenships remains in place. As Walia explains, "A prevailing assumption, even among some progressives, is that while blatant immigration restrictions are racist, *too much* immigration would 'taint' cultural values and 'flood' labor markets" (2021, 14). Walia continues, "But borders do not protect labor"; rather, they "manufacture divisions within the international working class."

The places that so many want to move from today are a map of Western European colonization and the globalized capitalist predation that followed it. Overdevelopment in the Global North has come at the cost of underdevelopment in the Global South. Unlike processes that extract resources and mobilize human labour to turn them into wealth while building skills, technology, and infrastructure in that same context, what economists refer to as "value-added" development, the current world system stands as a testament to the dynamics of exploitative wealth extraction from the majority world to enrich the minority.

When colonial powers were thrown out of Africa, Asia, the Caribbean, and elsewhere by anti-colonial movements, they did not leave behind a robust civil or industrial infrastructure because it was never their intention to build them. When those former colonial possessions tried to chart their own courses for development, they frequently found them blocked either by powerful states like Canada and the United States or by key institutions of neoliberal capitalism, like the World Trade Organization, World Bank, and International Monetary Fund (Engler 2009; Maynard 2017; Prashad 2008). These successor gatekeeper organizations were born precisely as the old colonial order was collapsing and have worked, by and large, to ensure that the same interests served by the old order would be protected in the new. But as John Munro reflects on in this chapter's first intervention, national liberation is not a dream so easily denied, and even when this dream was incompletely realized, it has continued to drive freedom struggles that have reshaped the global architecture of power and nurtured new possibilities for collective liberation.

NATIONAL LIBERATION — *JOHN MUNRO*

THE WAVE OF NATIONAL liberation that followed World War II was quite possibly the most important occurrence in world history since 1492, when the imperial system first became fully global. Beginning in the Philippines in 1946 and winding down in Angola and Mozambique in 1975, the achievement of formal independence from colonialism and the emergence of what was called the "Third World" irrevocably altered the world order. It is true that some territories in the Global South, such as Ethiopia, had never been colonized, while others, like Ireland, had won independence before World War II. Namibia did not experience decolonization until 1990, while Guam and Martinique remain governed by foreign powers. But it was during the three postwar decades that global geopolitics changed most dramatically. In 1945, the United Nations had fifty-one members, and world maps showed swaths of the Global South as possessions of the North.

Thirty years later, 144 countries were represented at the UN, and new cartographies presented a patchwork of formally sovereign polities. National liberation, in short, marked a momentous transformation in the workings of the world.

Like other global processes, national liberation did not happen all of a sudden. Indeed, the transformation of colonies into countries was not new to the twentieth century. Two early examples were the revolutions which created the first two independent countries in the Americas. With their Declaration of Independence, propertied white men in 1776 announced their intention to exit the British Empire. Their success ushered in the United States, though for Indigenous societies and enslaved people of African descent, the US offered something far short of sovereignty. Haiti gained independence from France in 1804, but events there had moved in a very different direction because, in contrast to the US, the Haitian Revolution was itself a revolt against slavery and anti-Black racism. Haitian sovereignty was curtailed by the heavy financial burden of economic debt to France for the loss of enslaved human "property," but for all their compromised circumstances, the independence of the United States and Haiti exemplified how independence from powerful empires could be fought for and won.

Over a century later, the conjuncture of World War I saw European imperialism beset by existential crisis at the very moment that it attained maximum spatial reach. Intellectuals, cultural workers, and activists throughout the Global South seized on this moment to push for decolonization. In 1919 alone, Indian civilians protested British colonialism at Amritsar, anti-imperialist demonstrators launched the May Fourth Movement in China, Egypt was engulfed in revolution against British rule, a major Pan-African Congress was held in Paris, and the Soviet Union, which became the world's first officially anti-imperialist power in 1917, held onto power against external and internal enemies. Although Europe had weakened itself during the war, and Europe's claims of civilizational superiority and scientific racism were rendered at best suspect by the mindless carnage of industrial trench warfare, the imperialist forces continued to hold the balance of power. The interwar decades were thus marked by dashed anticolonial hopes and the assumption of Germany's colonies by France and Britain.

World War II was different. Ongoing anticolonial activism that prefigures alternative futures, the sheer destructiveness of Nazi empire-building in Europe, and the further rise of the United States and the Soviet Union finally combined to begin the end of formal imperialism. In Algeria and Vietnam, huge anticolonial demonstrations took place on the very day that, respectively, victory over Germany then Japan was announced, and within two years of the war's end, Britain had relinquished the jewel in its imperial crown, creating the nations of India and Pakistan in the process. The bloodshed attending the conclusion of British Raj was not the only violence to accompany the coming of national liberation to the Global South. Again, Algeria and Vietnam stood out in scale and ferocity, but in Malaysia, Kenya, and Angola sovereignty also did not come without a fight.

Wondering, in an essay entitled "Yes, I Said 'National Liberation,'" what it would mean to move from "a radical vision of national liberation" to "a solidarity rooted in shared victimization," historian Robin Kelley evokes this concept's duality, its being both exemplar of epochal change and unfinished project. After the 1970s, the consolidation of neocolonialism and neoliberalism meant that indirect forms of rule of Global North over South, through financialization, extractivism, and direct military intervention, continued throughout and beyond the twentieth century, while in settler colonies Canada and Palestine, independence never really arrived and Indigenous Peoples remained subject to colonial forms of rule. And yet, by the 1970s, a massive transformation had been wrought in the world system, one that has also seen – through cultural transformation, migratory movement, and resistance – decolonization within the Global North. In the promise that such a transformation contains, the promise that liberatory forms of sovereignty could mean the dismantlement of mass incarceration, capitalism, heteropatriarchy, and white supremacy, national liberation remains a subject of more than mere historical curiosity.

SOCIAL MOVEMENTS AND THE RADICAL IMAGINATION

Human beings have and continue to experiment with many ways of organizing ourselves. Politics refers to that public space in society where we select leaders, settle disputes, identify problems and their possible solutions, and make decisions about how and on what terms we are going to live together. Most people see politics as a technocratic, elitist, and endlessly complicated and corrupt space, but it does not have to be any of these things. As with all the other social phenomena we've explored in this book, politics as we know it has been indelibly shaped by relations of ruling and the powerful interests they represent. For those of us living in the heart of the current globalized neoliberal capitalist order, it is profoundly difficult not to see the state everywhere we look, particularly because we have learned to conflate it with authority, order, regulation, and hierarchy, all things that seem intrinsic to modern life. As the late anarchist and anthropologist David Graeber (2004) urged, while it's right and appropriate to understand how the state works and how it came to be, it's also vital for us to explore all those forms of political organization that exist that are not states. It's tempting to romanticize such alternative forms of political organization, looking, for example, at radical political subcultures and countercultural and intentional communities as points of reference and inspiration. While these may draw our attention because they are dramatic, there are many alternatives that are more mundane and closer to hand. Sociologists and anthropologists have spent quite a lot of time exploring those alternatives. Social movement studies is a sub-field of political social science that examines non-institutionalized struggles to create social change. Researchers who study social movements and the individuals, groups, and organizations that make them up are interested in the ways social change is generated at the grassroots of society, not only by those with the most money and resources or are closest to the levers of power.

For serious observers of social movements, there are two basic truths that guide research about them. The first is that politics is not only the province of elites, parties, and formal institutions like parliaments but belongs also to those of us outside these gilded halls who practise politics in a diversity of ways, from prefigurative to contentious to insurrectionary and so much more. This first truth is the simple recognition that politics is not something that only happens in the spaces of the powerful but is woven through the fabric of our collective social life. It can look like a parliamentary debate, a backroom deal orchestrated between elites, a riot, a revolution, or a grassroots experiment in radically democratic social planning. The second truth is that grievances, no matter how deeply felt, are not enough to bring powerful social movements capable of driving social change into being. Mainstream media narratives to the contrary, movements don't simply "explode" into being out of nowhere and people do not sacrifice time and energy to organize and participate in them because they have "nothing left to lose." These clichés are not just wrong empirically, they also serve to reproduce the well-worn narrative that regular people are not capable of rational, intentional behaviour or politics. Movements are the product of organization and require careful, committed work before they coalesce. For those who study movements, this means we need to pay attention to how movements come to be, how and why people come together in struggle, and what counts as movement success and failure.

A *social movement* is an organized collective engaged in social action for a common project. These organized collectives are defined by three key elements: they are in a position of conflict, and act accordingly, with respect to those they identify as opponents; they are connected through dense, informal networks of communication; and they share a distinctive collective identity. Social movements are by no means necessarily social justice oriented, they can be conservative or transformative, radical or reformist, reactionary or revolutionary. They operate, at least in part, outside of established channels of political power and representation.

Social movements have long been objects of scholarly analysis with many important insights about politics and social change gained from this rich body of work. In the mid-20th century, collective behaviour theory cast social movements as little more than frenzied mobs, escape valves for the frustrations of the masses but far from real politics. Confronted by the inability of functionalist theory to make sense of what were clearly increasingly organized, intentional, and effective movements – particularly those of the new left of the 1960s, such as student, anti-war, Black power, and women's liberation movements (Epstein, 1991; Katsiaficas, 1987; Polletta, 2002) – researchers developed new analytical paradigms, including approaches that stressed political opportunity (Meyer and Minkoff, 2004; Piven and Cloward, 1977) and resource mobilization (McCarthy and Zald, 1977; Zald and McCarthy, 1979) models. These approaches took social movements seriously in ways that collective behaviour theory did not, but they also tended to reduce movements to being yet another political player in an already crowded field where the stakes of the game were influence and power in terms set by the established order. Others sought to map the social movement landscape in terms of a transition to a newer "postindustrial" capitalism (Melucci, 1996; Touraine, 1988), but all too often posited an untenable break between "old" (class-based and concerned with material redistribution) and "new" (identity-based and concerned with the nature of social life) movements. The new social movement paradigm underestimated the continuing importance of class conflict and the state and slid into a celebration of narrow identity politics that reproduced rather than critically exploring the commodified lifestyle individualism of neoliberal capitalism.

By the end of the millennium, social movement studies was much closer to a new synthesis than a paradigm war. Drawing on some of the best insights from previous generations, a new analytical perspective emerged that successfully combined a focus on structural factors relating to movements and contentious politics with a sincere engagement with their symbolic, affective, and subjective dimensions. Newer areas of study included emotion, identity, consciousness, and biography (Goodwin, Jasper, and Polletta, 2001; Jasper, 1999; Mansbridge and Morris, 2001; Polletta and Jasper, 2001); issue framing and meaning management (Benford and Snow, 2000; Olesen, 2005); networks and complexity theory (Arquilla and Ronfeldt, 2001; Keck and Sikkink, 1998); and transnationalism and globalization (Bandy and Smith, 2005; Della Porta, Kriesi, and Rucht, 2009). But in a field steeped in dominant understandings of what counts as politics, what its stakes are, and what success and failure mean, even an expanded field of inquiry left many blind spots.

What is missing, in the first place, is a willingness to understand movements, particularly radical ones, not only as engines of social change and vehicles for contentious political claims but as incubators of alternative social relations, laboratories for ways of living otherwise. But perhaps most importantly, many scholarly examinations of social movements fail to understand them as animated not only by grievances, material concerns, and a complex web of subjective and affective forces but by the radical imagination. Put simply, the *radical imagination* is a process by which we collectively map "what is," situate it as the result of "what was," and speculate on what "might be" (Haiven and Khasnabish 2014). At its root, it is the capacity to envision the world as it might be otherwise, and, as such, it is something we can only practise together. It isn't an individualized escape from reality; it is the spark of powerful social movements and is at the heart of struggles for social change.

All powerful and resilient social movements are animated by the radical imagination because struggling for social change makes no sense if you don't have a shared notion of how the world ought to be different. Movements don't merely push back against those things that make their members' lives unliveable; they fight for the world they want to see. For example, activists in Black, Indigenous, and queer liberation movements have not just fought against forms of oppression and violence directed at these groups; they have struggled to open up society beyond white supremacy, settler-colonialism, and heteropatriarchy so that all people can live liberated lives. While it's common to associate social movements with protest aimed at influencing power holders and changing specific laws or institutional practices, that's far from all that movements are involved in. When people organize themselves to take collective action to get what they need without asking the powerful for it, they are taking direct action. While the term "direct action" sounds dramatic, it doesn't have to be. Activists using their bodies, bike locks, and PVC tubing to blockade the entrances to a venue hosting a meeting of the global ruling class and so preventing the meeting from happening is direct action. So, too, is community members concerned about the lack of affordable, healthy food starting a community garden. In both cases, ordinary people are not begging the powerful for favours; they are asserting their agency. When movements do take direct action, however mundane or dramatic, such action can often offer a glimpse of the kind of society those people want.

Anarchists, adherents to the political ideology that is opposed to all forms of coercive authority and hierarchy, often talk about the importance of the means of struggle being equal to its hoped-for ends. That means if we want to live in a peaceful, democratic, egalitarian society, we can't use methods that involve coercion, terror, and random violence to get there. We cannot expect the society we create to magically be better than the tools used to create it. This does not preclude the legitimacy of armed struggle, insurrection, or revolution, but it demands that we do our utmost to align our practices with our principles. When means and ends align in the context of movement struggles, we are witnessing *prefigurative politics*. This refers to the practice of movement activists showing us the kind of world they want through their day-to-day organizing and activity. In this chapter's next intervention, Richard Day discusses movements building the world they want here and now through their own activity. This politics of prefiguration is one of the most important activities of social movements, and it's often hidden from view because it rarely registers in terms of policy changes or other metrics of conventional governance. Thinking about the way social movements offer glimpses of the world they want through their activity here-and-now also lets us think more complexly about what "winning" and "losing" means for social movements. In this way we might consider social movements as laboratories for socio-political, economic, and cultural alternatives, processes that allow us to experiment with ways of living otherwise.

PREFIGURATIVE POLITICS — *RICHARD DAY*

THE COMMON UNDERSTANDING OF politics in the mainstream of western societies is that we vote every four years or so, in the hope that the people we vote for will do the things we want them to do. Some of us are more committed than that, of course. We might encourage others to get out and vote, run for office ourselves, or try to influence the decisions of those who end up in office. But all this activity involves a series of disconnects between the actor and the action. We don't do the thing we want done; we ask someone else to do it for us — a disconnect at the level of who acts. That person is probably very far away from us, someone we don't know and never will know — a disconnect across space. And if the thing happens at all, it will only be after long, drawn out discussions and analyses, which make for a disconnect in time as well.

Prefigurative politics is about doing things differently, so as to reconnect us to ourselves and to each other. And the key to this different way of doing things is direct action. Rather than relying upon distant, bureaucratic entities like parliaments to decide what is to be done, we deliberate amongst ourselves. This can be via processes like affinity groups, in which a handful of people who know each other well get together to perform a specific, limited task, such as locking themselves down at a particular intersection as part of a larger protest, as occurred in Seattle in 1999 and Quebec City in 2001. Or it can involve a general assembly, in which hundreds, or even thousands, of people participate, such as the neighbourhood assemblies in Argentina after the insurrection of 2001, or the Occupy camps in North America in 2011–12.

Not only do we make our own decisions, but once we know what needs to be done, we take on the job ourselves, with the help of other people in our community and sometimes outside allies and supporters. The struggles of Indigenous Peoples against pipelines (Standing Rock, Trans Mountain, Line 9, Unist'ot'en), fish farms (Midsummer Island, Swanson Island), and uranium prospecting (Ardoch Algonquin and Shabot Obaadjiwan First Nations) can all be seen as prefiguring the return of the land to its traditional Indigenous keepers. These actions have also demonstrated certain possibilities for Indigenous-settler relations that go beyond mere recognition or reconciliation within the colonial, state-capitalist regime that currently dominates us all.

But perhaps the most important kind of change that prefigurative politics brings about is not political or economic, but personal and cultural. Once people have had a taste of what it's like to do things for themselves, it can be hard for them to accept the feelings of alienation and disempowerment they get from business and government as usual. They learn not only that they can look after themselves, but that it feels really good to do things that way. They get to know each other, they learn how to deal with their interpersonal issues, they rediscover all sorts of skills and powers that are fundamental to the human condition.

I've given a lot of examples that involve situations of protest, because this is where prefigurative politics is most visible in the mass media of mainstream societies today. But there are many other ways to work prefiguratively, like growing some of your own food and trading some of it with others, rather than going to the supermarket. Like talking with your neighbour about the eight-foot fence they are starting to build, rather than calling the bylaw enforcer. Or getting involved with local groups providing food, shelter, and other kinds of support to those who are not being served by the current social order. There is only one thing worse, in a society dominated by the colonial state and capital, than being included in its bestowal of benefits — and that is being excluded from them, for there is often nowhere outside of the system where one might seek support.

Finally, one of the most important things about prefigurative politics is that it doesn't follow any kind of "purity law." It's not perfect, it's not total, and there are many ways it can be pursued. Often it is mixed up with other modes of social change, such as pushing governments and corporations for reforms so that they are less destructive of our communities and the land upon which we all depend. This experimentation gives us more time to learn how to live. And it helps us to remember that the best way to live is not to be a docile servant in a world we don't believe in; nor is it to wait for the Revolution to occur, after which all will (apparently) be well. Rather, it is to live, here and now, as though the Revolution has already occurred.

While our authorized histories tend to be filled with accounts of great people (usually white men) doing great (and sometimes terrible, but still awe-inspiring) things, much of what we think of as central to our lives wasn't bestowed on us benevolently by the powerful but won by organized collectives of people. The abolition of slavery, the right to be free of arbitrary detention, women's right to vote, the eight-hour workday, unemployment insurance, environmental protections, all these things, no matter how partial and incomplete, were won by people organized in struggle (Featherstone 2012; McKay 2005; Zinn 2005).

While many people express disillusionment, apathy, and pessimism in response to the status quo, building viable alternatives to it seems impossibly daunting. This sense of futility and the inevitability of the status quo is one of the most potent defence mechanisms of the dominant order. As we've already explored in this book, the stories of how ordinary people have come together to fight for and win what they need to live dignified lives are systematically denied to us by authorized histories, formal schooling, and a range of ruling-class myths that serve to mystify relations of ruling.

Another problem with envisioning alternatives is the belief that alternatives must be entirely and wildly different from where we are now and where we've come from. But perhaps the most interesting and viable alternatives lie not in some fantastic, utopian vision of the future but in living up to responsibilities we have abdicated. For those of us who live in settler-colonial nation-states like Canada, the United States, and Australia, the current society exists by virtue of the dispossession, violent displacement, and genocide of the original inhabitants of these territories. There is no way to move forward into a more just, democratic, and sustainable future without first collectively accounting and making amends for the foundational and ongoing violence of settler-colonialism that has been borne by Indigenous Peoples. Beyond this, in countries like Canada where colonial powers signed treaties – nation-to-nation agreements of coexistence and cooperation – with Indigenous Nations, realizing a more just future begins with settlers and the settler state living up to the relations enshrined in these treaties. As Sherry Pictou explores in this chapter's final intervention, respectful coexistence and political relationships based on the mutual recognition of autonomy and dignity are at the root of what treaty-making promises. Settler-colonialism won't allow this promise to be fulfilled, but justice, reconciliation, and a collective future beyond domination are all possible if settlers commit to recognizing themselves as treaty people and living up to the responsibilities that entails.

TREATIES AND TREATY-MAKING – *SHERRY PICTOU*

THROUGHOUT WHAT IS KNOWN today as Canada, various types of treaty agreements were made between Indigenous Nations and European settlers dating back to the seventeenth century. In recent decades, Indigenous legal contestations against how these treaties have been denied or ignored mark extensions of colonialism that many Indigenous struggles for social justice continue to be up against.

It is unfortunate that Indigenous Peoples are forced to rely on the very legal system that has and continues to manifest the subjection of treaties to its own laws— the very treaties that Canada is built on. While treaties were being ignored, some the most dehumanizing laws, such as the Indian Act of 1876, were created by settler Canada, which included making ceremonies illegal, forcing children to attend residential schools, and stripping generations of Indigenous women of their identity. For example, Indigenous women who married non-Indigenous men lost their legal "status'" as an Indigenous person. And though some laws have attempted to rectify this by reinstating status, they are limited to only 1951 and onwards.

Therefore, even though there have been several successful court cases upholding or reasserting the legitimacy of treaties and treaty rights, their implementation is confined to state-driven processes. These especially take on neoliberal forms of governance, property rights and resource extraction (as though ongoing social injustices are not violations of treaty). This political-legal framework deludes the important role treaties play in the creation of Canada or what allows Indigenous and settler people to live here. Just as significant, Indigenous perspectives of treaties and treaty-making, which have been in practice since before the arrival of Europeans, are often ignored altogether.

Indigenous groups made agreements with each other for enacting peace, war, and social and economic relations. The most notable examples of peace treaties are the Haudenosaunee or Iroquois Confederacy agreement known as the Great Law of Peace and the Haudenosaunee agreement post-European arrival with the Dutch, known as the Two Row Wampum. Wampum refers to wampum belts, which are in essence woven and beaded treaty story belts that were used to orate who the partners were and the terms of the relationship and obligations between those partners.

The Two Row Wampum and the Peace and Friendship Treaties (of the Mi'kmaq, Welastekwewiyik or Maliseet, Passamaquoddy, and Penobscot Peoples) are known as a "covenant chain" of treaties marking a process for renewing treaty relationships, or in other words, making living agreements. Further, many treaty obligations for fulfilling those agreements were not restricted to just humans but also to the land and sharing of land in a sustainable way to ensure access to food and water. This concept of reciprocity between human and natural worlds is expressed in many Indigenous languages. For example, in the Mi'kmaw language, the word *netuku-klimk* roughly translates to providing for your family and community by taking only what you need. Though the nature of treaties may differ throughout various stages in history, most Indigenous understandings of treaty consisted of reciprocal obligations to ensure the well-being of each other and with the promise of food or access to food as a premise for sharing the land. These understandings (though often disregarded) were carried over into treaty-making with settler society.

Therefore, for many Indigenous Peoples, treaties are not static or historical documents of past events. Instead, treaty represents the practice of renewing relations for maintaining the well-being of human worlds interdependently by also ensuring the well-being of natural worlds, on which life depends.

This concept of treaty is a departure from how current state-driven processes of treaty negotiations seek to bring a finality and certainty to treaty relations. In this context, certainty is the means for securing individual property rights for corporate interests, comprising a neoliberal (il)logic of achieving well-being by increased modes of capitalism under the guise of "closing the gap" of inequality. The concept of closing the gap touted by non-Indigenous and Indigenous leadership who have bought into this approach is debatable in practice because the market economy benefits only the corporate sector, while poverty is reproduced and heightened with ongoing government divestment in social, education, and health programs. Thus, if the intent of the settler state is to achieve neoliberal forms of property rights in treaty negotiations, how this includes "official" or "legal" ways to further dispossess Indigenous People from land must be considered. In other words, the treaty relationship is undergoing neoliberalization by de-humanizing relationships with land, creating the illusion that the human dimension of treaties is separate from land. This further obscures how the numbers of Indigenous bodies that continue to be violently disposed of — through the murdering of Indigenous women and children without any justice — are connected to the neoliberalization of treaties.

Just as significant, the neoliberalization of treaties undermines how enacting reciprocal living relations for sharing the land must extend beyond political-legal relations to include all Indigenous and settler people. This raises the question about how neoliberalism is enacted in settler society. How is settler society engaged in or consulted with about development, especially if that development is unsustainable? Though neoliberalization may take on multiple forms and its capitalistic outcomes impact race, class, and gender differently, its underlying objective remains the same: profitability at the expense of human and environmental well-being. It is in this context that a deeper understanding of treaties as a living practice of relations for sharing the land offer possibilities for broader Indigenous and settler engagement toward ensuring a practice of treaties that contributes to the well-being of all humans and the natural worlds in which we live. This will demand a high degree of mutual uncertainty, as opposed to certainty, in order to avoid reinscribing neoliberal extensions of colonialism and instead create true living treaty partnerships.

Sometimes we can only move forward by looking back. Respectful coexistence among different peoples isn't impossible; in fact, it has been common throughout the course of human history. Border imperialism, settler colonialism, white supremacy, and capitalist predation, among a host of other oppressive and exploitative relations, all rely on and entrench notions of humanity as violently, irredeemably sectarian. Those who rule over us in their own narrow interests desperately want us to invest in this nightmarish vision because their grotesque enrichment requires us to be pitted against one another. The ruling class fears nothing more than the solidarity of those they seek to dominate and exploit.

As Pictou reflects on in her intervention, processes of treaty-making are grounded in a mutual recognition of dignity and the legitimacy of autonomy by the parties involved. Treaties are agreements between equals, not contracts imposed by the powerful on their subordinates. Recognizing that my power cannot compel another to accede to my desires means I have to negotiate with them to set out the terms of our mutual coexistence, not coerce them into agreeing to my demands. While settler-colonialism has attempted to destroy such histories, the very existence of treaties testifies to the possibility of crafting relationships and institutional practices predicated on dignity and consent rather than domination. As the COVID-19 pandemic, which began in 2020, has reminded us, our modern world stands on incredibly shaky foundations, and we renounce our mutual responsibilities to each other and other life with which we share this planet at our great peril.

CONCLUSION

Anthropologist and medical doctor Paul Farmer once wrote, "An honest account of who wins, who loses, and what weapons are used is an important safeguard against the romantic illusions of those who, like us, are usually shielded from the sharp edges of structural violence" (2004, 308). Farmer urges us to put social research to work in a way that exposes social relations and institutions that perpetuate the daily, grinding suffering faced by so many in our world. Rather than creating victim narratives, or what anthropologist Philippe Bourgois (n.d.) calls a "pornography of violence," that submerge the real causes of violence and suffering beneath sensationalized accounts, these practitioners call for critical inquiry that exposes the real roots of exploitation and oppression. While we are understandably drawn to dramatic eruptions of mass violence, such focus draws us away from less spectacular but much more mundane, widespread, and impactful relations, institutions, and forms of organization that make people's lives unlivable. While mass shootings and genocide are certainly in urgent need of attention, so too are the ways we organize ourselves socially, politically, and economically that cast whole groups of people onto the cutting edges of this system.

Structural violence refers to these forms of violence that are widespread, impersonal, and systematic. It is directed against groups rather than individuals and aims to deny them their dignity and autonomy while facilitating systemic forms of oppression and exploitation. When police in Halifax, Nova Scotia, stop, check identification, and collect information on Black people at a rate six times higher than on white people, this is an example of structural violence. When women have their reproductive function subject to state control and surveillance and are also forced to bear the costs and consequences of the work of care for the young, infirm, and elderly, this is an example of structural violence. When Indigenous communities are forced to live with boil-water advisories for decades because the Canadian government can't be bothered to provide them with potable water, this is an example of structural violence.

As we've explored in this chapter there are many ways that hierarchy, inequality, and injustice are naturalized through the circulation of stories that make them seem inevitable and even necessary. As Black revolutionary Malcolm X said, "If you're not careful, the newspapers will have you hating the people who are being oppressed, and loving the people who are doing the oppressing." The stories we tell matter. In stratified societies, and particularly in large-scale societies like our own, adorned with the trappings of liberal democracy, the privileges and power of the ruling class are only rarely defended through repressive force. In such societies, the consent of the ruled is extracted through dominant institutions like the media, schools, organized religion, and civic and moral authorities. The ideological domination of one class over others is what the Italian communist and anti-fascist Antonio Gramsci referred to as "hegemony." We learn to talk about some people who have the audacity to cross borders in search of a better life as "illegals" without ever stopping to think about the legitimacy of our settler presence on Indigenous territory. We learn to accept and reproduce a society awash in inequality with dramatic effects on the lived experience of people at every conceivable level. We find homes in a society structured by violent and toxic gendered and racialized hierarchies that pit people against each other who ought to find common cause against their exploiters.

As we explored to start the chapter, assumptions about what counts as civilization affect how we interpret the archaeological record and understand our human past. We look for what we know, what we expect to find, what we have come to understand as natural, however much it might not benefit us. Not only does this make relations of ruling seem natural and inevitable, it makes alternatives seem absurd and unthinkable. But alternatives to the status quo are not impossible; the fact that society isn't static proves this. More than this, history is littered with examples of social movements that have been engines of social change and incubators for social innovation, what we might call laboratories for ways of living otherwise. Although much official history tells the story of powerful and influential people making important decisions and taking action, grassroots social action has shaped human societies in profound and enduring ways. In fact, as practices such as treaty-making should remind us, more just, peaceful, and sustainable futures may not lie in some fantastical futuristic vision but in living up to responsibilities we have abdicated. Many of the institutions, relations, and practices we have for so long taken for granted and seen as overwhelmingly powerful find themselves on increasingly shaky ground, their limits ever more exposed. Capitalism, democracy, and liberalism have never seemed so precarious. What will come next isn't easy to predict, but engaged social research can help us ask better questions and gather better evidence to inform our collective action. This is a fairly humble contribution, but it is a worthy one. As the anarchist and anthropologist David Graeber reminds us, "We have tools at our fingertips that could be of enormous importance for human freedom. Let's start taking some responsibility for it" (2004, 105).

KEY CONCEPTS

egalitarian societies: the most equal with the fewest divisions in status, power, and wealth between individuals and groups.

globalization: most commonly used in reference to some of the most prominent features of the post-World War II world and the global dominance of capitalism. Tellingly, globalization does not refer to the right of free movement for all people, but it certainly does refer to the ideology of allegedly free markets and the increasingly frictionless movement of capital, goods, and services across borders.

political organization: the ways in which societies are organized to plan group activities, make decisions, select leadership, and settle disputes within and outside the group.

prefigurative politics: the practice of movement activists showing the kind of world they want through their day-to-day organizing and activity.

radical imagination: the process by which we collectively map "what is," situate it as the result of "what was," and speculate on what "might be." At its root, it is the capacity to envision the world as it might be otherwise and, as such, it is something we can only practice together.

ranked societies: those in which status and prestige are unevenly distributed but wealth and power remain equal.

social movement: an organized collective engaged in social action for a common project. These organized collectives are defined by three key elements: they are in a position of conflict with respect to those they identify as opponents; they are connected through dense, informal networks of communication; and they share a distinctive collective identity.

social orders: how people organize themselves collectively beyond the sphere of kin relations, roughly divided according to whether they are egalitarian, ranked, or stratified.

state: a bureaucratic apparatus that exercises political sovereignty over its defined territory, collects taxes, and monopolizes the legitimate use of violence within its own borders.

stratified societies: those marked by significant differences in status, wealth, and power between individuals and group

REFERENCES

Abramovich, Alex. 2016. "Preventing, Reducing and Ending LGBTQ2S Youth Home-lessness: The Need for Targeted Strategies." *Social Inclusion* 4, 4: 86–96. https:// <doi.org/10.17645/si.v4i4.669>.

Alfred, Taiaiake. 2005. *Wasáse: Indigenous Pathways of Action and Freedom*. Peter-borough: Broadview Press.

___. 2016. "The Great Unlearning." Envision: The Big Picture. December 15. <envi-sionthebigpicture.com/news/2017/1/7/the-great-unlearning>.

Anderson, Benedict. 2006. *Imagined Communities: Reflections on the Origin and Spread of Nationalism*, second edition. London and New York: Verso.

Anti-Defamation League. n.d. "Swastika." <adl.org/education/references/hate-sym-bols/swastika>.

Appadurai, Arjun. 1996. *Modernity at Large: Cultural Dimensions of Globalization*. Minneapolis: University of Minnesota Press.

Arquilla, John, and David Ronfeldt. 2001. *Networks and Netwars*. Santa Monica: Rand.

Asch, Michael. 2015. "Anthropology, Colonialism and the Reflexive Turn: Finding a Place to Stand." *Anthropologica* 57: 481–489.

ASHG. 2018. "ASHG Denounces Attempts to Link Genetics and Racial Suprem-acy." *American Journal of Human Genetics* 103, 5: 636. <doi.org/10.1016/j. ajhg.2018.10.011>.

Ayres, Jeffrey McKelvey. 1998. *Defying Conventional Wisdom: Political Movements and Popular Contention against North American Free Trade*. Studies in Compar-ative Political Economy and Public Policy. Toronto and Buffalo: University of Toronto Press.

Bakhtin, Mikhail. 1981. *The Dialogic Imagination: Four Essays*, translated by Caryl Emerson and Michael Holquist. Austin: University of Texas Press.

Bandy, Joe, and Jackie Smith, eds. 2005. *Coalitions across Borders*. Lanham, MD: Rowman & Littlefield.

Bannerji, Himani. 2016. "Ideology." In *Keywords for Radicals*, edited by A.K. Thompson, K. Fritsch, and C. O'Connor. Oakland, CA: AK Press.

References

Barrouquere, Brett. 2018. "FBI: Hate Crime Numbers Soar to 7,106 in 2017; Third Worst Year since Start of Data Collection." <splcenter.org/hate-watch/2018/11/16/fbi-hate-crime-numbers-soar-7106-2017-third-worst-year-start-data-collection>.

BBC. n.d. "Religion: Religions." <bbc.co.uk/religion/religions/>.

Bear Nicholas, Andrea. 2011. "Linguicide: Submersion Education and the Killing of Languages in Canada." *Briarpatch*, March 1. <briarpatchmagazine.com/articles/view/linguicide>.

Beiser, Vince. 2015. "The Deadly Global War for Sand." *Wired*, March 26. <wired.com/2015/03/illegal-sand-mining/>.

Benford, Robert, and David Snow. 2000. "Framing Processes and Social Movements: An Overview and Assessment." *Annual Review of Sociology* 26: 611–39.

Bhambra, Gurminder K. 2016. "Postcolonial Reflections on Sociology." *Sociology* 50, 5: 960–966. <doi.org/10.1177/0038038516647683>.

Bhambra, Gurminder K., Dalia Gebrial, and Kerem Nişancıolu. 2018. *Decolonising the University*. London: Pluto Press. <library.oapen.org/bitstream/id/0b692853-23af-49ad-83a9-6844dca1dc1d/1004145.pdf>.

Bishop, Anne. 2002. *Becoming an Ally: Breaking the Cycle of Oppression in People*. Halifax, NS: Zed Books and Fernwood Publishing.

Bourgois, Philippe. n.d. "The Power of Violence in War and Peace." Accessed February 9, 2022. http://istmo.denison.edu/n08/articulos/power.html.

Bury, Jeffrey, and Anthony Bebbington. 2013. "New Geographies of Extractive Industries in Latin America." In *Subterranean Struggles: New Dynamics of Mining, Oil, and Gas in Latin America*, 27–66. Austin: University of Texas Press.

Butler, Judith. 1988. "Performative Acts and Gender Constitution: An Essay in Phenomenology and Feminist Theory." *Theatre Journal* 40, 4: 519. <doi.org/10.2307/3207893>.

___. 2004. *Undoing Gender*. New York: London: Routledge.

Canadian Institutes of Health Research, Natural Sciences and Engineering Research Council of Canada, and Social Sciences and Humanities Research Council of Canada. 2018. *Tri-Council Policy Statement: Ethical Conduct for Research Involving Humans 2018* <https://ethics.gc.ca/eng/policy-politique_tcps2-eptc2_2018.html>.

Canadian Women's Foundation. n.d. "The Facts about Gender Based Violence in Canada." Canadian Women's Foundation. <canadianwomen.org/the-facts/gender-based-violence/>.

Carrington, Damian. 2016. "The Anthropocene Epoch: Scientists Declare Dawn of Human-Influenced Age." The Guardian, August 29. <theguardian.com/environment/2016/aug/29/declare-anthropocene-epoch-experts-urge-geologi-

cal-congress-human-impact-earth>.

Carroll, A, L.R. Mendos, and International Lesbian, Gay, Bisexual, Trans and Intersex Association. 2017. "State-Sponsored Homophobia: A World Survey of Sexual Orientation Laws: Criminalization, Protection and Recognition." Geneva: ILGA.

Castoriadis, Cornelius. 1987. *The Imaginary Institution of Society*, translated by Kathleen Blamey. Cambridge: MIT Press.

___. 1997. *World in Fragments: Writings on Politics, Society, Psychoanalysis, and the Imagination*, edited & translated by David Ames Curtis. Meridian. Stanford, CA: Stanford University Press.

CBC News. 2015. "Abuse, Trauma Leads Women in Prison to Cry Out for Help." January 6. <cbc.ca/news/health/abuse-trauma-leads-women-in-prison-to-cry-out-for-help-1.2891680.

___. 2019. "Why Incels Are a 'Real and Present Threat' for Canadians." *The Fifth Estate*, January 27. <cbc.ca/news/canada/incel-threat-canadians-fifth-estate-1.4992184.

Centers for Disease Control and Prevention. 2021. "Adverse Childhood Experiences (ACES)." May 21. <cdc.gov/violenceprevention/aces/index.html>.

Chatterton, Paul. 2010. "So What Does It Mean to Be Anti-Capitalist? Conversations with Activists from Urban Social Centres." *Urban Studies* 47, 6: 1205–1224. <doi.org/10.1177/0042098009360222>.

Collier, George. 1999. *Basta!: Land and the Zapatista Rebellion in Chiapas*, revised edition. Oakland: Food First Books.

Combahee River Collective. n.d. "History Is a Weapon: The Combahee River Collective Statement." <historyisaweapon.com/defcon1/combrivercoll.html>.

Conant, Jeff. 2010. *A Poetics of Resistance: The Revolutionary Public Relations of the Zapatista Insurgency*. Oakland: AK Press.

Conway, Janet. 2004. *Identity, Place, Knowledge: Social Movements Contesting Globalization*. Halifax, NS: Fernwood.

Coulthard, Glen Sean. 2014. *Red Skin, White Masks: Rejecting the Colonial Politics of Recognition*. Minneapolis: University of Minnesota Press.

Crenshaw, Kimberle. 1989. "Demarginalizing the Intersection of Race and Sex: A Black Feminist Critique of Antidiscrimination Doctrine, Feminist Theory and Antiracist Policies." *University of Chicago Legal Forum* 1: 139–167.

Crines, Andrew. 2017. "The Fight Against the 'Post-Truth' and 'Fake News Era.'" *HuffPost UK*. February 16. <huffingtonpost.co.uk/dr-andrew-crines/the-fight-against-the-pos_b_14763806.html>.

Daschuk, James W. 2013. *Clearing the Plains: Disease, Politics of Starvation, and the Loss of Aboriginal Life*. Regina: University of Regina Press.

References

Davis, Angela Y. 2003. *Are Prisons Obsolete?* Open Media Book. New York: Seven Stories Press.

Della Porta, Donatella, Hanspeter Kriesi, and Dieter Rucht. 2009. *Social Movements in a Globalizing World*. Basingstoke: Palgrave Macmillan.

Dixon, Chris. 2014. *Another Politics: Talking across Today's Transformative Movements*. Berkeley: University of California Press.

Du Bois, W.E.B. 2017. *The Souls of Black Folk*. Brooklyn, NY: Restless Books.

Durr, Andy. 1988. "William King of Brighton: Co-Operation's Prophet." In *New Views of Co-Operation*, edited by S. Yeo. New York: Routledge.

Dwivedi, Supriya. 2019. "Our National Silence on Bill 21." *The Walrus* [blog]. October 18. <thewalrus.ca/our-national-silence-on-bill-21/>.

"Early Social Research and Martineau." 2021. Social Science LibreTexts, February 20. <socialsci.libretexts.org/Bookshelves/Sociology/Introduction_to_Sociology/Book%3A_Sociology_(Boundless)/01%3A_Sociology/1.02%3A_The_History_of_Sociology/1.2C%3A_Early_Social_Research_and_Martineau>.

Economist. 2008. "Building BRICs of Growth." *The Economist*, June 5. <economist.com/finance-and-economics/2008/06/05/building-brics-of-growth>.

____. 2017. "An Improbable Global Shortage: Sand." *The Economist*, March 30. <economist.com/finance-and-economics/2017/03/30/an-improbable-global-shortage-sand>.

Edgar, Andrew, and Peter Sedgwick (eds.). 2005. *Cultural Theory: The Key Concepts*. London: Routledge.

Ehrenreich, Barbara, and Arlie Russell Hochschild (eds.). 2004. *Global Woman: Nannies, Maids, and Sex Workers in the New Economy*. New York: Metropolitan Books/Holt.

Ellison, Treva. 2017. "Is It More Acceptable to Be Transgender than Transracial?" OZY, June 6. <ozy.com/pov/is-it-more-acceptable-to-be-transgender-than-transracial/78947>.

Ellwood, Wayne. 2010. *The No-Nonsense Guide to Globalization*, third edition. Toronto, ON: New Internationalist/Between the Lines.

Engler, Yves. 2009. *The Black Book of Canadian Foreign Policy*. Vancouver: Fernwood Pub./Red Pub.

Epstein, Barbara. 1991. *Political Protest and Cultural Revolution Nonviolent Direct Action in the 1970s and 1980s*. Berkeley: University of California Press.

Epstein, Rachel. 2012. "Queer Parenting in Canada: Looking Backward, Looking Forward." In *Queerly Canadian: An Introductory Reader in Sexuality Studies*. Toronto: Canadian Scholars' Press.

Eriksen, Thomas Hylland. 2010. *Small Places, Large Issues: An Introduction to Social and Cultural Anthropology*, third edition. London: Pluto Press.

Eschner, Kat. 2017. "Four Things that Happen When a Language Dies." Smithsonian, February 21. <smithsonianmag.com/smart-news/four-things-happen-when-language-dies-and-one-thing-you-can-do-help-180962188/>.

Evans, Robert. 2019. "Shitposting, Inspirational Terrorism, and the Christchurch Mosque Massacre." Bellingcat, March 15. <bellingcat.com/news/rest-of-world/2019/03/15/shitposting-inspirational-terrorism-and-the-christchurch-mosque-massacre/>.

Fanon, Frantz. 1982. *Black Skin, White Masks*. New York: Grove Press.

Farmer, Paul. 2004. "An Anthropology of Structural Violence." *Current Anthropology* 45, 3: 305–325. <doi.org/10.1086/382250>.

Farsetta, Diane, and Daniel Price. 2006. "Fake TV News: Widespread and Undisclosed." PR Watch, March 16. <prwatch.org/fakenews/execsummary>.

Fawaz, Ramzi. 2016. *The New Mutants: Superheroes and the Radical Imagination of American Comics*. New York; London: New York University Press.

Featherstone, David. 2012. *Solidarity: Hidden Histories and Geographies of Internationalism*. London; New York: Zed Books.

Federici, Silvia. 2003. *Caliban and the Witch : Women, the Body and Primitive Accumulation*. New York; London: Autonomedia; Pluto.

___. 2012. *Revolution at Point Zero: Housework, Reproduction, and Feminist Struggle*. Oakland, CA: PM Press.

Federici, Silvia, and Arlen Austin (eds.). 2018. *The New York Wages for Housework Committee 1972–1977: History, Theory and Documents*. Brooklyn: Autonomedia.

Finchelstein, Federico. 2017. *From Fascism to Populism in History*. Oakland, CA: University of California Press.

Finkler, Kaja. 2001. "The Kin in the Gene." *Current Anthropology* 42, 2: 235–263. <doi.org/10.1086/320004>.

Foran, John (ed.). 2003. *The Future of Revolutions: Rethinking Radical Change in the Age of Globalization*. London; New York: Zed Books.

Foucault, Michel. 1995. *Discipline and Punish: The Birth of the Prison*, translated by Alan Sheridan. New York: Vintage Books.

Frampton, Caelie, Gary Kinsman, A.K. Thompson, and Kate Tilleczek (eds.). 2006. *Sociology for Changing the World: Social Movements/Social Research*. Black Point, NS: Fernwood Publishing.

Gander, Kashmira. 2019. "California Man Puts Giant Swastika in His Front Yard, Neighbors Are Offended, Worried about Property Value." Newsweek, June 6. <newsweek.com/california-man-puts-giant-swastika-front-yard-1442471>.

Gangestad, Steven W., and Martie G. Haselton. 2015. "Human Estrus: Implications for Relationship Science." *Current Opinion in Psychology* 1 (February): 45–51.

<doi.org/10.1016/j.copsyc.2014.12.007>.

Gaudet, Maxime. 2018. "Police-Reported Hate Crime in Canada, 2016." *Juristat* 38, 1: 31.

Geertz, Clifford. 1973. *The Interpretation of Cultures: Selected Essays*. New York: Basic Books.

Ghabrial, Sarah. 2008. "Access to Abortions." *Section15.Ca*. <section15.ca/features/people/2008/09/16/access_to_abortions/.

Gibson-Graham, J.K. 2006. *A Postcapitalist Politics*. Minneapolis: University of Minnesota Press.

Gilly, Adolfo. 1998. "Chiapas and the Rebellion of the Enchanted World." In *Rural Revolt in Mexico: US Intervention and the Domain of Subaltern Politics*, edited by Daniel Nugent. Durham: Duke University Press.

Gilmour, Jared. 2019. "'A Lot of Regret:' California Man Hides Swastika Landscaping with Blankets — for Now." *The Sacramento Bee*, June 12. <sacbee.com/news/california/article231497228.html>.

Giroux, Henry A. 2002. *Breaking in to the Movies: Film and the Culture of Politics*. Malden, MA: Blackwell Publishers.

Goodman, Amy, and David Goodman. 2007. *Static: Government Liars, Media Cheerleaders, and the People Who Fight Back*. New York; London: Hyperion.

Goodwin, Jeff, James Jasper, and Francesca Polletta. 2001. *Passionate Politics: Emotions and Social Movements*. Chicago: University of Chicago Press.

Goodwin, Kim. 2018. "Mansplaining, Explained in One Simple Chart." BBC, July 29. <bbc.com/worklife/article/20180727-mansplaining-explained-in-one-chart>.

Government of Canada. 2020. "Annual Report of the Office of the Correctional Investigator 2014–2015 — Office of the Correctional Investigator." Office of the Correctional Investigator, April 16. <oci-bec.gc.ca/cnt/rpt/annrpt/ann-rpt20142015-eng.aspx>.

Graeber, David. 2004. *Fragments of an Anarchist Anthropology*. Chicago: Prickly Paradigm Press.

___. 2013. *The Democracy Project: A History, a Crisis, a Movement*. New York: Spiegel & Grau.

Gramsci, Antonio. 1985. *Selections from the Prison Notebooks of Antonio Gramsci*, translated by Quintin Hoare. New York: International Publ.

Graveland, Bill. 2016. "Police Say Increasing Domestic Abuse in Calgary Tied to Economic Downturn." *Globe and Mail*, January 11. <theglobeandmail.com/news/alberta/police-say-economic-downturn-tied-to-increasing-domestic-abuse-in-calgary/article32622377/.

Guardian. 2013. "Margaret Thatcher: A Life in Quotes." *The Guardian*, April 8. <theguardian.com/politics/2013/apr/08/margaret-thatcher-quotes>.

Hackett, Conrad, and David McClendon. 2017. "Christians Remain World's Largest Religious Group, but They Are Declining in Europe." *Pew Research Center* [blog]. April 5. <pewresearch.org/fact-tank/2017/04/05/christians-remain-worlds-largest-religious-group-but-they-are-declining-in-europe/>.

Haiven, Max. 2014. *Crises of Imagination, Crises of Power: Capitalism, Creativity and the Commons*. London; New York: Halifax; Winnipeg: Zed Books; Fernwood Publishing.

Haiven, Max, and Alex Khasnabish. 2014. *The Radical Imagination: Social Movement Research in the Age of Austerity*. Halifax; London: Zed Books/Fernwood Publishing.

Hall, Stuart. 2007. "Encoding, Decoding." In *The Cultural Studies Reader*, edited by Simon During. New York: Routledge.

Hardt, Michael, and Antonio Negri. 2000. *Empire*. Cambridge, MA: Harvard University Press.

Harman, Chris. 2000. "Anti-Capitalism: Theory and Practice." *International Socialism: A Quarterly Journal of Socialist Theory*. <pubs.socialistreviewindex.org.uk/isj88/harman.htm>.

Harvey, Neil. 1998. *The Chiapas Rebellion: The Struggle for Land and Democracy*. Durham: Duke University Press.

Haworth, Robert H., and John M. Elmore (eds.). 2017. *Out of the Ruins: The Emergence of Radical Informal Learning Spaces*. Oakland, CA: PM Press.

Hemingway, Alex, and Michal Rozworski. 2020. "Canadian Billionaires' Wealth Skyrocketing amid the Pandemic." *Policy Note*, September 16. <policynote.ca/billionaires-wealth/>.

Hett, Benjamin Carter. 2018. *The Death of Democracy: Hitler's Rise to Power and the Downfall of the Weimar Republic*. New York: Allen Lane. <overdrive.com/search?q=21B19C75-2F59-423A-B661-503DD5945C2B>.

Hirst, Martin. 2017. "Towards a Political Economy of Fake News." *The Political Economy of Communication* 5, 2: 82–94.

Holloway, John. 2002. *Change the World without Taking Power: The Meaning of Revolution Today*. London: Pluto Press.

___. 2010. *Crack Capitalism*. London: Pluto.

Horkheimer, Max, and Theodor W. Adorno. 2002. *Dialectic of Enlightenment: Philosophical Fragments*, edited by Gunzelin Schmid Noerr. Stanford, CA: Stanford University Press.

Hunt, Allcott, and Matthew Gentzkow. 2017. "Social Media and Fake News in the 2016 Election." *Journal of Economic Perspectives* 31, 2: 211–236.

James, C.L.R. 1989. *The Black Jacobins: Toussaint L'Ouverture and the San Domingo Revolution*. New York: Vintage Books.

References

Jasper, James. 1999. *The Art of Moral Protest: Culture, Biography, and Creativity in Social Movements*. Chicago: University of Chicago Press.

Jones, A.G., and N.L. Ratterman. 2009. "Mate Choice and Sexual Selection: What Have We Learned since Darwin?" *Proceedings of the National Academy of Sciences* 106 (Supplement 1): 10001–8. <doi.org/10.1073/pnas.0901129106>.

Jones, J.P. 2010. "Fake News vs. Real News: The Case of The Daily Show and CNN." In *Entertaining Politics: Satiric Television and Political Engagement*. Lanham, MD: Rowman & Littlefield.

Juris, Jeffrey. 2008. *Networking Futures: The Movements against Corporate Globalization*. Durham: Duke University Press.

Karpowitz, Christopher F., Tali Mendelberg, and Lee Shaker. 2012. "Gender Inequality in Deliberative Participation." *American Political Science Review* 106, 3: 533–547. <doi.org/10.1017/S0003055412000329>.

Katsiaficas, George. 1987. *The Imagination of the New Left: A Global Analysis of 1968*. Boston: South End Press.

Keck, Margaret, and Kathryn Sikkink. 1998. *Activists beyond Borders: Advocacy Networks in International Politics*. Ithaca: Cornell University Press.

Kelley, Robin. 2002. *Freedom Dreams: The Black Radical Imagination*. Boston: Beacon Press.

Khaldarova, Irina, and Mervi Pantti. 2016. "Fake News: The Narrative Battle over the Ukrainian Conflict." *Journalism Practice* 10, 7: 891–901. <doi.org/10.1080/17512786.2016.1163237>.

Khasnabish, Alex. 2008. *Zapatismo beyond Borders: New Imaginations of Political Possibility*. Toronto: University of Toronto Press.

____. 2010. *Zapatistas: Rebellion from the Grassroots to the Global*. London: Zed Press.

Kimmel, Michael S. 2015. *Angry White Men: American Masculinity at the End of an Era*. New York: Nation Books.

Kingsnorth, Paul. 2004. *One No, Many Yeses: A Journey to the Heart of the Global Resistance Movement*. London: Free Press.

Kirby, Alex. 2016. "Rise in Plunder of Earth's Natural Resources." *Climate News Network* [blog]. July 23. <climatenewsnetwork.net/rise-in-plunder-of-earths-natural-resources/>.

Klein, Naomi. 2000. *No Logo: Taking Aim at the Brand Bullies*. Toronto: Knopf Canada.

____. 2002. *Fences and Windows: Dispatches from the Front Lines of the Globalization Debate*. Toronto: Vintage Canada.

Knight Foundation. 2018. "American Views: Trust, Media and Democracy." Knight Foundation. January 16. <knightfoundation.org/reports/american-views-trust-media-and-democracy/>.

Know Your Meme. "Mansplaining." n.d. https://knowyourmeme.com/memes/mansplaining.

Kuhn, Thomas S., and Ian Hacking. 2012. *The Structure of Scientific Revolutions*, fourth edition. Chicago; London: University of Chicago Press.

Larsen, C.S. 2003. "Equality for the Sexes in Human Evolution? Early Hominid Sexual Dimorphism and Implications for Mating Systems and Social Behavior." *Proceedings of the National Academy of Sciences* 100, 16: 9103–4. <doi.org/10.1073/pnas.1633678100>.

Leroux, Darryl. 2018. "Self-Made Métis." *Maisonneuve*, November 1. <maisonneuve.org/article/2018/11/1/self-made-metis/>.

Linebaugh, Peter. 2008. *The Magna Carta Manifesto: Liberties and Commons for All.* Berkeley: University of California Press.

Linebaugh, Peter, and Marcus Rediker. 2000. *The Many-Headed Hydra: Sailors, Slaves, Commoners, and the Hidden History of the Revolutionary Atlantic.* Boston: Beacon Press.

MacIntosh, H., K.D. Reissing, and H. Andruff. 2010. "Same-Sex Marriage in Canada: The Impact of Legal Marriage on the First Cohort of Gay and Lesbian Canadians to Wed." *Canadian Journal of Human Sexuality* 19, 3: 79–90.

Mackenzie, Hugh. 2017. "Throwing Money at the Problem: 10 Years of Executive Compensation." Canadian Centre for Policy Alternatives. <policyalternatives.ca/sites/default/files/uploads/publications/National%20Office/2017/01/Throwing_Money_at_the_Problem_CEO_Pay.pdf>.

Maeckelbergh, Marianne. 2009. *The Will of the Many*. London: Pluto Press.

Mansbridge, Jane, and Aldon Morris, eds. 2001. *Oppositional Consciousness: The Subjective Roots of Social Protest*. Chicago: University of Chicago Press.

Marantz, Andrew. 2019. *Antisocial: Online Extremists, Techno-Utopians, and the Hijacking of the American Conversation*. New York: Viking.

Marcos, Subcomandante Insurgente. 2002. "Testimonies of the First Day." In *The Zapatista Reader*, edited by Tom Hayden. New York: Thunder's Mouth Press.

___. 2004. "The Seven Loose Pieces of the Global Jigsaw Puzzle (Neoliberalism as a Puzzle)." In *¡Ya Basta!: Ten Years of the Zapatista Uprising*, edited by Žiga Vodovnik. Oakland: AK Press.

Marcuse, Herbert. 1964. *One-Dimensional Man: Studies in the Ideology of Advanced Industrial Society*. Boston, MA: Beacon Press.

Marlowe, Frank W., and J. Colette Berbesque. 2012. "The Human Operational Sex Ratio: Effects of Marriage, Concealed Ovulation, and Menopause on Mate Competition." *Journal of Human Evolution* 63, 6: 834–842. <doi.org/10.1016/j.jhevol.2012.09.004>.

Maynard, Robyn. 2017. *Policing Black Lives: State Violence in Canada from Slavery to the Present*. Halifax: Fernwood Publishing.

McCarthy, John, and Mayer Zald. 1977. "Resource Mobilization and Social Movements: A Partial Theory." *The American Journal of Sociology* 82, 6: 1212–41.

McGlade, Christophe, and Paul Ekins. 2015. "The Geographical Distribution of Fossil Fuels Unused When Limiting Global Warming to 2°C." *Nature* 517 (January): 187–190.

McKay, Ian. 2005. *Rebels, Reds, Radicals: Rethinking Canada's Left History*. Toronto: Between the Lines.

McNair, Brian. 2018. *Fake News: Falsehood, Fabrication and Fantasy in Journalism*. New York: Routledge.

McNally, David. 2002. *Another World Is Possible : Globalization and Anti-Capitalism*. Winnipeg: Arbeiter Ring Publishing.

Mehta, Pankaj. 2014. "There's a Gene for That." <jacobinmag.com/2014/01/theres-a-gene-for-that>.

Melucci, Alberto. 1996. *Challenging Codes: Collective Action in the Information Age*. Cambridge Cultural Social Studies. Cambridge: Cambridge University Press.

Meyer, David, and Debra Minkoff. 2004. "Conceptualizing Political Opportunity." *Social Forces* 82 (June): 1457–92. https://doi.org/10.1353/sof.2004.0082.

Midnight Notes Collective. 2001. *Auroras of the Zapatistas: Local and Global Struggles of the Fourth World War*. Brooklyn: Autonomedia.

Mies, Maria. 1986. *Patriarchy and Accumulation on a World Scale: Women in the International Division of Labour*. London: Zed Books.

Mignolo, Walter. 2011. *The Darker Side of Western Modernity: Global Futures, Decolonial Options*. Latin America Otherwise: Languages, Empires, Nations. Durham: Duke University Press.

Miller, Niki A., and Lisa M. Najavits. 2012. "Creating Trauma-Informed Correctional Care: A Balance of Goals and Environment." *European Journal of Psychotraumatology* 3, 1: 17246. <doi.org/10.3402/ejpt.v3i0.17246>.

Mills, Charles W. 1997. *The Racial Contract*. Ithaca: Cornell University Press.

Moore, Jason W. 2015. *Capitalism in the Web of Life: Ecology and the Accumulation of Capital*. New York: Verso.

___ (ed.). 2016. *Anthropocene or Capitalocene? Nature, History, and the Crisis of Capitalism*. Oakland, CA: PM Press.

Morris, Ruth. 1999. *Why Transformative Justice?* Toronto: Rittenhouse.

___. 2000. *Stories of Transformative Justice*. Toronto: Canadian Scholars' Press.

Mosendz, Polly. 2015. "Family Accuses NAACP Leader Rachel Dolezal of Falsely Portraying Herself as Black." Newsweek, June 12. <newsweek.com/family-accuses-naacp-leader-rachel-dolezal-falsely-portraying-herself-black-342511>.

Moyser, Melissa, and Amanda Burlock. 2018. "Time Use: Total Work Burden, Unpaid Work, and Leisure." Statistics Canada, July 30. <www150.statcan.gc.ca/n1/pub/89-503-x/2015001/article/54931-eng.htm>.

Mumford, Lewis. 1964. *The Myth Of The Machine: The Pentagon of Power*. <archive.org/details/in.ernet.dli.2015.214098>.

Muñoz Ramírez, Gloria. 2008. *The Fire & the Word: A History of the Zapatista Movement*. San Francisco: City Lights Books.

NCTR n.d. "About/NCTR." <nctr.ca/about/>.

Niemi, Rami. 2018. "Fake News 2.0: AI Will Soon Be Able to Mimic Any Human Voice." *Wired UK*, August 1. <wired.co.uk/article/fake-voices-will-become-worryingly-accurate.

Nocella, Anthony J. 2011. "An Overview of the History and Theory of Transformative Justice." *Peace and Conflict Review* 6, 1.

Notes from Nowhere (ed.). 2003. *We Are Everywhere: The Irresistible Rise of Global Anticapitalism*. New York: Verso.

Olesen, Thomas. 2005. *International Zapatismo: The Construction of Solidarity in the Age of Globalization*. London: Zed Press.

Ortner, Sherry B. 2017. "Social Impact without Social Justice: Film and Politics in the Neoliberal Landscape." *American Ethnologist* 44, 3: 528–359. <doi.org/10.1111/amet.12527>.

Owen, David. 2017. "The World Is Running Out of Sand." *New Yorker*, May 22. <newyorker.com/magazine/2017/05/29/the-world-is-running-out-of-sand>.

Panofsky, Aaron, and Joan Donovan. 2019. "Genetic Ancestry Testing among White Nationalists: From Identity Repair to Citizen Science." *Social Studies of Science*, July 2. <doi.org/10.1177/0306312719861434>.

Patel, Raj. 2009. *The Value of Nothing: How to Reshape Market Society and Redefine Democracy*. New York: Picador.

Paul, Daniel N. 2006. *We Were Not the Savages: Collision between European and Native American Civilizations*, third edition. Halifax, NS: Fernwood Publishing.

Paxton, Robert O. 2004. *The Anatomy of Fascism*. New York: Vintage Books.

Pew Research Center. 2017. "The Changing Global Religious Landscape." *Pew Research Center's Religion & Public Life Project* [blog]. April 5. <pewforum.org/2017/04/05/the-changing-global-religious-landscape/>.

Piven, Frances, and Richard Cloward. 1977. *Poor People's Movements : Why They Succeed, How They Fail*. New York: Pantheon Books.

Pizzigati, Sam. 2018. "The World Would Be a Better Place Without the Rich." *Jacobin*, October 17. <jacobinmag.com/2018/10/rich-people-philanthropy-inequality-wealth>.

Polletta, Francesca. 2002. *Freedom Is an Endless Meeting: Democracy in American Social Movements*. Chicago: University of Chicago Press.

References

Polletta, Francesca, and James Jasper. 2001. "Collective Identity and Social Movements." *Annual Review of Sociology* 27: 283–305.

Prashad, Vijay. 2008. *The Darker Nations: A People's History of the Third World*. New York; London: New Press.

Price, David H. 2011. *Weaponizing Anthropology : Social Science in Service of the Militarized State*. Edinburgh: AK Press.

Prontzos, Peter G. 2019. "The Concept of 'Race' Is a Lie." *Scientific American* Blog Network. <blogs.scientificamerican.com/observations/the-concept-of-race-is-a-lie/>.

Quammen, David. 2020. "We Made the Coronavirus Epidemic." *New York Times*, January 28. <nytimes.com/2020/01/28/opinion/coronavirus-china.html>.

Rediker, Marcus. 2004. *Villains of All Nations: Atlantic Pirates in the Golden Age*. Boston: Beacon Press.

____. 2007. *The Slave Ship: A Human History*. New York: Viking.

Reeve, Elspeth. 2016. "Alt-Right Trolls Are Getting 23andme Genetic Tests to 'Prove' Their Whiteness." *Vice News* [blog], October 9. <news.vice.com/en_us/article/vbygqm/alt-right-trolls-are-getting-23andme-genetic-tests-to-prove-their-whiteness>.

Reilly, Ian. 2013. "From Critique to Mobilization: The Yes Men and the Utopian Politics of Satricial Fake News." *International Journal of Communication* 7: 1243–64.

____. 2018. "F for Fake: Propaganda! Hoaxing! Hacking! Partisanship! And Activism! In the Fake News Ecology." *The Journal of American Culture* 41, 2: 139–152. <doi.org/10.1111/jacc.12834>.

Reinsborough, Patrick, and Doyle Canning. 2010. *Re:Imagining Change: How to Use Story-Based Strategy to Win Campaigns, Build Movements, and Change the World*. Winnipeg: Fernwood Publishing.

Reuters. 2018. "Canada Hate Crimes Up 47% as Muslims, Jews and Black People Targeted." *The Guardian*, November 29. <theguardian.com/world/2018/nov/29/canada-hate-crimes-rise-muslims-jews-black-people>.

Reynolds, Matt. 2018. "Technology Can't Rescue Us from AI-Generated Fake News." *Wired UK*, September 1. <wired.co.uk/article/fake-images-video-nvidia-news-online-twitter-facebook-digital-forensics>.

Richie, Beth. 2012. *Arrested Justice: Black Women, Violence, and America's Prison Nation*. New York: New York University Press.

Richmond, Brian, and J. Colette Berbesque. 2001. "Origin of Human Bipedalism: The Knuckle-Walking Hypothesis Revisited." *Year Book of Physical Anthropology* 44: 70–105.

Roediger, David R. 2007. *The Wages of Whiteness: Race and the Making of the Amer-

ican Working Class. London; New York: Verso.

____. 2017. "Making Solidarity Uneasy: Cautions on a Keyword from Black Lives Matter to the Past." In *Class, Race, and Marxism*. New York; London: Verso.

Roitman, Janet L. 2013. *Anti-Crisis.* Durham: Duke University Press.

Ross, John. 2000. *The War against Oblivion: Zapatista Chronicles, 1994–2000.* Monroe, ME: Common Courage Press.

Rubin, G.S. 1984. "Thinking Sex: Notes for a Radical Theory of the Politics of Sexuality." In *Pleasure and Danger: Exploring Female Sexuality*, edited by C. Vance. Boston: Routledge & K. Paul.

Rymer, Russ. 2012. "Vanishing Voices." *National Geographic*, July 1. <nationalgeographic.com/magazine/2012/07/vanishing-languages/>.

Sachs, Jeffrey Adam. 2018. "There Is No Campus Free Speech Crisis: A Close Look at the Evidence." Niskanen Center, April 27. <niskanencenter.org/there-is-no-campus-free-speech-crisis-a-close-look-at-the-evidence/>.

Sahlins, Marshall. 2011a. "What Kinship Is (Part One)." *Journal of the Royal Anthropological Institute* 17, 1: 2–19.

____. 2011b. "What Kinship Is (Part Two)." *Journal of the Royal Anthropological Institute* 17, 2: 227–242.

Sassen, Saskia. 2014. *Expulsions: Brutality and Complexity in the Global Economy.* Cambridge, MA: Belknap Press of Harvard University Press.

Schneider, David. 2004. "What Is Kinship All About?" In *Kinship and Family: An Anthropological Reader*, edited by Robert Parkin and Linda Stone. Malden, MA: Blackwell Pub.

Scott, James C. 2017. *Against the Grain: A Deep History of the Earliest States.* New Haven: Yale University Press.

Section 15.ca. 1997. "Women Take the Right to Vote." May 30. <section15.ca/features/news/1997/05/30/women_take_right_vote/>.

Sen, Jai (ed.). 2017. *The Movements of Movements. Part 1: What Makes Us Move?* Challenging Empires Series, volume 4. Oakland, CA; New Delhi: PM Press; OpenWord.

Sheff, Elisabeth. 2011. "Polyamorous Families, Same-Sex Marriage, and the Slippery Slope." *Journal of Contemporary Ethnography* 40, 5: 487–520. <doi.org/10.1177/0891241611413578>.

Sherwood, Harriet. 2018. "Religion: Why Faith Is Becoming More and More Popular." *The Guardian*, August 27. <theguardian.com/news/2018/aug/27/religion-why-is-faith-growing-and-what-happens-next>.

Shingler, Benjamin. 2019. "Quebec's Religious Symbols Ban Causes 'irreparable Harm,' Teachers Tell Court." CBC, September 25. <cbc.ca/news/canada/montreal/quebec-teachers-religious-symbols-ban-1.5297120>.

Silverman, Craig, and Jeremy Singer-Vine. 2016. "The True Story behind the Biggest Fake News Hit of the Election." *BuzzFeed News*, December 16. <buzzfeed-news.com/article/craigsilverman/the-strangest-fake-news-empire.

Sitrin, Marina. 2012. *Everyday Revolutions: Horizontalism and Autonomy in Argentina*. London; New York: Zed Books.

Small, Meredith F. 1993. *Female Choices: Sexual Behavior of Female Primates*. Ithaca, NY: Cornell University Press.

Snyder, Kieran. 2014. "How to Get Ahead as a Woman in Tech: Interrupt Men." Slate Magazine, July 23. <slate.com/human-interest/2014/07/study-men-interrupt-women-more-in-tech-workplaces-but-high-ranking-women-learn-to-interrupt.html>.

Snyder, Timothy. 2016. *Black Earth: The Holocaust as History and Warning*. New York: Tim Duggan Books.

Solnit, David (ed.). 2004. *Globalize Liberation: How to Uproot the System and Build a Better World*. San Francisco: City Lights Books.

____. 2009. "The Battle of the Story of the Battle of Seattle." In *The Battle of the Story of the Battle of Seattle*, edited by David Solnit and Rebecca Solnit. Oakland, CA: AK Press.

Solnit, David, and Rebecca Solnit. 2009. *The Battle of the Story of the Battle of Seattle*. Edinburgh Oakland, CA: AK Press.

Solnit, Rebecca. 2012. "Men Explain Things to Me." Guernica, August 20. <guernicamag.com/rebecca-solnit-men-explain-things-to-me/>.

Springer, Simon. 2020. "Toilet Paper Wars and the Shithouse of Capitalism." *Common Dreams*, March 15. <commondreams.org/views/2020/03/15/toilet-paper-wars-and-shithouse-capitalism>.

Staggenborg, Suzanne. 2012. *Social Movements*. Don Mills, ON: Oxford University Press.

Stanyon, R., S. Consigliere, and M.A. Morescalchi. 1993. "Cranial Capacity in Hominid Evolution." *Human Evolution* 8, 3: 205–216. <doi.org/10.1007/BF02436715>.

Statistics Canada. 2013. "2011 National Household Survey Profile - Province/Territory." <www12.statcan.gc.ca/nhs-enm/2011/dp-pd/prof/details/page.cfm?Lang=E&Geo1=PR&Code1=01&Data=Count&SearchText=Canada&SearchType=Begins&SearchPR=01&A1=Religion&B1=All&Custom=&TABID=1.

____. 2017a. "The Daily — Police-Reported Crime Statistics, 2016." July 24. <www150.statcan.gc.ca/n1/daily-quotidien/170724/dq170724b-eng.htm>.

____. 2017b. "Census in Brief: Same-Sex Couples in Canada in 2016." August 2. <www12.statcan.gc.ca/census-recensement/2016/as-sa/98-200-x/2016007/98-

200-x2016007-eng.cfm>.

___. 2017c. "Census in Brief: Young Adults Living with Their Parents in Canada in 2016." August 2. <www12.statcan.gc.ca/census-recensement/2016/as-sa/98-200-x/2016008/98-200-x2016008-eng.cfm>.

___. 2017d. "Portrait of Households and Families in Canada." August 2. <www150.statcan.gc.ca/n1/pub/11-627-m/11-627-m2017024-eng.htm>.

___. 2017e. "The Daily — Families, Households and Marital Status: Key Results from the 2016 Census." August 2. <www150.statcan.gc.ca/n1/daily-quotidi-en/170802/dq170802a-eng.htm>.

Stauber, John C., and Sheldon Rampton. 1995. *Toxic Sludge Is Good for You: Lies, Damn Lies, and the Public Relations Industry*. Monroe, ME: Common Courage Press.

Stechyson, Natalie. 2019. "Dads Are Happier than Moms, and It Might Be Because They Play More: Study." 2019. *HuffPost*, February 6. <huffpost.com/archive/ca/entry/dads-happier-than-moms-study_a_23663122?utm_source=headtop-ics&utm_medium=news&utm_campaign=2019-02-07>.

Steffen, Will, Wendy Broadgate, Lisa Deutsch, et al. 2015. "The Trajectory of the Anthropocene: The Great Acceleration." *The Anthropocene Review* 2, 1: 81–98. <doi.org/10.1177/2053019614564785>.

Stote, Karen. 2015. *An Act of Genocide: Colonialism and the Sterilization of Aborigi-nal Women*. Black Point, NS; Winnipeg: Fernwood Publishing.

Subramanian, Samanth. 2017. "Inside the Macedonian Fake News Complex." *Wired*, February 15. <wired.com/2017/02/veles-macedonia-fake-news/>.

TallBear, Kim. 2013. "Genomic Articulations of Indigeneity." *Social Studies of Sci-ence* 43, 4: 509–33. <doi.org/10.1177/0306312713483893>.

Tang, Jackie, Nora Galbraith, and Johnny Truong. 2019. "Living Alone in Canada." Statistics Canada, March 6. <www150.statcan.gc.ca/n1/pub/75-006-x/2019001/article/00003-eng.htm>.

Taub, Amanda. 2017. "The Real Story About Fake News Is Partisanship." *New York Times*, January 11. <nytimes.com/2017/01/11/upshot/the-real-story-about-fake-news-is-partisanship.html>.

Taylor, Astra, Carla Blumenkranz, Keith Gessen, et al. (eds.). 2011. *Occupy!: Scenes from Occupied America*. London: Verso.

Taylor, Charles. 2004. *Modern Social Imaginaries*. Durham: Duke University Press.

Third Eye Collective. 2017. "Fear of a Black Feminist Nation." *Third Eye Collective* [blog]. April 30. <thirdeyecollective.wordpress.com/2017/04/30/fear-of-a-black-feminist-nation/>.

Thornes, Robin. 1988. "Change and Continuity in the Development of Cooperation, 1827–1844." In *New Views of Co-Operation*, edited by S. Yeo. New York: Routledge.

References

Touraine, Alain. 1988. *Return of the Actor: Social Theory in Postindustrial Society.* Minneapolis: University of Minnesota Press.

Tremblay, M. 2016. "Introduction." In *Queer Mobilizations.* Vancouver: UBC Press.

Truscello, Michael. 2020. *Infrastructural Brutalism: Art and the Necropolitics of Infrastructure.* Infrastructures. Cambridge: The MIT Press.

United Nations Office on Genocide Prevention and the Responsibility to Protect. n.d. <un.org/en/genocideprevention/genocide.shtml.

Uprichard, Lucy. 2019. "What Is Quebec's Secularism Law – and How Does It Affect Women?" *Chatelaine*, November 6. <chatelaine.com/news/quebec-secularism-bill-21-women/>.

Uyehara, Mari. 2018. "The Free Speech Grifters." *GQ*, March 19. <gq.com/story/free-speech-grifting>.

Vancouver Aboriginal Transformative Justice Services Society. n.d. "What Is Transformative Justice." <vatjss.com/what-is-transformative-justice>.

Vaughan, Adam. 2016. "Human Impact Has Pushed Earth into the Anthropocene, Scientists Say." *The Guardian*, January 7. <theguardian.com/environment/2016/jan/07/human-impact-has-pushed-earth-into-the-anthropocene-scientists-say>.

Veracini, Lorenzo. 2016. "Colonialism." In *Keywords for Radicals: The Contested Vocabulary of Late-Capitalist Struggle*, edited by Kelly Fritsch, Clare O'Connor, and AK Thompson. Chico, CA: AK Press.

Walia, Harsha. 2013. *Undoing Border Imperialism.* Oakland, CA: AK Press.

___. 2021. *Border and Rule: Global Migration, Capitalism and the Rise of Racist Nationalism.* Halifax, NS: Fernwood Publishing.

Warner, Michael. 2000. *The Trouble with Normal: Sex, Politics, and the Ethics of Queer Life.* Cambridge, MA: Harvard University Press.

Wartzman, Rick. 2020. "'We Were Shocked': RAND Study Uncovers Massive Income Shift to the Top 1%." Fast Company, September 14. <medium.com/fast-company/we-were-shocked-rand-study-uncovers-massive-income-shift-to-the-top-1-a4970c2e0863>.

Wilson, Shawn. 2009. *Research Is Ceremony: Indigenous Research Methods.* Black Point, NS: Fernwood Publishing.

Wolf, Eric R. 2010. *Europe and the People without History.* Berkeley: University of California Press.

Womack, John. 1999. *Rebellion in Chiapas: An Historical Reader.* New York: New Press.

Wong, Sam. 2016. "Marks of the Anthropocene: 7 Signs We Have Made Our Own Epoch." *New Scientist*, January 7. <newscientist.com/article/dn28741-marks-of-the-anthropocene-7-signs-we-have-made-our-own-epoch/>.

Wood, Lesley J. 2014. *Crisis and Control: The Militarization of Protest Policing*. Toronto: Between the Lines.

Wrangham, Richard. 2009. *Catching Fire: How Cooking Made Us Human*. New York: Basic Books.

Yglesias, Matthew. 2018. "Everything We Think about the Political Correctness Debate Is Wrong." *Vox*, March 12. <vox.com/policy-and-politics/2018/3/12/17100496/political-correctness-data>.

Yong, Ed. 2020. "How the Pandemic Defeated America." *The Atlantic*, September. <theatlantic.com/magazine/archive/2020/09/coronavirus-american-failure/614191/>.

Young, S.B., and S. Boyd. 2006. "Losing the Feminist Voice? Debates on the Legal Recognition of Same Sex Partnerships in Canada." *Feminist Legal Studies* 14, 2: 219–240.

Zald, Mayer, and John McCarthy (eds.). 1979. *The Dynamics of Social Movements: Resource Mobilization, Social Control, and Tactics*. Cambridge, MA: Winthrop.

Zhang, Sarah. 2016. "Will the Alt-Right Promote a New Kind of Racist Genetics?" *The Atlantic*, <theatlantic.com/science/archive/2016/12/genetics-race-ancestry-tests/510962/>.

Zinn, Howard. 2005. *A People's History of the United States: 1942–Present*. New York: Harper Perennial Modern Classics.

INDEX

Index